CHRIST
CRUCIFIED

Donald Macleod's work is always stimulating, sometimes provocative, and never less than excellent. This is a contribution to thought on the atonement that is both timely and incisive. It should be required reading for students, theologians, ministers and anyone interested in learning more about the stupendous atoning work of Christ.
Robert Letham, Director of Research and Senior Lecturer in Systematic and Historical Theology, Wales Evangelical School of Theology, Bridgend

This book explores 'The Way of the Cross' from the Gospel narratives and then examines 'The Word of the Cross' as it is explained in the rest of the New Testament. Donald Macleod writes with careful analysis and persuasive clarity about the great issues that have absorbed the attention of preachers and scholars throughout the ages, including substitution, expiation, propitiation, reconciliation, satisfaction, redemption and victory. In the tradition of Stott, Packer, and other evangelical leaders, he provides a theology of the atonement for the general reader, argued from Scripture, but helpfully engaging with debates about the meaning and significance of biblical affirmations about the cross.
David G. Peterson, emeritus faculty member, Moore College, Sydney

Donald Macleod has written a welcome and convincing exposition of the cross of Christ. He skilfully blends biblical exegesis and engagement with systematic theologians to produce a robust defence of the classic evangelical view of penal substitution which anticipates objections, places it in a wide framework, and implicitly rebukes sloppy thinking. His clear style makes this book not only a 'must read' on this topic but also a joy to read and an educative treat.
Derek Tidball, Visiting Scholar, Spurgeon's College, London

Those who have heard Donald Macleod preach or who have read his writings will know that the crucified Christ is, of all theological topics, his forte. He has both dazzling insight matched by a way with words which together serve to bring out aspects of the person and work of Christ with memorable beauty. Thus, it is a pleasure to be able to commend this book. If you are familiar with Donald's work, you know what to expect and know that you will be challenged and edified. If you have never read him before, you are in for a treat.
Carl R. Trueman, Paul Woolley Professor of Church History, Westminster Theological Seminary, Philadelphia USA

CHRIST
CRUCIFIED

Understanding
the Atonement

DONALD
MACLEOD

ivp

INTER-VARSITY PRESS
Norton Street, Nottingham NG7 3HR, England
Email: ivp@ivpbooks.com
Website: www.ivpbooks.com

First published 2014
Reprinted 2014

British Library Cataloguing in Publication Data
A catalogue record for this book is available from the British Library.

ISBN: 978-1-78359-101-5

Set in Monotype Garamond 11/13pt
Typeset in Great Britain by CRB Associates, Potterhanworth, Lincolnshire
Printed and bound in Great Britain by Ashford Colour Press Ltd, Gosport, Hampshire

Inter-Varsity Press publishes Christian books that are true to the Bible and that communicate the gospel, develop discipleship and strengthen the church for its mission in the world.

Inter-Varsity Press is closely linked with the Universities and Colleges Christian Fellowship, a student movement connecting Christian Unions in universities and colleges throughout Great Britain, and a member movement of the International Fellowship of Evangelical Students. Website: www.uccf.org.uk.

CONTENTS

PREFACE

Any first-century missionary who prided himself on rapport with his audience would have kept silent about the cross. It was a 'most vile death', and the idea that the Son of God could save the world by dying would have seemed both scandalous and ridiculous.

Things are no different in the twenty-first century. Yet from first-century Corinth to modern Korea, the story of the cross, and the doctrine of penal substitution, have brought peace to millions who have faced the truth about themselves, and light, joy and power to drifting lives.

In my case, if I may paraphrase the dying words of John Knox, this is where I first cast my anchor; though the surrounding theological seas have always had their own fascinations it is this rock that really matters. I owe it everything, and all that remains now is to see it from within the veil.

It is hard to know where to draw the line when it comes to acknowledgements. All the books I have ever read, all the preachers I have ever heard, and all the believers I have ever met, have made their own contribution to this volume. I have tried, however, to keep quotations to a minimum, and some of the omissions will seem very strange. But it is precisely to such works as John Stott's *The Cross of Christ*[1] and James Packer's *What Did the Cross*

---

1. John Stott, *The Cross of Christ* (Leicester: IVP, 1986) [20th anniversary edition 2006].

Achieve?[2] that my debt is greatest: so great that had I returned to them in the course of preparing this volume it might well have ended up as no more than a rewrite of theirs. I had to maintain some semblance of independence.

I am especially grateful to Dr Philip Duce, Senior Commissioning Editor (Theological Books) at Inter-Varsity Press, for his patience, encouragement and guidance. He not only homed in expertly on blemishes, but allowed me to expand certain sections (my idea of the perfect editor).

Donald Macleod

2. James I. Packer, *What Did the Cross Achieve?: The Logic of Penal Substitution*, Tyndale Biblical Theology Lecture, 1973, repr. in *The Collected Shorter Writings of J. I. Packer*, vol. 1 (4 vols., Carlisle: Paternoster Press, 1998–99), pp. 85–124.

ABBREVIATIONS

ANF   Ante-Nicene Fathers, 10 vols.: <http://www.ccel.org/fathers.html>

BAGD   W. Bauer, *A Greek English Lexicon of the New Testament and Other Early Christian Literature*, tr. William F. Arndt and F. Wilbur Gingrich (2nd ed., Chicago: University of Chicago Press, 1958)

ESV   English Standard Version

ET   English translation

Gk   Greek

Institutes   John Calvin, *Institutes of the Christian Religion*, 2 vols., ed. John T. McNeill, tr. Ford Lewis Battles, Library of Christian Classics (Philadelphia: Westminster, 1960)

KJV   King James Version

Lat.   Latin

Luther's Works Martin Luther, *Luther's Works*, 55 vols., tr. and ed. various (Saint Louis: Concordia Publishing House, 1955–86)

LXX   Septuagint

NASB   New American Standard Bible

NIV   New International Version

NPNF   Nicene and Post-Nicene Fathers: <http://www.ccel.org/fathers.html>

NRSV   New Revised Standard Version
RV   Revised Version
TDNT   G. Kittel and Gerhard Friedrich (eds.), *Theological Dictionary of
                the New Testament*, 10 vols., tr. and ed. Geoffrey W. Bromiley
                (Eerdmans: Grand Rapids, 1965–76)

PART I

THE WAY OF THE CROSS

1. A MAN OF SORROWS

The apostles clearly saw it as their duty not only to proclaim the cross, but to explain it. St Paul, for example, speaks of both the word (*logos*) of the cross (1 Cor. 1:18) and the word (*logos*) of reconciliation (2 Cor. 5:19). Yet the cross is not in the first instance a doctrine, but a fact, and no interpretation of the fact can make the suffering of Christ more or less awful than it actually was. Whether we speak of the cross as penal, piacular, expiatory, propitiatory, vicarious, substitutionary, exemplary, liberating or conquering makes no difference to what Jesus had to endure. The cross remains a fact. With this fact the church, and indeed the whole world, has to reckon; and with this fact all our thinking about the atonement must begin.

The centrality of the cross

The story of the cross is proclaimed in all four canonical Gospels, and the first thing that strikes us is how much space it occupies in the overall narrative. Mark, for example, devotes eight of his sixteen chapters to the last fateful journey following Peter's confession at Caesarea Philippi, and one-fifth of his material is taken up with the story of the crucifixion itself. The same focus on the cross appears in Matthew, who again makes the confession at Caesarea Philippi pivotal. In Luke, Caesarea Philippi is placed in chapter 9, while no fewer than four-and-a-half chapters (19:28 – 23:56) are devoted to events between the triumphal entry and the resurrection. John omits all reference to key events such as the baptism, the temptations, the transfiguration and the institution of the Lord's Supper, concentrating, from chapter 7 onwards, on Jesus' last visit to Jerusalem. He devotes chapters 13 to 17 to the last night of Jesus' life, and two chapters (18–19) to the crucifixion.

It is clear from these details that the evangelists had no interest in writing conventional biographies of Jesus. His childhood, adolescence, education and early manhood, so central to modern biography and psychology, are passed over in almost total silence. Instead, the proportions of the Gospel narratives underline the centrality of the cross in the evangelists' understanding of Jesus' mission; and that understanding was derived from Jesus himself. In Mark 10:45, for example, he declared that the very reason for his coming was to give his life as a ransom for many, and according to John 10:18 the commission he had received from the Father was to lay down his life. From this point of view the Gospels strike exactly the same note as St Paul: 'We preach Christ crucified' (1 Cor. 1:23). Precisely for this reason, the proportions we find in the Gospels become the criterion for all interpretations of Christianity. However important the teaching of Jesus, it was not there that his primary significance lay. It lay in his death. Muslims may glory in the teaching of their prophet. Christians glory in the death of theirs (Gal. 6:14).

The climax of his suffering

A word of caution is needed here, however. The centrality of the cross must not beguile us into ignoring a second striking feature of the story of the passion: the cross was but the climax of Jesus' suffering. His whole life, from the cradle to the tomb, was suffering. The principle underlying this was that from the moment of his birth Jesus was identified with sinful humanity, and all the circumstances of his life reflected the fact that he was bearing the sin of the world (John 1:29). In solidarity with us, he was 'the Man of Sorrows' (Isa. 53:3, KJV).

This is not to say that his life was one of unrelieved gloom. There were moments when he rejoiced in spirit (Luke 10:21), there was the satisfaction of doing his Father's will and there was the constant anticipation of 'the joy that was set before him' (Heb. 12:2). But none of this detracts from the fact that his whole life involved suffering. The tension is underlined by the circumstances of his birth. At one level its glory is attested by the miracle of the virgin conception and such other signs as the acclamation of the angels, the adoration of the shepherds and the visit of the Magi. At another, the details paint a picture of lowliness, poverty and exclusion. The condescension already implicit in the incarnation is aggravated by his being laid in a manger and by all that was implied in the fact that there was no room in the inn.[1] Shortly afterwards, the family are forced to flee to Egypt. On their return, they have to reside in Nazareth, out of which there could come nothing good (John 1:46). In the eyes of the Jewish elite this would forever define him as a provincial. He clearly had few educational opportunities; in later life, in fact, people were well aware that he had never had a formal education and were amazed that nevertheless he could teach (John 7:15). The Christian imagination has lingered lovingly over the image of him as a carpenter, and the image itself has cast lustre over that noble trade. But nothing is heard of Joseph after Jesus' visit to the temple at the age of twelve, and his total absence from the accounts of the public ministry strongly suggests that Jesus lost his father at an early age.

Once the public ministry commences, the pressures and privations are immediately obvious. They begin with the temptations in the desert, underlining the fact that though Jesus was free from sin he was not free from temptation. On the contrary, he was tempted just like ourselves 'in every way' (Heb. 4:15). Behind the phraseology, sanitized by centuries of quotation, lies the harsh reality that Jesus was dogged and harassed by the Prince of Darkness throughout his life. But there were more mundane pressures as well, and they clearly took their toll, even of his physical appearance: so much so that he could be taken for a fifty-year-old (John 8:57) when he was scarcely thirty. He was poor beyond our imagining, owning only the clothes he stood in; homeless, without a pillow for his head; oppressed by crowds demanding a sign and plying him with endless questions; often exhausted, as when he lay dead to the world in the stern of a tiny fishing boat caught in the eye of a fearful storm (Mark 4:38). He was misunderstood by his family, who feared for his sanity; pursued by the sick and their desperate relatives; stalked by the Pharisees with their undisguised hostility and their sly coadjutors with their entrapping conundrums (Mark 12:13). His whole life followed a pattern of rejection: rejection in 'his own country', Nazareth; rejection by the religious establishment; rejection by public opinion, always fickle; and rejection, at last, by his disciples, who all forsook him and fled.

---

1. The general meaning of *katalyma* is 'lodging-place', sometimes more specifically a 'guest room', as rendered by the newer NIV and some other recent versions (Luke 2:7). However, the translation 'inn' remains firmly embedded in the traditional Christmas narrative and is retained by ESV, NRSV and NASB.

Add to these the sheer horror of life among sinners for one so morally and spiritually sensitive. We skip lightly over the words, 'made his dwelling among us' (John 1:14), forgetting that he had come 'from highest bliss, down to such a world as this'[2]: a world where he was surrounded on all sides by the sights of misery and wickedness, the sounds of profanity and blasphemy, and the stench of poverty, death and corruption.

That had been the story so far. Pontius Pilate was the climax, not the commencement, of his suffering. It is tempting to surmise that because of Jesus' inner strength he was able to rise easily above such pressures and continue on his way unruffled and serene. But Jesus' endurance and courage were not those of the insensitive and unfeeling. The pressure hurt, and sometimes there were tears (John 11:35), sometimes anger (Mark 3:5), and sometimes an almost mortal sorrow (Mark 14:34). This is what undergirds the sympathy highlighted in Hebrews 4:15: Jesus was tested in every way, just as we are.

Dawning realization

Yet apart from the divine identity of the sufferer and his remaining sinless despite the full force of temptation there is little that is unique in the catalogue of Jesus' sufferings prior to Gethsemane. They express his solidarity with us, but do not set him apart from us. What sets him apart is his cross: not only *a* cross, but *his* cross, a road no-one had travelled before and no-one has travelled since. The full horror of it would have dawned on Jesus only gradually, and only carefully and gradually did he introduce the subject to his disciples. His mother doubtless shared with him the mysterious words spoken to her at the annunciation. These had made plain his messianic destiny, as had the words spoken by Elizabeth (Luke 1:42–43) and by Simeon (Luke 2:29–32), but they had also made plain that he would be 'a sign spoken against'; and Mary had been warned of a sword that would one day pierce her soul (Luke 2:35).

We can be sure, too, that Mary had introduced him to the prophets. He would have read his own destiny in their delineations of the Messiah, not least in those neglected passages which spoke so clearly of his suffering and death. He may at first have pondered, like the Ethiopian eunuch, 'Who is the prophet talking about, himself or someone else?' (Acts 8:34); or, like the angels, probed the great predictions of the suffering of Messiah and the glory that would follow, wondering to what, and to when, and to whom they referred (1 Pet. 1:11). As

---

2. 'See amid the winter's snow', Edward Caswall (1814–78).

he read, the Spirit of his Father would have guided him and led him to the core truths of messianic suffering: that one day he would be led like a lamb to the slaughter; that he was called to give his life a ransom for many; that the sword of Yahweh would strike him; and that at the end even his heavenly Father would forsake him.

Jesus embarked on his public ministry with these thoughts already firmly impressed on his mind, and his forebodings may well have been conformed at his baptism, when the voice from heaven spoke words which were at one level so comforting, at another so disturbing. Here the Father acknowledges him as his beloved Son, but in words clearly reminiscent of the command to Abraham: 'Take your son, your only son, whom you love – Isaac . . . and sacrifice him . . . as a burnt offering on a mountain that I will show you' (Gen. 22:2). He was to be God's Isaac. The words of John the Baptist, spoken shortly afterwards, confirmed that this was indeed the path Jesus was to tread. He was the Lamb of God, bearing the sin of the world (John 1:29).

From the very beginning of his public ministry Jesus' own utterances betray not only the expectation of a violent death, but his perception that this death was the very heart and purpose of his mission. The earliest recorded reference to it is in Mark 2:20. In the context, Jesus is being challenged as to why his disciples never fast. He answers with a rhetorical question: how can the guests fast while the bridegroom is still with them? But he adds, 'the day will come when the bridegroom will be *taken from* them, and on that day they will fast'. This verb, *apairō*, occurs twice in the Septuagint version of Isaiah 53:8, referring to the violent death of the Servant:

By oppression and judgment he was *taken away*.
   Yet who of his generation protested?
For he was *cut off* from the land of the living;
   for the transgression of my people he was punished.

Though the word does not always imply the use of force, the context here clearly requires it; and its use by Jesus makes plain that he set out on his mission fully aware that it would end violently.

Peter's confession at Caesarea Philippi marks a watershed, Jesus judging that the time has now come to speak explicitly of his violent end: 'The Son of Man must suffer many things and be rejected by the elders, the chief priests, and the teachers of the law, and . . . be killed and after three days rise again' (Mark 8:31–32). The sequel is fascinating. Peter finds the whole concept of messianic suffering abhorrent, just as he would later find the idea of the foot washing (John 13:8), and says, in effect, 'Don't talk such rubbish!' Jesus' response is sharp, almost harsh, as if Peter had touched a raw nerve: 'Get behind me, Satan!' The disciple's words clearly presented a temptation, a temptation with which Jesus was already wrestling and which would come to its climax in Gethsemane (Mark 14:36). How plausible, for a moment, must Peter's argument have seemed! He was the Messiah; the Messiah should not suffer; he could bypass the suffering, then! It all seemed so logical, and to think that it came from a disciple! It was its very plausibility that made Jesus angry and drew from him the harshest rebuke he ever directed at an individual. Later, as they make their way through Galilee, Jesus brings up the same subject again (Mark 9:32), but the disciples still don't understand, and they are afraid to ask. 'Possibly,' comments C. E. B. Cranfield, 'they understood enough to know that to know more would be painful. Possibly they could see that the subject was painful to Jesus himself.'[3]

In the Gospel of John the clearest allusion Jesus makes to his impending death is in chapter 12: 'Unless a grain of wheat falls to the ground and dies, it remains only a single seed. But if it dies, it produces many seeds' (12:24). The most remarkable thing about these words is their context: 'The hour has come for the Son of Man to be glorified' (John 12:23). This is the paradox of the cross. 'Without the "death" of the seed,' wrote C. H. Dodd, 'no crop: without the death of Christ, no world-wide gathering of mankind.'[4] By dying, Christ brings life to millions. By dying, he is glorified. This is linked to John's use of the verb, *hypsoō*. In Philippians 2:9 Paul uses it (with the prefix *hyper*) to express the hyper-exaltation of Jesus, but John uses it of his crucifixion. This is particularly clear in John 12:32, 'I, when I am *lifted up* from the earth, will draw all people to myself.' John himself adds the explanatory comment, 'he said this to indicate the kind of death he was to die'. It would involve, quite literally, his being lifted up. The following verse makes plain how the crowd understood the words: 'We have heard from the Law that the Messiah will remain for ever, so how can you say, "The Son of Man must be lifted up"?' They clearly heard the words as if they meant, 'the Son of Man must be hanged'. Yet, as Carson points out, John has chosen this precise verb because it is ambiguous.[5] Jesus is not only 'lifted up' on the cross, he is also 'lifted up' (exalted) to glory. The point of contact between the idea of crucifixion and the idea of exaltation is clear enough. The cross involves physical elevation and for that very reason becomes

---

3. C. E. B. Cranfield, *The Gospel According to Saint Mark: An Introduction and Commentary* (Cambridge: Cambridge University Press, 1959), p. 306.

4. C. H. Dodd, *The Interpretation of the Fourth Gospel* (Cambridge: Cambridge University Press, 1968), p. 372.

5. D. A. Carson, *The Gospel According to John* (Leicester: IVP, 1991), p. 444.

a symbol of the personal spiritual elevation of the Messiah. But it is not mere symbolism. Through the cross Jesus will return (bringing human nature with him) to the glory he had with the Father before the world was (John 17:5). This is why, on the eve of the crucifixion, Jesus can pray that the Father would glorify the Son, and he would do so because 'the hour' had come: the hour when the Father would glorify his name (John 17:1).

The story of the foot washing is also prefaced by a reference to 'the hour': Jesus knew that 'the hour had come for him to leave this world and go to the Father' (John 13:1). The foot washing as such does not contain any direct allusion to the cross. It is an acted parable to highlight what is meant by the attitude or 'mindset' (Phil. 2:5) of a servant: the willingness to perform the lowest-grade task for our equals and even for our supposed inferiors. It is precisely in this attitude that Jesus, knowing that he had come from God and was returning to God (John 13:3), is at his most 'matchless, God-like and divine'.[6] This immediately relates it to the cross. There is no service that Jesus is not prepared to render, whatever the cost, and Jesus now fully appreciates the cost. He must love 'to the end' (*eis telos*). This is the point of no return, where he knows the price of love and steels himself to face it. Love will not merely wash feet. It will lay down its life.

All of this gradually-dawning realization finally overwhelms Jesus in Gethsemane. But before Gethsemane comes the transfiguration and it is important to see it in its original context, closely linked to the cross. During his earthly ministry Jesus' divine identity was normally veiled by his human form and by his low, servile condition. Now for a brief moment the veil is removed, his whole appearance changes and the underlying *morphē* of the divine briefly breaks through the veil of the human. The disciples become, as Peter reminds us, eye-witnesses of his majesty (2 Pet. 1:16). This is why A. M. Ramsey preferred to speak of the *glorification* rather than of the *transfiguration* of Jesus.[7] He and his disciples are given a glimpse of the glory which was his even while he was on earth, and this is reinforced by the voice from heaven, 'This is my Son, whom I love' (Mark 9:7). The same voice had spoken to Jesus on the threshold of his public ministry (Mark 1:11) and now, as he sets his face toward Calvary, he is reminded once again who he is; and reminded, too, of the Father's love and approbation. When the crowd around the cross mocks (Mark 15:29), he must remember the voice which came from heaven and which gave him honour and

---

6. From 'Great God of wonders!', Samuel Davies, 1769.

7. Arthur Michael Ramsey, *The Glory of God and the Transfiguration of Christ* (London: Longmans, Green and Co., 1949), p. 101.

glory (2 Pet. 1:17). It is as if Abba were saying, 'Son, in all you are now going to face, never forget who you are, never forget that I love you, and never forget how proud I am of you.' Whatever the pain of his ordeal, it would be a pain in which the Father would share.

Yet it is not only the underlying *divine* glory of Jesus that is revealed in the transfiguration. It is also a revelation of the *human* glory (*morphē*) that lies beyond the cross. At Caesarea Philippi he had told his disciples that he would be killed, but he had also told them that after three days he would rise again (Mark 8:31). Now, here on the mountain, he, and they, have a glimpse of his resurrection glory, and a glimpse, too, of the resurrection glory of his people. But this, too, belongs firmly to the psychology of the moment. It is part of the Father's ministry of encouragement. He will not die in vain.

The appearance of the heavenly visitors, Moses and Elijah, also belongs to the ministry of encouragement. Immediately after Peter's confession at Caesarea Philippi Jesus introduced the subject of his death, but Peter wanted to hear not a word of it. This gives particular point to the words, 'Listen to him!' (Mark 9:7). The attitude of the heavenly visitors differs completely from that of the disciples. The cross is all Moses and Elijah want to talk about, though Luke's account of their conversation is extraordinary. He summarizes it as a conversation about his 'departure' (using the word *exodos*) and refers to it as something Jesus was to accomplish, or 'bring to fulfilment' (Luke 9:31). The dismissive attitude of the disciples would have brought profound discouragement to Jesus; the interest of the heavenly visitors would have lifted his heart. The cross was what all heaven was talking about. Even the angels were fascinated (1 Pet. 1:12).

Slow motion

The fourth fascinating feature of the story of the passion is that when it comes to Good Friday the Gospels go into slow motion. They have passed over in silence whole decades of Jesus' life, and even when they pick up the threads of the public ministry there are weeks and months of which they say nothing. We are even left in considerable uncertainty as to the length of Jesus' ministry. Mark implies at least two years. John mentions three Passovers, but does not exclude the possibility that there may have been more. Some of the early church fathers limited the ministry to one year only.

But when it comes to the crucifixion we have the sequence frame by frame; almost, indeed, an hourly bulletin. There is one remarkable parallel to this change of tempo: the account of creation in Genesis 1. This account covers the events of billions of years in twenty-five verses, and summarily covers the emergence of vast heavenly bodies in the throwaway line, 'he also made the stars' (v. 16). But when it comes to the creation of the human species, the pace instantly changes. God pauses to deliberate, resolves to create humans in his image, does it, blesses them and then gives them the great mandates to procreate, to colonize the whole earth and to act as servants and custodians of creation. Of all species, the human race alone is singled out, and over it alone does the story linger.

The reason is simple enough. Humankind is the centre of the story, and the account of the preceding six 'days' serves merely to set the scene for the history of the redemption of our species. It is for the same reason that the crucifixion narrative goes into slow motion. It is the pivot on which the world's redemption turns, and it involves such a sequence of separate events that we assume, instinctively, that they must have occupied several days. Instead we find to our astonishment that they all occurred on one day; and the events of that one single day are reported in meticulous detail.

Our printed Bibles do not, unfortunately, highlight the significance of Mark 14:17, where the evangelist introduces his account of the Last Supper with the words, 'when evening came'. Unpretentious though they sound, they are of huge moment. The Jewish day began with the sunset, and this 'evening' marks the beginning of Good Friday. Fifteen hours later, Jesus would be crucified, but these intervening hours would themselves be crammed with drama: the Last Supper, Gethsemane, the betrayal, the arrest and the trial; then the crucifixion, followed by the entombment. From the Last Supper to his burial, a mere twenty-four hours; and so detailed is the account of his last few hours that we know exactly what happened at 9 o'clock in the morning (the third hour), at midday (the sixth hour) and at 3 o'clock in the afternoon (the ninth hour). Against the background of the previous indifference to chronology, such detail is remarkable, and serves to underline once again the evangelists' concentration on Jesus' death.

The Last Supper

The day began (on what would be our Thursday evening) with the Last Supper. The earliest written account is that of St Paul in 1 Corinthians 11:23–34, but there are parallels in all three synoptics, and though the accounts contain slight variations in wording they constitute one coherent narrative. That narrative itself has bred many different discourses. Here we limit ourselves to the light which the Last Supper sheds on the death of Christ, and particularly on his own understanding of that death.

It is clear, first of all, that Jesus saw his death as, in the most formal sense, a sacrifice. We know from the synoptics that the Last Supper was a Passover meal,[8] and in all probability Jesus had long seen himself as the Passover lamb. At the very beginning of his ministry John the Baptist had introduced him as 'the Lamb of God' (John 1:29), and Paul reminds the Corinthians that 'Christ, our Passover lamb, has been sacrificed' (1 Cor. 5:7). The fact that he offers no elaboration suggests that the idea was already familiar to the Christian community.

It is in this Passover context that Jesus refers separately to his body and to his blood (we should remember that the blood was always treated separately in the sacrificial liturgy). In both Matthew and Mark the bread-saying is limited to 'this is my body', but Paul's account adds the words, 'for you': 'This is my body, which is for you' (1 Cor. 11:24). This points clearly to the vicarious nature of his sacrifice. The body *is* for the benefit of his disciples. The bread, interpreted as 'my body', has already been broken, and this detail ('the fraction') has long been regarded as an essential step in the liturgical administration of the Lord's Supper. The practice gains some support from the fact that some manuscripts add the word 'broken' (*klomenon*) in 1 Corinthians 11:24: 'This is my body, which is *broken* for you.' Most modern editors, however, regard this as a later addition.[9] There is, besides, the fact to which Jeremias draws attention: the breaking of bread was 'an established phrase for the action of the Jewish head of the household in the grace before meals'.[10] We see Jesus himself performing this action when, in feeding the five thousand, he 'gave thanks and broke the loaves' (Mark 6:41). Similarly, when he shared a meal with the two disciples he met on the road to Emmaus, he 'took bread, gave thanks, *broke* it and began to give it to them' (Luke 24:30).

In view of this we need to be cautious in asserting that the 'breaking' is a theologically significant detail. On the other hand, Luke's account of the bread-saying does contain the significant (and undisputed) word, 'given' (*didomenon*): 'This is my body given for you' (Luke 22:19). This is certainly sacrificial language, reminiscent of John's statement (John 3:16) that 'God so loved the world that he *gave* his one and only Son'. The same idea occurs, with a hint of even greater intensity, in Romans 8:32: 'He who did not spare his own Son,

---

8. For the evidence for this see Joachim Jeremias, *The Eucharistic Words of Jesus* (London: SCM Press, 1966), pp. 15–88.

9. See the brief summary of the evidence in Bruce M. Metzger, *A Textual Commentary on the Greek New Testament: A Companion Volume to the United Bible Societies' Greek New Testament* (3rd ed., London/New York: United Bible Societies, 1975), p. 562.

10. Jeremias, *Eucharistic Words of Jesus*, p. 174.

but gave him up (*paredōken*) for us all . . .' Both passages point to a priest-hood of God the Father, 'giving' or 'giving up' his only Son. There may be an echo of the same idea in the chronological detail with which Paul introduces his account of the Last Supper; it took place, he says, 'on the night he was *betrayed*'. This is the same verb, *paradidōmi*, as is used in Romans 8:32. Did Paul intend it as a double entendre? The night of the Last Supper was both the night on which Jesus was 'betrayed' by Judas and the night on which he was 'delivered up' by God the Father.

The sacrificial nature of Jesus' death is set forth even more clearly in the cup-saying: 'This cup is the new covenant in my blood; do this, whenever you drink it, in remembrance of me' (1 Cor. 11:25). The immediate point of com-parison between the cup and the blood is the red colour of the wine, and the metaphor was an old one. Genesis 49:11, for example, refers to 'the blood of grapes' and Deuteronomy 32:14 speaks of 'the foaming blood of the grape'. In the context of the cross, however, Jesus' reference to blood is particularly striking: crucifixion was bloodless, yet all three synoptics record Jesus declaring that his blood is to be 'poured out' (Mark 14:24 and parallels). This echoes Isaiah 53:12, which speaks of the Servant 'pouring out' his life unto death. In homicide, the slayer sheds blood (Gen. 9:6). Here, Jesus sheds his own, laying down his life for his sheep (John 10:17) in accordance with the will of the Father. His death is neither martyrdom nor tragedy, but the climactic act of his obedience (Phil. 2:8).

The cup-saying also makes clear the link between the death of Jesus and the covenant: 'this cup is the new covenant in my blood', or, in its synoptic form, 'this is my blood of the covenant' (Mark 14:24). The exodus had been explicitly rooted in God's remembering his covenant with Abraham, Isaac and Jacob (Exod. 2:24), and this covenant was renewed after the escape from Egypt, when God promised to send his angel to lead Israel into the promised land (Exod. 23:20) and they in turn promised to comply with the stipulations laid down in the book of the covenant (Exod. 24:7). This covenant was ratified by sacrificial blood (Exod. 24:5), and now Jesus speaks of a 'new' covenant, also to be ratified by blood: his own blood. Jeremiah had spoken of such a 'new' covenant (Jer. 31:31–34) and at its heart lay the promise of forgiveness: 'I will forgive their wickedness and will remember their sins no more' (Jer. 31:34). This is echoed in Matthew's version of the cup-saying: 'This is my blood of the covenant, which is poured out for many *for the forgiveness of sins*' (Matt. 26:28). This phrase-ology quickly became standard in the early church, where the blood of Christ became synonymous with his death and the death came to be linked specifically to forgiveness (Eph. 1:7), redemption (Eph. 1:7; Rev. 1:5) and expiation (Rom. 3:25; Heb. 2:17). The forgiveness of sins no longer rests on the blood of bulls and goats, but on the blood of the Mediator: a point fully developed later by the writer to the Hebrews (Heb. 9:11 – 10:18).

But can we be more specific about the precise relation between the death of Jesus and the covenant? One thing that is clear is that Jesus' whole mission is set in the context of the covenant. He was not sent into the world by the imperious command of the Father, nor as a self-appointed volunteer. He came by virtue of the agreement between the Father, the Son and the Holy Spirit to act together for the salvation of humanity. Admittedly, the word 'covenant' is applied to his mission only infrequently, yet it is clear that in his chosen capacity as the Servant he operates within rules of engagement agreed between all three divine persons prior to his coming. This is why he can speak of a work given him to do (John 17:4), and of a 'command' to lay down his life (John 10:18). This is why with his last breath he can cry, 'It is finished!' (John 19:30). Even the schedule of his mission has been agreed beforehand, hence his several references to 'the hour', as in the opening words of the high-priestly prayer: 'Father, the hour has come' (John 17:1). Events moved at a pre-agreed pace. But the covenant contains not only stipulations. It also contains promises. He will be upheld by the Father and anointed with the Spirit (Isa. 42:1); when his work is finished he will be glorified (John 17:1); and after his ascension God will pour out his Spirit to empower his church for the work of mission (Acts 1:4; 2:33).

The death of Jesus also *seals* the covenant. In the Old Testament, covenants were almost invariably ratified by sacrifice, hence the standard Hebrew phraseology, 'to *cut* a covenant' (*kārat běrît*). This is seen at its most dramatic in the story of the inauguration of the original covenant between God and Abraham (Gen. 15:7–20). On the Lord's instructions, Abraham sacrificed a heifer, a goat and a ram, cut them in pieces and arranged them in two rows. A divine theophany (a smoking brazier with a flaming torch) then passed between the pieces. This ritual proclaimed the seriousness of the commitment for both parties. God is the initiator, but there is a solemn bond of mutual obligation, each party invoking upon himself the covenant curse (symbolized by the sacrificed animals) should he violate the covenant.

The covenant significance of the death of Jesus should probably be seen against this background. It is a pledge of the divine seriousness: the one who did not spare his own Son (Rom. 8:32) will, surely, give us all things. But it is also beckoning us into something deeper. The covenant, the divine law, *has* been broken, but it is the non-violator, the one who has not broken it, who takes upon himself the curse (Gal. 3:13) and thereby seals and pledges his love.

But the blood of Jesus not only seals the covenant, it secures all the blessings to which God is pledged. It is the ransom price, it has been paid in full, and it lies at the heart of the church's doxology: 'To him who loves us and has freed [loosed] us from our sins by his blood . . . be glory and power for ever and ever!' (Rev. 1:5–6). He is the one who dies in the place of the many; the holy one judged in the place of the guilty. But all this presupposes a prior agreement: not one worked out by negotiation between God and man, but one finalized in eternal counsel between the Father, the Son and the Holy Spirit. This counsel provides the indispensable framework for Jesus' work of atonement. It is within this framework that the Son accepts the office of redeemer, undertaking to act as our representative and our substitute, but this already presupposes love and goodwill on God's part. He concedes that the one may take the place of the many. But he goes further. He ordains that he himself will not only *provide* the ransom, but will *become* the ransom (in the person of his Son): '*autos hilasmos!*' writes John in 1 John 2:2. He himself is the expiatory sacrifice. He will bear the whole cost.

Finally, Jesus' words at the Last Supper make plain that there must be a taking as well as a giving, and a drinking as well as a pouring out: 'Take and eat . . . Drink from it, all of you' (Matt. 26:26–27). His body and blood avail nothing except through faith. But such a faith also implies total satisfaction with the divine covenant. There is nothing in God's plan of salvation that we would want out, and there is nothing out that we would want in. We can be saved only on God's terms; and faith is delighted with the terms.

Gethsemane

The supper over, Jesus goes with his disciples to Gethsemane, moving 'over there' to pray with Peter, James and John (Matt. 26:36–37). Here, as we noted earlier, the gradually-dawning realization of what was involved in his messianic destiny finally becomes almost total clarity, and the burden of knowledge and foreboding suddenly becomes overwhelming. The language used by Mark and the other synoptists makes plain the unimaginable depth and intensity of his emotions. His soul is filled with grief. The word *perilypos* itself points to deep sadness ('My soul is exceeding sorrowful', Mark 14:34, KJV), but here it is intensified by the addition, 'unto death'. The burden of grief was life-threatening, and associated with it were distress and agitation. The verb *ademonein* suggests bewilderment, anxiety and near-panic, the feelings of somebody asking, 'How am I going to cope?' The strongest word of all is the one which the KJV renders 'sore amazed' (v. 33). The best clue to its meaning is that it is also used in Mark's account of the resurrection to express the feelings of the awestruck women at the tomb when they find the body of Jesus gone and the empty tomb guarded by an angel. It is the feeling we experience in the presence of the unearthly, the uncanny and the utterly eerie. In Gethsemane Jesus knew that he was face to face with the unconditionally holy, that absolutely overwhelming might that condones nothing, cannot look on impurity and cannot be diverted from its purpose. What would it do to him?

But the vocabulary of emotion is not the only indicator of Jesus' distress. There are other indicators as well, such as the fact, for example, that he took with him his three closest friends, Peter, James and John. It is as if he dreaded being alone and begged the simple human comfort of having other people near him: 'Please don't leave me alone!' There is the fact, too, that he asked them to pray for him. Nothing could more graphically highlight the reality of the incarnation and the sense of dependence that went along with it. But neither should we lose sight of the paradox of the Son of God, the Almighty Maker of heaven and earth, asking mortals to remember him in their prayers. Equally remarkable is the detail mentioned by Luke, 'an angel from heaven appeared to him and strengthened him' (Luke 22:43). How the angel 'strengthened' him we can only speculate, but perhaps it bore some relation to the point made by Peter in 1 Peter 1:12, 'even angels long to look into these things'. Though the angels had no direct or personal interest in the redemptive mission of the Son of God, yet they watched the progress of his love with amazement, as it descended ever deeper into its unimaginable cost. What must they have thought as they saw their beloved Maker distraught? This must, surely, be as bad as it would get! But no! Worse was to follow: immolation, death and a heart-rending 'why?' as Abba forsook him. Whatever, the angel's would be the last word of comfort Jesus would hear, till it was all over. Then the angels, too, though owing nothing to his blood, would join in the great chorus of praise: 'Worthy is the Lamb, who was slain, to receive power and wealth and wisdom and strength and honour and glory and praise!' (Rev. 5:12).

But the supreme indicator of the anguish of Gethsemane is the prayer offered by Jesus. Everything about it is remarkable: the fact that he doesn't gently kneel, but throws himself to the ground; the fact that he prays three times; his 'anguish' (Greek *agōnia*) as he literally wrestles with God; the sweat of blood, signalizing the terrible intensity of his struggle (Luke 22:44). Above all, there is the prayer itself, 'Abba, everything is possible for you. Take this cup from me. Yet not what I will, but what you will' (Mark 14:36). Why is the prayer not answered? Why does the cup not pass? He is still able to call God 'Abba', still conscious of the special filial relationship and of Abba's affection, goodwill and approbation. This should remind us that for all its darkness Gethsemane is not yet *the* darkness. It is but the shadow of Calvary. At the last there will be no 'Abba', but only the almost despairing *'Eloi'*.

His wish, what he asks for, is clear: 'Take away this cup. Let it pass.' This is what he wants; wanted with all his soul and with all his strength. He wanted God's will to be different. He asks, 'Could there not be some other way?' He knows it is God's will, 'the cup Abba has given him'. 'But, Abba, could I have another cup, a different cup?' For a moment he stands with the millions of his people who have found God's will almost unendurable, shrunk from the work given them to do, shuddered at the prospect of the race set before them and prayed that God would change his mind. But solidarity is not the main thing here. This is not a road less trodden. It is a road never trodden, before or since: the cup of the one man, the Son of God. He shudders; hesitates. For a moment the whole salvation of the world, the whole of God's determinate counsel, hangs in the balance, suspended on the free, unconstrained decision of this man. There is dread here and bewilderment and awe and self-doubt, and fear (Heb. 5:7).

It is impossible as we sit in the gallery of history not to be aware of the contrast between the discomposure of Jesus and the composure of thousands of his martyred followers as they faced the prospect of certain, and cruel, death. When Dietrich Bonhoeffer was executed at Flossenbürg concentration camp in April 1945, the camp doctor (who didn't know who he was) watched him take off his prison garb, kneel on the floor and pray. 'I was most deeply moved,' he wrote, 'by the way this unusually lovable man prayed, so devout and so certain that God heard his prayer.'[11] Why, then, is Jesus so distraught? It can only be because he is facing more than martyrdom and more than death.

There is one Old Testament story which offers some slight parallel: Moses meeting with Yahweh on Mount Sinai (Exod. 19:16–19). 'The sight was so terrifying that Moses said, "I am trembling with fear"' (Heb. 12.21). The reason lay in the stark terror of the scene confronting him, the holiness of God symbolized by uncanny physical phenomena: a thick cloud, smoke, lightning, earth tremors, a fearful trumpet-blast, a voice like thunder and the direst warnings that anyone who so much as touched the mountain would perish. Here was the supreme Old Testament revelation of God as an absolute over-whelming might, the Wholly Other who brooks no disobedience and no familiarity. And here was the ultimate in 'creature-feeling': a sense of the infinite qualitative divide between humanity and deity, a sense of total vulnerability, a sense of nothingness and of defenceless fragility.

What Jesus dreads in Gethsemane is his own imminent encounter with the holy. But we have to be careful here. The 'holy' is not just an item in a series

---

11. Eberhard Bethge, *Dietrich Bonhoeffer: A Biography*, rev. and ed. Victoria J. Barnett (Minneapolis: Fortress Press, 1989), p. 928.

which reads 'betrayal, arrest, trial, condemnation, crucifixion, death' and then, 'encounter with the holy'. The holy (the hand of God) is in everything at Calvary, just as it was in the thunder, lightnings and tremors of Sinai. But it is equally true that the physical, observable events, for all their horror, do not exhaust the curse. Like Moses, Jesus has a rendezvous with God, but there is one almighty difference. He is not here merely to receive the Law, but to suffer its curse. There will be pain indeed, and he shrinks from that. There will be an awful loneliness, and he shrinks from that. There will be the virulent, hellish demonic, and he shrinks from that. And there will be dying and death (and its taste), and he shrinks from that. But there will be more, and it doesn't help that he doesn't yet know what. The curse: what will it mean? The full ransom price: what will it mean? Forsaken by God: what does that mean? The thunder and lightning of unmitigated divine judgment, condemning sin in his tiny, frail body: what will that mean?

Gethsemane is apprehension: an apprehension of the awfulness of what is still unknown. The imagination of Jesus fixes on it, but in its unfolding it will be even more dreadful than the worst forebodings of his imagination. And there is, besides, the crushing weight of responsibility. So much hinges on his seeing it through. Suppose he fails?

But Gethsemane is more than the dread of suffering. It is itself suffering; part of the road he had to walk and part of the price he had to pay, part, indeed, of the cup itself. His obedience included having to cope with the fear of death as well as with death itself. And here as nowhere else Jesus is tested: tested in his love, in his faith and in his courage. Here Satan shows him, not all the kingdoms of the world as in a previous temptation, but the full cost of his love, and here he presses home the questions: Is it worth it? Are they worth it?

There is, however, one further crucial point. Gethsemane is not the supreme moment of atonement. The 'it is finished!' must wait. In the meantime, it is, 'Rise, let us go!' It is the prelude to the great redeeming act, not the act itself, and we have to ask why. Why was Gethsemane not enough? Why did there have to be a Calvary as well? And why do Calvary, the cross, the death, the blood, become the great central reality of Christianity? Gethsemane so beautiful; Golgotha so unutterably ugly!

Suppose, for example, that the redeeming power of Christ lay, as some have argued, in his vicarious repentance; that he entered fully into our sin, made its shame his own shame, confessed it to God and said 'amen!' to God's condemnation. Why, then, is the atonement not complete at Gethsemane? Here, after all, is complete submission: 'not my will, but yours be done' (Luke 22:42). Where, after this point, does Jesus utter any words remotely suggesting repentance? It may be said in answer that he expressed his remorse (*our* remorse) by meekly submitting to the sentence. But that implies that there *was* a sentence, that the cross was set in a context of justice, that justice was executed on Jesus, and that that execution of justice is the basis of our forgiveness. For Jesus to say 'amen!' to the divine condemnation is not merely to express his general sorrow for sin. It is to say 'amen!' to the need for expiation and propitiation; 'amen!' to the divine sword of justice; 'amen!' to God's right to damn him, notwithstanding his submission. He will atone, not by repenting in the place of others, but by dying for them.

Arrest and trial

Having prayed for the third time Jesus returned to the disciples. He had asked them to watch and pray. Instead, he once again found them sleeping. On his two previous returns, he had excused them: 'The spirit is willing, but the flesh is weak' (Mark 14:38). But now his 'hour' has come and the time for watching and praying is over. The betrayer is at hand (Mark 14:42). The word for 'betrayer' is *paradidous*, and we have already noted its ambivalence. The corresponding verb is used in Romans 8:32, referring to God not sparing his own Son, but 'delivering him up' for us all. Judas's traitorous act is God the Father's priestly act. The arresting party itself consists of Israel's finest: the chief priests, the teachers of the law, and the elders. They are emphatically men of the Torah, yet they are blind to its message and blind to their own Messiah. In a few hours they will hand him over to 'men without the Law' (Acts 2:23[12]) to be tried, condemned and slain.

The betrayal and arrest are followed by the trial. Two things stand out here.

First, it was fourfold: before the Sanhedrin (the Jewish Supreme Council, presided over by the high priest); before Pilate; before Herod; and finally back to Pilate again. We must bear in mind that every detail of the passion is specifically ordained by God the Father as an integral element in his own all-encompassing priestly act of sacrificing his beloved Son. The fourfold trial is an indispensable part of the ritual, certifying the Lamb as one 'without blemish or defect' (1 Pet. 1:19). It involved both the civil and the religious authorities and it culminated in Pilate's unambiguous verdict, 'I find no basis for a charge against this man' (Luke 23:4). And even in all the horrors he experiences as his passion comes to its climax, Jesus' integrity shows through.

---

12. See NIV footnote.

He conducts himself impeccably, without a word of lament against God or bitterness towards men: 'Father, forgive them, for they do not know what they are doing' (Luke 23:34).

The second striking feature of the trial is the role of Pilate. It was no accident. On the contrary, as Calvin noted, it was a key detail precisely because of his position as governor.[13] It was not enough for Christ to suffer any kind of death. It had to be a judicial death involving an arraignment, an accusation and a condemnation. Pilate, the authority established by God (Rom. 13:1), is the symbol and executor of a judicial process by which Jesus was formally found guilty and formally sentenced. He was not murdered by an assassin or lynched by a mob or killed in an accident. He was convicted by a judge, after due process, and judicially executed. Pilate, as the servant (*diakonos*, Rom. 13:4) of God, speaks forth the divine condemnation of the sinner, Jesus. Yet, as Calvin also remarks, Jesus was acquitted by the same lips as condemned him:[14] 'I find no basis for a charge against this man' (Luke 23:4). Here, human justice condemns itself. The criminal is on the bench, not in the dock, just as in the person of Caiaphas the blasphemer is the one at the altar, not the one on the cross. Calvary exposes the corruption which is endemic to human justice. The judge acquits the prisoner, and then sentences him to be flogged and crucified.

The crucifixion

The Gospel accounts of the crucifixion are remarkably restrained, possibly because the process was all too familiar to the original readers, but also because the writers have no interest in satisfying morbid, prurient interest in the details of an execution. The original spectators derived no spiritual benefit from witnessing it in all its gruesome detail and we today would be little the better for knowing 'exactly how it was done'. It would amount, at best, to no more than knowing Christ 'according to the flesh' (2 Cor. 5:16, ESV).

One of the most helpful studies of the background is Martin Hengel's *Crucifixion in the Ancient World*.[15] This form of punishment was not, as is often assumed, peculiar to the Romans. It was also practised in India, Assyria, Germany and Britain; even, indeed, by the Celts, 'who offered their criminals in this way

---

13. *Institutes*, II:XVI, 5.

14. Ibid.

15. Martin Hengel, *Crucifixion in the Ancient World and the Folly of the Message of the Cross* (Philadelphia: Fortress Press, 1977).

as a sacrifice to their gods'.[16] By the time of Jesus, it was taboo among the Jews as a form of punishment (probably because of its brutal use by the Romans in their 'pacification' of Judea), but the Jews had resorted to it in past ages, particularly as a punishment for high treason.

In all these cultures, the cross was seen as a deliberately degrading and obscene form of punishment, 'in which the caprice and sadism of the executioners were given full rein'.[17] There were, literally, no limits. Once the condemned man was handed over, the soldiers could torture, humiliate and violate as they pleased; but not all the blame for the barbarism should be laid on the executioners; crucifixion, as Hengel points out, 'satisfied the primitive lust for revenge and the sadistic cruelty of individual rulers and of the masses'.[18] Nor did such vengefulness and cruelty die with the passing of ancient civilizations. To quote Hengel yet again, crucifixion is but one specific expression of the inhumanity which is always dormant within human beings and which finds expression today in constant calls for popular justice and harsher treatment of offenders: 'It is a manifestation of trans-subjective evil, a form of execution which manifests the demonic character of human cruelty and bestiality.'[19]

Against this background, it is hard to resist the conclusion that, horrific though Jesus' sufferings were, there was an overruling divine restraint which forbade the worst excesses of crucifixion. There is no record of any particularly sadistic acts on the part of the soldiers, who seem to have concentrated on the essentials of their task, while an overseeing providence ensured that not a bone of Messiah's body was broken (John 19:36). Clearly, while the Son of Man must suffer, the Father set limits to the indignities he had to endure, and this extended even beyond his death. His body was honourably entombed rather than left to rot on the cross as was common, and it suffered no decomposition. Once he had breathed his last, the humiliation was over and from that point onwards the whole trajectory was reversed. From Bethlehem onwards his path had been a steady descent into the abyss, but from the moment he shouts, '*tetelestai!*' (John 19:30), the trajectory is upwards. His body lies, indeed, in the tomb, but his soul is in paradise (Luke 23:43), and after the briefest of 'three days' come resurrection and then enthronement.

Christian devotion almost invariably refers to the place of crucifixion as 'Calvary'. The word, however, does not occur in the New Testament. It was

---

16. Hengel, *Crucifixion*, p. 23.
17. Ibid., p. 25.
18. Ibid., p. 89.
19. Ibid., p. 87.

introduced into Christian tradition by the Vulgate (late fourth century), which used the Latin *calvariae* to translate Luke's reference to 'the place called the Skull' (Luke 23:33). It has the advantage of being much more euphonious than the harsh gutturals of 'Golgotha' (Mark 15:22; Matt. 27:33), and well adapted to the purposes of poetry and hymnody. But in that very euphony lies a danger. It is easy to sanitize the cross, rob it of its horror and imagine Calvary as a place of serene, evocative spirituality. Anyone who has visited both the Church of the Holy Sepulchre and Gordon's Calvary (the Garden Tomb) is instantly aware of the temptation to 'prefer' the latter as the site of the crucifixion. Quiet, peaceful and beautiful, it feels much more like a holy place, conducive to meditation and prayer. The Church of the Holy Sepulchre is a complete contrast: noisy, tourist-infested and exuding all that is worst about religion. Yet there is cogent evidence that this was the site of the crucifixion (though inside modern Jerusalem it lay outside the walls of the ancient city),[20] and it is no accident that it was (and is) a horrid, ugly place. The late Dr George Macleod of Iona expressed it memorably: 'Jesus was not crucified in a Cathedral between two candles, but on a cross between two thieves; on the town garbage heap . . . at the kind of place where cynics talk smut, and thieves curse, and soldiers gamble.'[21] God had chosen the site, and the atmosphere. The act was barbaric; the site, with the detritus of previous executions still lying around, horrific; the procedure a shambles. But precisely because it was all these things it dramatized the ugliness of sin while at the same time proclaiming the Son of God a despised, accursed nobody for whom there lay beyond the cross only the horrors of hell. We cannot, dare not, reduce the cross to a crucifix or Golgotha to a rose garden. The aesthetics of the crucifixion are in keeping with its criminality.

Once at Golgotha, the Gospels note two details: they stripped him naked, and 'they offered him wine mingled with myrrh, but he did not take it' (Mark. 15:23). Both of these were standard procedures. What is interesting is that Jesus declined the mixture offered to him, a concoction routinely prepared by pious Jerusalem women and offered to condemned men as an anaesthetic to dull the senses and deaden the pain. Why did Jesus decline it? No explanation is offered, but we should remember that even on the cross Jesus was still 'on service' and needed to be in full possession of his faculties. At any moment an urgent need or claim might arise, as when one of the two men crucified with him suddenly

---

20. See, for example, the literature cited in Raymond E. Brown, *The Gospel According to John (XIII-XXI): Introduction, Translation, and Notes*, The Anchor Yale Bible (New Haven: Yale University Press, 1970), p. 899; and D. A. Carson, *John*, pp. 609–610.

21. George F. Macleod, *Only One Way Left* (Glasgow: The Iona Community, n.d.), p. 38.

said, 'Jesus, remember me when you come into your kingdom'. Jesus is instantly alert and instantly reassuring: 'Today, you will be with me in paradise' (Luke 23:42–43). In the same way, Jesus in his dying moments is equally solicitous for his mother, commending her to the care of John, the beloved disciple (John 19:26–27). He loved and served to the end.

But quite apart from his having to be available for others, Jesus is also engaged in a titanic spiritual struggle. It was, after all, the hour and the power of darkness (Luke 22:53), the prince of the world present in all his force and cunning, hell doing all in its power to subdue and destroy the Son of God. What force there must have been in the taunt, 'Come down from the cross!' and in the thought (clearly somewhere in Jesus' mind) that he could send for twelve legions of angels. Moment by moment he must repel Satan's insidious suggestions, summon all his own strength, choose the pain and continue his journey into the terrifying unknown.

But above all, Jesus must 'taste' death: not simply die, but taste it (Heb. 2:9). This is why he took a long time dying, and this is why he had to die un-anesthetised. He had to walk, as his people do, through the valley of the shadow of death, tasting the fear of it and the encroachments of it and the power of it, and then yielding himself to it consciously and deliberately. His life did not ebb away, slowly and peacefully, ending with a pathetic death-rattle. Instead, he shouts in triumph, 'It is finished!', and then dismisses his spirit into the loving hands of God his Father (Luke 23:46).

2. FROM THE THIRD TO THE NINTH HOUR

From the moment of the immolation the tempo of the narrative slows down yet again, particularly in Mark, who gives us three-hourly bulletins as the passion of Jesus moves to its climax. He records that that the crucifixion took place at the third hour (nine o'clock in the morning by our time), and mentions four specific details.

The charge

First, the charge on which Jesus was condemned: 'The king of the Jews' (Mark 15:26). Formally, and in Pilate's eyes, this was a political charge. Jesus was guilty of sedition, and the governor ordered this precise wording in order to make a political point. The Jews wanted it altered: 'Don't write, "The King of the Jews", but that this man claimed to be king of the Jews' (John 19:21). Pilate refused. The Jews had humiliated him by forcing him to condemn an innocent man, and he would exact revenge by this gesture of contempt for the whole Jewish nation. He nailed the nation to the cross.

But beneath the charge of sedition lay something deeper. In Jewish eyes, Jesus was not merely a seditionist, but a messianic pretender: 'We have a law, and according to that law he must die, because he claimed to be the Son of God' (John 19:7). The law in question is probably the one laid down in Leviticus

24:16, 'anyone who uses the name of the LORD blasphemously is to be put to death'. The precise blasphemy in Jesus' case was that he called God his father, thus making himself equal with God (John 5:18). Jesus did not deny the charge, though he did explicitly deny that his kingship was political. His kingdom was not of this world (John 18:36). He would rule by his Spirit, not by the sword. But that he was a king in the pre-eminent spiritual sense Jesus never denied, even when the denial might have saved his life. When Caiaphas demanded, 'Tell us if you are the Messiah, the Son of God,' Jesus calmly replied, 'You have said so'; to make his meaning unmistakeably clear, he added, 'from now on you will see the Son of Man sitting at the right hand of the Mighty One and coming in the clouds of heaven' (Matt. 26:63–64). Not even the grim horror of his circumstances could obliterate his messianic consciousness. God *is* his Father: had he not made such a claim he would never have been crucified. He was condemned for what he taught, and what he taught was not simply the universal fatherhood of God and the universal brotherhood of man, but his own absolute deity. He was the Messiah, the Son of God, the promised King.

John records that the charge was written in three languages, Aramaic (the language of the populace), Latin (the language of the administration) and Greek (the language of the Empire). It is difficult to be sure that this trilingual form has any special theological significance. It was certainly not unique. It occurs in reports of other executions, no doubt as a deterrent to others who might be planning a similar crime. In Jesus' case, there was no real crime, and Pilate's real concern, as we have seen, was to hold the entire Jewish nation up to ridicule.

It remains true, nonetheless, that the charge proclaimed a fact. The Crucified One was indeed the Messiah, the King of the Jews, and the heathen governor is unwittingly proclaiming that fact. God's providence, as Calvin points out, governed Pilate's pen and 'dictated to him this commendation of the Gospel, even though he did not understand what he wrote. By the same secret moving of the Spirit it came about that the title was proclaimed in three languages . . . the Lord showed by this prelude that the time was already at hand when the name of the Son should be made known everywhere'.[1]

The underlying theological fact is that the dying of Christ is a kingly act, not merely in the sense that he dies royally and with dignity, but in the sense that his dying is his supreme achievement for his people: the act by which he conquers their foes, secures their liberty and establishes his kingdom. This, of course, was completely hidden from Pilate but, as Joseph Ratzinger points out, the

---

1. John Calvin, *The Gospel According to John 11-21 and the First Epistle of John*, tr. T. H. L. Parker, Calvin NT Commentaries (Grand Rapids: Eerdmans, 1994), p. 178.

death sentence he passed on Jesus 'became with paradoxical unity the "profes-sion of faith"'.[2] It is precisely as the crucified criminal that Jesus is the Christ, the King; and the cross, as we shall see later, is the scene of his victory. Any attempt to obviate the scandal by dressing him in the fashions of the age (any age) is a betrayal.

Between two thieves

A second detail recorded by both Matthew and Mark is that Jesus was crucified between two other criminals, one on his right and one on his left. The same fact is recorded by Luke though with slightly different wording. All three accounts stress the word 'with'; they were crucified *along with* Jesus. Some manuscripts of Mark 15:28 insert at this point the words, 'and the scripture was fulfilled which says, "He was counted with the lawless ones"', but the evidence for these words at this point is poor, and modern editions of the New Testament omit them. However, the Scripture referred to is Isaiah 53:12, and this verse is certainly quoted by Jesus himself just before he goes to Gethsemane: 'It is written, "And he was numbered with the transgressors"; and I tell you that this must be fulfilled in me. Yes, what is written about me is reaching its fulfilment' (Luke 22:37). There is no doubt about the authenticity of this passage, nor about the authen-ticity of the original words of Isaiah, and we must take them with complete seriousness. The truth they point to, Jesus' solidarity with sinners, did not begin at the cross; it had been a fact throughout his life. He had made himself notorious as the friend of tax collectors and sinners and repeatedly allowed himself to be compromised by associating with people of dubious reputation. But here at the cross the solidarity climaxes. He is not merely *among* his two co-accused. He is *together with* them; and he is together with them specifically in their character as transgressors and criminals.

The full force of this is brought out in the original wording of Isaiah: he was numbered with the transgressors *'for he bore the sin of the many'*. It is not a matter of mere association or even, ultimately, of mere solidarity, as if he were just taking the position of a sinless one forced to endure the company of sinners. He identifies completely. He lets himself be reckoned as a sinner, and dealt with as a sinner; and not only by men, but by God. He has come to redeem sinners, but the way he will redeem them is by taking their sins as his own and becoming

---

Joseph Ratzinger, *Introduction to Christianity*, tr. J. R. Foster and Michael J. Miller (San Francisco: Ignatius Press, 2000 [1969]), p. 206.

accursed in their place (Gal. 3:13). By hanging him in the middle, wrote Calvin, 'they gave Him first place as though he were the thieves' leader'.[3] Luther, ever more graphic, put it even more strongly: 'He bore the person of a sinner and of a thief – and not of one but of all sinners and thieves . . . And all the prophets saw this, that Christ was to become the greatest thief, murderer, adulterer, robber, desecrator, blasphemer, etc., that has ever been anywhere in the world.'[4] Here, on the cross, he not only bears, but *is* (2 Cor. 5:21) the sin of the world; and so here, in solemn divine equity, the sword falls.

The chorus of derision

Linked to this is a third detail, the chorus of derision. In Mark's account (followed closely by Matthew) there are three disparate but representative groups of mockers. First, there are the passersby: ordinary people coming in to the city early in the morning for their daily business. Then there are the chief priests (Matthew includes the teachers of the law and the elders), and, finally, those crucified with him. The whole of humanity is here. The common people are here, stripped of the romance that attributes special insight to an unsophisticated peasantry. They see no sign of kingship in the crucified one. The world's power, learning and religion are equally blind. And at the other end of the scale, stand his co-condemned. However death concentrated their minds, they had no compunction about adding to the torment of their fellow-sufferer. There was nothing about him which could enable mere human insight, at any point on the social, academic or religious scale, to recognize Jesus for who he was. The veil, the *incognito*, was complete. He was dying to save the world, but he died not to a chorus of gratitude but to a chorus of mockery.

There is more to the taunts and sneers than ordinary human hostility. They attack Jesus at the very foundation of his obedience: his faith in God. 'He trusts in God,' they cry, 'let God rescue him now' (Matt. 27:43). The wording is very close to that of Psalm 22:8, 'He trusts in the LORD; let the LORD rescue him', a psalm Jesus himself will quote at the height of his agony. But the jibe also recalls

---

3. John Calvin, *A Harmony of the Gospels of Matthew, Mark and Luke, Volume III, and the Epistles of James and Jude*, tr. A. W. Morrison, Calvin's NT Commentaries (Grand Rapids: Eerdmans, 1995), p. 197.

4. Martin Luther, 'Lectures on Galatians, 1535, Chapters 1-4', in *Luther's Works*, vol. 26, p. 277.

Psalm 42:3, 'Where is your God?' Where is your God *now*? How, in these circumstances, can Jesus continue to believe that God delights in him and that in his own time he will vindicate him? On the face of things, the mockers are right: his circumstances make a mockery of his faith, and the taunts and sneers make their own contribution to that final impression of utter divine rejection expressed in the cry, 'My God, my God, why have you forsaken me?' (Mark 15:34). Far from being God's beloved, he is a worm (Ps. 22:6).

But the mockery is also one of the final assaults of the tempter. At the beginning of Jesus' ministry Satan had attacked him specifically on the basis of his identity: '*If* you are the Son of God' (Matt. 4:3; Luke 4:3). Here he uses the same approach: 'If you are the Messiah, if you are the Son of God, come down from the cross!' (Matt. 27:40). For Jesus, the force of the temptation must have been almost overwhelming. He had saved others, he could save himself. He could come down from the cross. He could end the agony: the excruciating thirst, the awful strain on his arms, the searing pain in his lacerated back. He could silence the roaring lions and the snarling dogs (Ps. 22:13, 16). He could end his silence, show who he really was, and let them see his glory. He could; and yet he couldn't, because as Calvin comments, if he had shown his sonship in *their* way he would have shown only that he was not God's Son: 'The proof which the wicked demand of Christ is such that by showing Himself to be Son of God He must cease to be Son of God. The terms on which He took on mortal flesh were to secure, by the sacrifice of his death, the reconciliation of men with God the Father. To show Himself Son of God He had to hang on the cross.'[5] He had come to do his Father's will: this was his Father's will. He had come to save the world: the price of that salvation was his blood. He must therefore, and with unflagging resolution, choose the cross: the next moment of the agony, and the next, and the next, until the last, because only his will, and only his sense of divine sonship, keeps him there, finishing the work given him to do. For now, crucifixion is what it means to be the faithful Son of God: that with which, in a dreadful paradox, God is well pleased.

But precisely because he is well pleased, God himself will answer the mockers, take him down from the cross and give him glory; and when he does so, he will also expose the duplicity of the mockers. They had said, 'Come down now from the cross, and we will believe in him' (Matt. 27:42). He came down, but they broke faith even with their own sneers. They still did not believe. Instead, the resurrection itself is mocked (Acts 17:32).

---

5. Calvin, *Harmony of the Gospels*, p. 199.

The three hours' darkness

Three hours pass: hours of unimaginable torture, but affording little insight into Jesus' soul. Then at the sixth hour (noon) darkness comes over the whole land. All three synoptic Gospels record this fact, which suggests they clearly thought it significant. Yet none offer any explanatory comment. It covered 'the whole land', and although the phrase can sometimes mean 'the whole earth', the prevailing view in the Christian tradition has been that here it refers only to Israel. One reason for this is that the voluminous records of the period contain no reference to any such darkness in other lands. Another is that at that time such a darkness would have had no significance for half the globe, the southern hemisphere being already in darkness. But perhaps the most pertinent comment is that of Calvin: 'While the sun shone elsewhere, Judea was plunged into shadow: this made the prodigy more notable.'[6]

The darkness was clearly supernatural. It happened at high noon, and it was the Passover, the time of the full moon, when there was no possibility of an eclipse. It is notable, too, that the darkness was no brief, momentary phenomenon. It lasted for three hours. Nor is it helpful to suggest that it could have been caused by, for example, a black sirocco (a dust-bearing wind originating in eastern deserts and blowing across the Mediterranean). The fact is, the sun failed, and no further explanation is needed than a divine *fiat*: 'But here is the finger of God, a flash of the will that can.'[7]

But what could the darkness mean? One possibility is that it was a tribute to the majesty of Christ, the Father marking the death of his Son with a public and visible mark of distinction just as he had signalled his birth by means of the star that rested over Bethlehem. Here, however, the sign is not a light, but darkness. It was in these terms that Joel had described the Day of the Lord, 'a day of darkness and gloom, a day of clouds and blackness' (Joel 2:2). Amos had spoken similarly: '"In that day," declares the Sovereign Lord, "I will make the sun go down at noon and darken the earth in broad daylight"' (Amos 8:9). Both prophets were speaking of apocalyptic judgment and apocalyptic sorrow, and from this point of view, the darkness at Golgotha is entirely appropriate. Here, at the cross, sin is being judged, condemned in the flesh of Jesus (Rom. 8:3), and here sin is being exposed in all its darkness. Unbelief, ignorance, injustice, inhumanity and deicidal hatred are all here, and the darkness is

---

6. Calvin, *Harmony of the Gospels*, p. 207.

7. From Robert Browning's poem, 'Abt Vogler', in *The Poems of Robert Browning* (London: Oxford University Press, 1905), p. 635.

God's verdict: the expression of his displeasure, as if he must hide it from his eyes.

But perhaps the darkness is not only the darkness of aversion and judgment. Perhaps it is also the darkness of sorrow. Amos had spoken of the Day as 'a time like mourning for an only son' (Amos 8:10), and from this point of view the darkness suggests not only God's abhorrence of the crucifixion, but his sorrow over it. One ingredient in this may have been his sorrow over the depths to which man, made in his own image, could sink. But is this all? Is God, too, 'mourning for an only Son'? And what of the angels? We know they have knowledge of things below, that there is joy among them when a sinner repents; and we know that they were watching the drama unfolding outside Jerusalem on Good Friday (1 Pet. 1:12). Was it with sorrow as well as astonishment that they strained their eyes to watch the mystery of the dying of the Son of God?

There is a remarkable passage on the darkness at Calvary in the *Communion Sermons* of the seventeenth-century Scottish theologian, Samuel Rutherford:

> Darkness was all in Judea when our Lord suffered. And why? Because the Candle that lighted the sun and the moon was blown out. The God-head was eclipsed, and the world's eye was put out. He took away the sun with him, as it were, to another world, when he that was the world's sun was put out. When he went out of the earth, the sun would not stay behind Him. Sun, what ails thee? 'I have not will to shine when my Lord is going to another world.' As if the sun had said to Jesus, 'Lord, if Thou be going to another world, take me with you.'[8]

Can any of this be reduced to propositional Christian doctrine? Rutherford was not alone in suggesting the idea of nature sympathizing with its Maker. It is in these terms that the commentator, Alfred Plummer, for example, understands the darkness at the cross: 'The sympathy of nature with the sufferings of the son of God is what seems to be indicated in all three [Gospel] accounts.'[9] Milton, in his poem, 'On the Morning of Christ's Nativity', similarly portrays nature as sensitive to its Maker, hiding her 'guilty face with innocent snow',

---

8. *Fourteen Communion Sermons by the Rev. Samuel Rutherford*, with a Preface and Notes by Rev. Andrew A. Bonar (Glasgow: Charles Glass & Co., n. d.), pp. 286–287.

9. Alfred Plummer, *A Critical and Exegetical Commentary on the Gospel according to S. Luke*, International Critical Commentary (5th ed., Edinburgh: T&T Clark, 1922), p. 537.

Confounded, that her Maker's eyes
Should look so near upon her foul deformities.[10]

But we need to be careful here. Nature is no autonomous personal agent possessed of emotional intelligence. It is, as John C. Lennox points out, no more than 'every physical thing that is'.[11] Any idea, therefore, of 'Nature' expressing empathy with its Maker is misplaced. The real agent behind the darkness at Golgotha is God, and Rutherford's contemporary and friend, David Dickson, expressed this well, portraying the 'eclipse' of the sun as parallel to the eclipse involved in the *kenosis* of the divine Son. God, says Dickson, veiled the glory of creation, 'not suffering the creatures to show their glory where their Maker is suffering the extremity of shame'.[12] Here the Light of the world is being extinguished, the Life dies and the Logos is silenced. Of these paradoxes the darkness is the portent, as if the universe itself trembled on the brink of chaos while the one who holds it together (Col. 1:17) devoted all his strength to the titanic task of redemption. It is as if the Light was left with no energy to shine and the Logos bereft of the strength to speak. Eventually, the very Life would be extinguished.

But is the 'eclipse' a portent, above all, of the darkness in Jesus' soul? Surrounded by treachery, rejection, injustice, irrational hatred and barbaric cruelty, he is like the remnant of old, walking in a darkness where there is no light (Isa. 50:10). Just how dark becomes clear at the ninth hour (3 o'clock in the afternoon, our time), when Jesus utters his cry of dereliction, 'My God, my God, why have you forsaken me?'

Jesus' words from the cross

The cry of dereliction is the only utterance from the cross recorded in the Gospels of Matthew and Mark. Others are reported, however, by Luke and John (though neither records the cry of dereliction).

The first recorded word was his prayer for the executioners, 'Father, forgive them, for they do not know what they are doing' (Luke 23:34). Here, God is

---

10. Written 1629 and first published in *Poems of Mr. John Milton* (1645).

11. John C. Lennox, *God's Undertaker: Has Science Buried God?* (Oxford: Lion, 2009), p. 28.

12. David Dickson, *A Brief Exposition of the Evangel of Jesus Christ according to Matthew* (repr., Edinburgh: Banner of Truth, 1981 [1647]), p. 396.

still 'Father' (probably 'Abba' in the original utterance). Clearly, the bond of loving intimacy is still strong and unshaken. To the prayer he appends a reason, 'they do not know what they are doing'. His divine glory is completely eclipsed, or at least hidden from human eyes, and they have no idea who he is and therefore no idea of the scale of the evil in which they are involved. They have seen none of his miracles. They have heard none of his preaching. They have overheard none of his prayers. Even more than the arch-persecutor, Saul of Tarsus, they are acting ignorantly, in unbelief (1 Tim. 1:13).

The next word is addressed to 'the penitent thief': 'Truly I tell you, today you will be with me in paradise' (Luke 23:43). We know that at first he was as hostile to Jesus as his fellow criminal (Mark 15:32). Clearly, then, some profound forces of spiritual renewal had been at work, and Jesus' own demeanour was probably one of them. No-one ever again came to faith in such circumstances. Here was a faith able to see the glory of Jesus at its most hidden, stripped not only of divine majesty but of human dignity: helpless, battered, bloodied, mortal, derided. The cross had blown away the faith of the disciples and killed their hopes. But this man, at the lowest point of Jesus' *kenōsis*, when the veil is thickest and the messianic identity most obscured, proclaims him king, and prays, 'Jesus, remember me when you come into your kingdom' (Luke 23:42).

Jesus, instantly alert, replies, 'I tell you the truth, today you will be with me in paradise' (Luke 23:43). These are words of profound import, for two reasons.

First, they make plain that at this point in his agony there is still a degree of calm in Jesus' soul. He has not yet reached the point where he feels forsaken by God. Instead, he is still confident of 'the joy set before him' (Heb. 12:2). Before the day is over, he will be in paradise. But there are greater depths of bitterness still to come.

Secondly, the words shed light on the question where Jesus was between his death and his resurrection. Discussion of this issue has been complicated by the statement of the Apostles' Creed that he descended into 'hell', a statement on which Calvin is surprisingly defensive, not only because of his respect for the creed but also because he views it as of central theological importance: 'If any persons have scruples about admitting this article into the Creed, it will soon be made plain how important it is to the sum of our redemption: if it is left out, much of the benefit of Christ's death will be lost.'[13]

When it comes to the meaning of the article, Calvin goes off in an unexpected direction. He dismisses the idea that 'hell' (*hades*) means merely the grave or the

---

13. *Institutes*, II:XVI, 8.

sepulchre. Why should the creed repeat in obscure language what it had already said so plainly in the statement that he was 'buried'? He also dismisses the idea that the language of the creed refers to Christ's descending to the limbo of the Fathers (*limbus patrum*): a place between heaven and hell where (according to Roman Catholic teaching) the righteous souls of the Old Testament were detained until, after his death, Christ went and preached to them the message of redemption. Calvin argues, instead, that the descent into hell took place *before* the death of Jesus. To the objection that this reverses the order of the creed, which mentions the descent *after* the burial, he replies that the first three details ('crucified, dead and buried') refer to what Christ suffered in the sight of men, whereas the descent into hell refers to what he suffered in the sight of God. This overlaps with another distinction, between what Christ suffered in his body and what he suffered in his soul. It is to the latter, according to Calvin, that the descent into hell refers: 'The point is, that we might know not only that Christ's body was given as the price of our redemption, but that he paid a greater and more excellent price in suffering in his soul the terrible torments of a condemned and forsaken man.'[14]

Calvin completes his interpretation by virtually identifying the descent into hell with the cry of dereliction, 'My God, my God, why have you forsaken me?' (Matt. 27:46). We shall return to this later. In the meantime we simply note that on this interpretation the descent into hell is perfectly consistent with his promise, 'today, you will be with me in paradise'. The descent refers to his suffering on the cross; paradise indicates his condition after it. The word 'paradise' occurs twice elsewhere in the New Testament. In Revelation 2:7 it is the location of the tree of life; in 2 Corinthians 12:4 it is the place to which Paul was 'caught up' to enjoy 'visions and revelations'. It was to this paradise, where one sees what no earthly eye can see, that Jesus would welcome 'the dying thief' before the day was done.

We must not forget, however, that in death the body of Christ was separated from his soul or spirit. His body continued under the power of death until the third day, although, as we have seen, the power of death over him was limited even then: his body suffered no decomposition. Yet for this brief interval, death and the grave held him, and held him publicly, for the whole moral universe to see. He not only died, but continued in the *state* of death for a time. He was clinically dead, his body inanimate and separated from his soul (although still united to his divine person; it is the body of the Son of God that lies in the grave). But while his body lay inert in the grave, his soul was in paradise, at rest,

14. *Institutes*, II:XVI, 10.

rejoicing in the approbation of the Father, adored by the angels, acclaimed by the redeemed and at perfect peace with the outcome of his mission.

'Woman, behold your son'

It was around this same time, and certainly before the ninth hour, that Jesus addressed his mother and the Apostle John (her nephew): "'Dear woman, here is your son," he said to his mother; and to the disciple, "Here is your mother." From that time on, [John] took [Mary] into his home' (John 19:26–27). The words lack the drama of Jesus' words to the 'dying thief', but they highlight, once again, his sensitivity to others, even at the height of his own pain. They also highlight one of the most striking human features of the passion narrative: the loyalty of the group of women who had followed him from Galilee 'to care for his needs' (Matt. 27:55). Here, at the end, according to John's account, there are four of them: Jesus' mother, Mary; her sister (possibly Salome), the wife of Zebedee and mother of the apostles James and John; Mary, the wife of Clopas; and Mary Magdalene. Earlier (Mark 3:31–35) Jesus had seemed to minimize the importance of family ties, yet here are his mother, his aunt and his cousin with him to the very last. The courage of the women is of the highest order. All the disciples had deserted Jesus and fled (Matt. 26:56), but the women remained; and though they initially watched 'from a distance' (Mark 15:40), as the end approaches they are standing 'near the cross' (John 19:25). For his mother, the pain must have been close to unendurable, yet she could not but watch.

On the face of things, the words reflect Jesus' natural solicitude for his mother, but Roman Catholic scholars have argued that they have a deeper, ecclesiological meaning. John, they say, is a symbol for the church and Jesus' words are an announcement that Mary is the mother of the church. Now that he is gone she is charged with caring for it, and the church, in turn, is charged with honouring her as a child would honour a parent.[15]

This is not an interpretation which would have occurred to the ordinary Christian reader. It savours, instead, of that impatience with the literal sense which bred a passion for allegory among pre-Reformation interpreters of Scripture. It is also a convenient alternative for those who question the factual historicity of this (and many other) portions of John's narrative and regard it as a creative supplement to the tradition. Yet history is what John purports to be narrating, and in its context the episode makes perfect psychological and

---

15. See, for example, Brown, *John (XIII – XXI)*, pp. 922–927.

cultural sense. Jesus has already shown his concern for the executioners and for the penitent criminal. It was only natural, then, that he should show at least equal concern for his mother, of whose substance he had been born, who had nourished and nurtured him in his tender years and who was now facing the intellectual, emotional and social cost of his disgraceful death. It may seem strange that Jesus entrusted her to his cousin, John, rather than to his brothers. But John was there; his brothers were not. Very likely they were still back home.

Besides, it is very likely that at this point his brothers still did not believe in him. He could be sure, however, of John, the beloved disciple. Mary, for her part, disappears into virtual obscurity. By the time John faced his own personal tribulations in Ephesus and Patmos she had probably passed away, but the excesses of Roman Catholic devotion must not blind us to all that we owe her. God had not asked her consent before enfleshing himself in her womb, but she had acquiesced meekly and reverently in what he had done. She had borne the disgrace of a 'scandalous' pregnancy, she had known the pain of labour as she had brought the Messiah into the world, she had had to flee as a refugee to Egypt, and she had had to take up residence in what was then the disreputable town of Nazareth. She had taught Jesus all that a child could learn at its mother's knee, including what the angel had told her as to his identity and his unique destiny. She had introduced him to the scriptures which had foretold that he must suffer many things before entering into his glory (Luke 24:26). She had borne faithful witness to him on such occasions as the wedding at Cana in Galilee. She had suffered as she saw him break taboos and offend the establishment. How often she must have wished that he could just be like other men and hold his peace! And now she stands by him in his final moments, steeling herself to gaze on that 'sacred head sore wounded'[16] and assuring him by her very presence that she, at least, was not ashamed.

The cry of dereliction

We return to the synoptic account. It is now the ninth hour, the land is still in darkness, and Jesus has reached the lowest point in his humiliation and the most awful moment of his agony. The physical pain is no worse than before, perhaps less, but his soul is in torment: 'My God, my God, why have you forsaken me?' (Matt. 27:46; Mark 15:34). The words are from Psalm 22, a reminder that what Jesus suffers was not without its parallels in the lives of prophets and patriarchs,

---

16. Hymn by anon, tr. Paul Gerhardt and James W. Alexander.

or even in the lives of Christian believers. But the parallels do not make for identity. Jesus stands where no-one ever stood before or since, knowing himself the bearer of the sin of the world, destined to pay the price for its redemption (Mark 10:45), and now drinking the bitterest dregs of the cup which had so discomposed him in Gethsemane. In its very nature, the spiritual content of this climax of his suffering is inaccessible to us. Even he himself had to appropriate the words of the psalmist, as if he could find no words of his own; and perhaps *no* human words could express what his 'hell' meant.

The most striking thing is the form of address: '*Eloi*' (this is Mark's Aramaic; Matthew gives the Hebrew '*Eli*'). This is the only occasion, even on the cross, when Jesus does not invoke God as 'Father'. In Gethsemane, for all its anguish, he had held fast to this: 'Abba, everything is possible for you' (Mark 14:36). Even in the moment of his immolation he retained this sense of his own divine sonship: '*Father*, forgive them, for they do not know what they are doing' (Luke 23:34). And by the end, after the dereliction, he has recovered it: 'Father, into your hands I commit my spirit' (Luke 23:46). Clearly, the forsakenness is only a moment in the long journey from the third to the ninth hour; for much of the time Jesus remained in communion with his Father. But now comes a moment of well-nigh unsustainable awfulness. Abba is out of reach, not listening. The intimacy is broken: an intimacy that had never been broken before. It was a breach for which nothing could have prepared Jesus. Like Abraham and Isaac going up to Mount Moriah (Gen. 22:2), Father and Son had gone up to Calvary together, and throughout his life Jesus had been assured that he was not alone, but that the Father was with him. Even at the cross, his Father, like his mother, had been there. But now, at the ninth hour, Abba was not there, and Jesus can say only 'Eloi!' God is certainly there, but not as Abba. There is now no sense of his own divine sonship, no sense of God's love and no sense of his Father's approval. God is not hearing him. He cries, but there is no answer, and God even seems to mock his trust (Ps. 22:8). Trouble is near, but there is no one to help (Ps. 22:11). There are no comfortable scriptures to fill his mind, nor any assurance of ultimate victory, nor any vision of a redeemed multitude too great to count. At every other time of crisis, Abba had spoken great words of encouragement: 'This is my son, whom I love' (Mark 1:11; 9:7). How he needed these words now! But no such words came. He hears only the derision of the spectators, the curses of the soldiers and the whispers of the Prince of Darkness. He is on his own.

But did the forsakenness involve more than loss and deprivation? It clearly did. In everything he saw around him, and everything he heard, there was the hand of God. It was the Father who was delivering him up (Rom. 8:32) and everything spoke of *his* anger. That anger was no additional fact or circumstance. It was *in* the circumstances: in the pain, in the loneliness, in Satan's whispers and in heaven's deafness; and under that anger his identity contracted to the point where the whole truth about him was that he was the sin of the world. He was carrying it, heaven held him answerable for it, and he *was* it. It was here, all of it, in his body (1 Pet. 2:24), being condemned in his flesh (Rom. 8:3); because of it he was a doomed and ruined man, *korban*, devoted to destruction. God's pure eyes could not look on him, nor heaven entertain his cry. 'Christ cried, "Is there not a word, dear Father, not a look?" And He answers, "No, not a look for a world."'[17]

Yet, somehow, there is no despair. Even at the lowest point, in the black hole of dereliction, faith and hope still breathe, as they must, for unbelief and despair are sin, and would have rendered his sacrifice void. Faith must walk where there is no light (Isa. 50:10). Even when Jesus cannot say 'Abba!', he can say 'Eloi', *my* God: the God he loves and serves and still, somehow, trusts. Maybe this is what he dreaded as he trembled in Gethsemane, that his mind would break in an unbearable anxiety of separation, when he realized that Abba was out of sight and out of hearing. But in the end, though hope may not burn, it flickers, even in the darkness.

Yet there is a 'why?'. It is not the 'why?' of protest or self-pity, but the 'why?' of the Righteous One, conscious of personal innocence and knowing that not even Holiness itself can find a spot in him. But it is also the 'why?' of a unique sufferer who has momentarily lost sight of the great divine purpose which his suffering was progressing, and asking, like the great Afro-American spiritual, 'Lord, how come me here?' Let us remember that Jesus' human mind was finite and that at any one moment he could be in possession of only some, not all, of the facts. Had the great mutual undertakings and promises of the covenant of redemption slipped out of his mind? Had he lost sight of what he had earlier known so clearly: that his life would be a ransom for many (Mark 10:45)? Had he forgotten that he had a future as well as a present, a rising again as well as a dying? Almost certainly, for a moment. All he 'knows' is that he is a 'worm and not a man' (Ps. 22:6); and his faith is a question, not an answer: 'why?'

Does the Father, too, suffer loss?

There remains the question whether there is anything in God the Father corresponding to the forsakenness of God the Son. Does the Father, too, suffer loss, or is the pain of Calvary confined entirely to the Son?

---

17. Rutherford, *Fourteen Communion Sermons*, p. 124.

Clearly, the unity of the divine Trinity remains unbroken throughout the passion. Even while the Father is angry with the Mediator, the Son is still the beloved and still fully involved in all the external acts (the *opera ad extra*) of the Trinity. Just as it was true that in his infancy he was still the eternal Logos, performing all his cosmic functions as the one in whom all things consist (Col. 1:17), so in the darkness and desolation of Golgotha he was still carrying the universe on his shoulders (Heb. 1:3). But this very fact of the trinitarian unity has profound implications for the traditional Christian doctrine of divine impassibility. If it is true at the human level that where one member of the church suffers all other members suffer with her, must the same not be true of the Trinity? The Son, we remember, is one and the same in substance (*homoousios*) with the Father. 'They' are not only generically identical, but numerically one. It is the one only and eternal God who is enfleshed in Jesus, the son of Mary of Nazareth; and though the Father is not the divine person who suffers on the cross, he is one with the sufferer, and must therefore suffer with him, though in his own way.

Besides, there is the fact of the *perichoresis*. Not only are God the Father and God the Son one and the same in substance and being, but they dwell in and around each other. The Father is in the Son and the Son in the Father (John 14:10; 17:21). The trinitarian persons are not three separate gods. On the contrary, where the One is, the Three are. The Three, then, are at Calvary, suffering not only *from* the sin of the world, but suffering *for* it. The Son's passion cannot be external to the Father and the Holy Spirit. They are in it, as they embrace and include the Son. The pain of the cross is the pain of the triune God.

This accords with the fact that it is to the love of the Father that the New Testament characteristically ascribes the work of atonement. This is clearly the message of John 3:16: 'God so loved the world that he gave his one and only Son.' The force of this passage clearly hinges on two facts: first, the divine identity of the crucified one; and, secondly, the divine identity of the one who delivered him up. It is the Lord of Glory, the beloved Son, who hangs on the cross; and it is the divine Father who has given him up. This, surely, implies that the Father bore, with the Son, the cost of our redemption? How, otherwise, could the cross be an exposition of *his* love? If he sacrificed his Son impassively, as a priest might sacrifice a pigeon, where is the sacrifice for *him*? And why does the New Testament so often express the relation between the Father and the Son in language reminiscent of Abraham sacrificing Isaac? Abraham was called to sacrifice his son, his only son, whom he loved (Gen. 22:2); God so loved the world that he gave *his* only Son (John 3:16; 1 John 4:9). Abraham did not spare his son, his only son (Gen. 22:16); God did not spare his own Son, but delivered him up for us all (Rom. 8:32).

In view of such echoes, we are surely justified in concluding that there was a continuity between the pain suffered by the human father and the pain suffered by the divine. Otherwise we are called to live lives of gratitude (Rom. 12:1) for a pity that cost God nothing: the Unmoved Mover was unmoved by the death of his Son on the cross.

The prophet Hosea offers another parallel to God's emotional involvement at Calvary. God is faced with the challenge of chastising Israel. She fully deserves it, but God hesitates:

> How can I give you up, Ephraim?
> How can I hand you over, Israel?

God is in turmoil. He cannot go through with it:

> My heart recoils within me;
> my compassion grows warm and tender.
> I will not execute my fierce anger;
> I will not again destroy Ephraim;
> for I am God and no mortal.
> (Hos. 11:8–9, NRSV)

'There was something holding Jehovah back from judgement,' wrote Dr. Campbell Morgan.[18] But what? His heart was turned over. It was in a state of upheaval, an upheaval of divine pity and sorrow. His compassions were kindled, convulsing: 'My compassions are in spasm,' is Campbell Morgan's paraphrase. It is a picture of love in agony.

All this is part of the wider post-Great War discourse on divine passibility,[19] and it is interesting to see Campbell Morgan unhesitatingly endorsing the sentiment that 'God is the chief Sufferer in the universe'.[20] He even quotes lines from the hymn 'There's a wideness in God's mercy':

---

18. G. Campbell Morgan, *Hosea: The Heart and Holiness of God* (London: Marshall, Morgan and Scott, n.d.), p. 129.
19. See, for example, J. K. Mozley, *The Impassibility of God: A Survey of Christian Thought* (Cambridge: Cambridge University Press, 1926).
20. Campbell Morgan, *Hosea*, p. 131.

There is no place where earth's sorrows
Are more felt than up in Heaven.[21]

But if the prospect of disciplining his wayward people caused God such angst, how could he have given up his Son to the cross with detachment and equanimity? Here, if anywhere, is love in agony. Here, if anywhere, is a sorrow keenly felt in heaven. And here, if anywhere, God is the chief sufferer.

But what loss could the Father have suffered in the forsakenness of the Son? The narrative offers no explicit answer, but the cry of dereliction itself presupposes a suspension in the ordinary intercourse between the Father and the Son. In the words of an interesting textual variant on Hebrews 2:9, Jesus tastes death 'without God' (*chōris theou*: a variant on *chariti theou*). They are 'not talking'. If the Son can no longer call God 'Abba', then, equally, the Father can no longer hear him speak in the accustomed terms of loving adoration. The intercourse between them is suspended, or at least limited to the Son's cry of lament; and it would break any father's heart.

And God's, too, if we are made in his image.

The last words

But the cry of dereliction was not to be Jesus' last word, nor was he to die forsaken; nor, yet again, in a state of exhausted weakness, his life ebbing slowly away. All three synoptists record that at the end Jesus cried out with a 'great' voice (Mark 15:37; Matt. 27:50; Luke 23:46), a sign that there was strength to the last. Neither Matthew nor Mark record what he actually said, but Luke does, and so, too, does John, though neither gives the full content of the cry.

John records but one word, *tetelestai*: 'It is finished' (John 19:30). The same word occurs a few verses earlier (v. 28) as part of John's own narrative: 'Later, knowing that everything *had now been finished*.' This was certainly part of what Jesus meant by his last cry. He had now completed every stage of his passion. But the reference is to more than the series of events which unfolded at Calvary. The *tetelestai* embraces his life's work and points to the completion of his mission. Now he can say, not proleptically, but as a matter of genuine accomplishment, 'I have completed the work you gave me to do' (John 17:4). He has drunk the cup and paid in full the ransom needed to redeem his people. He can say what the high priest of Judaism could never say, 'It's done! Finished! Nothing more

---

21. Frederick W. Faber, 1854.

is needed'. Now and for all time coming this one act of perfect obedience and sacrifice would determine humanity's relation to God.

And yet there is work to be done beyond the *tetelestai*. He has glorified the Father on earth, and in response the Father will glorify him (John 17:1); not, however, in order to an existence of self-indulgent ease, but so that, with all the new power and authority of his throne, he will continue his work as redeemer, giving eternal life to all those the Father has given him (John 17:2).

Luke omits the *tetelestai*, as he does the cry of dereliction. He does, however, record what were probably the last words spoken by Jesus on the cross, 'Father, into your hands I commit my spirit' (23:46). Here, again, Jesus uses one of the psalms (31:5) to express his own thoughts and feelings, but he modifies the original wording in two significant ways.

First, he changes the tense of the verb 'commit'. In the original, it is future: 'Into your hands I *will* commit my spirit'. The psalmist, praying to be saved from death, promises (himself?) that when death eventually comes he will commit his spirit into the hands of God. For Jesus, death is not future, but imminent. He is dying now; and in his dying moment he commits his spirit into the hands of God.

But quite apart from the tense, the verb used (*paratithēmi*) is significant in itself. It underlines the fact that Jesus dies voluntarily. He is not, like the psalmist, praying to be delivered from death. John uses the same verb (*paradidōmi*) that Paul uses when he speaks of God *delivering up* his own Son (John 19:30; Rom. 8:32). Jesus delivered up his spirit. The language here is reminiscent of Isaiah 53:12, 'he poured out his life unto death', and fully justifies Raymond E. Brown's comment, 'death does not come till he signifies his readiness'.[22]

The plain import of this is that Jesus himself decided when to stop breathing. Augustine exclaims in wonder:

> Who can thus sleep when he pleases, as Jesus died when He pleased? Who is there that thus puts off his garment when he pleases, as He put off His flesh at His pleasure? Who is there that thus departs when he pleases as He departed this life at His pleasure? How great the power, to be hoped for or dreaded, that must be his as judge, if such was the power he exhibited as a dying man![23]

Yet, as a man, Jesus had no absolute sovereignty over his own life, no inherent right to lay it down, and certainly no inherent right to squander it. His dying is

---

22. Brown, *John (XIII – XXI)*, p. 930.

23. Augustine, *Homilies on the Gospel of John*, Tractate CXIX, 6 (NPNF, vol. VII).

justified only as an act of obedience. It is through the Son's choice that the Father completes his own priestly action and delivers up his Son; as Calvin points out, this voluntariness, this willing self-offering, is a key element in the atoning significance of Christ: 'truly, even in death itself his willing obedience is the important thing because a sacrifice not offered voluntarily would not have furthered righteousness . . . no proper sacrifice could have been offered unless Christ, disregarding his own feelings, subjected and yielded himself wholly to his Father's will.'[24]

Jesus' second modification of the language of Psalm 31 is his use of the word 'Father': '*Father*, into your hands I commit my spirit.' In the original, the psalmist's address is to 'Yahweh, God of faithfulness'. At that stage in revelation, no individual Israelite ever addressed God as 'Father', but this is exactly what Jesus did, possibly using the Aramaic 'Abba', or a related term. What it underlines is that the moment of desolation is now past. Normal relations have been restored between the Father and the Son. No longer does God present himself merely as 'El', the eternal power and god-ness who finds sin repellent and cannot even acknowledge the cries of his sin-bearing Son. Now, once again, he is 'Abba', who loves him and is well, well pleased. The darkness is past, and the favour of his righteous Father shines once again and gives him peace. The spirit of Jesus is honoured to be welcomed into such hands, and the hands are honoured to receive such a precious spirit. The battle is over, the victory won, and Jesus dies calm, serene and triumphant.

These final utterances recorded by Luke and John are totally incompatible with the idea that after he breathed his last there lay before Jesus a hazardous descent into the underworld, there to complete his expiation of sin and his conquest of Satan. His dying completes his obedience, and his death, in and of itself, destroys the one who has the power of death (Heb. 2:14). The cross brings the triumph (Col. 2:15), and beyond it nothing more is required. He goes from Golgotha to paradise, into the arms of a proud and loving Father.

The piercing of Jesus' side

The crucifixion narrative is precisely that, a narrative, and though it presupposes a rationale for the death of Christ (a doctrine of the atonement) it does not itself provide it. It does, however, record three incidents which,

---

24. *Institutes*, II:XVI, 5.

while strictly historical, were also significant pointers to the meaning of Jesus' death.

First, the piercing of Jesus' side (John 19:34). The normal Roman practice was to allow the prisoner to die slowly, often over a period of days, and then to leave the bodies on the cross to be consumed by the vultures. To the Jews, however, this was abhorrent. The Torah laid down (Deut. 21:23) that a body must not hang on a tree overnight: 'Be sure to bury it that same day, because anyone who is hung on a pole is under God's curse.' In the case of Jesus, there was an additional factor: the following day (our Saturday) was a special (literally 'great') sabbath, the first day of the Feast of Unleavened Bread (Exod. 12:16). On such a day, more than ever, it was imperative that the land should not be defiled by a corpse hanging on a gibbet. The fact carries its own poignancy. Jesus had been born as 'the holy one' (Luke 1:35). Now, hanging on the cross, the Torah declared that he defiled the land. His body was the body of the Son of God, but now it was an accursed thing, and its visible presence near the holy city on such a special sabbath intolerable.

It is against this background that the Jewish leaders approached Pilate requesting that the three bodies be taken down. This meant that their deaths had to be hastened, and there was a routine procedure for this: smashing the legs of the victims with a heavy mallet (*crurifragium*). This quickly resulted in asphyxiation, the bodies having no purchase to enable them to breathe. When the soldiers came to Jesus, however, it appeared that he was already dead, surprisingly quickly, they thought. But just to make sure, one of them stabbed him with a spear; not just a prick, but forceful enough to cause a wound into which Thomas could later be invited to insert his hand (John 20:27).

There was an instant rush of blood. John, who was an eyewitness, not only records the fact, but does so with unusual solemnity: 'The man who saw it has given testimony, and his testimony is true. He knows that he tells the truth, and he testifies to it so that you also may believe' (John 19:35). The reason for such emphasis is clear: while the medical details are uncertain (the narrative does not even tell us which side was stabbed), the blood and water were clear proof that the body of Jesus was not, as the Docetists claimed, a mere appearance or phantom. It was a real body, and his death was a real death. For John, it was imperative to be absolutely clear on this. The saving power of Jesus' ministry lay not in his teaching, nor in his example, nor in his influence, but in his dying. The Lamb had to be slain (John 1:29; Rev. 5:6), and John wants us to be in no doubt that he *was* slain. He has redeemed us from our sins 'by his blood'. For John, no less than for Paul, it is the death of Jesus that secures our salvation. We wash our robes in the blood of the Lamb (Rev. 7:14).

The tearing of the curtain

The second incident which marks the death of Jesus is noted by all three synoptists: 'The curtain of the temple was torn in two from top to bottom' (Matt. 27:51; Mark 15:38; Luke 23:45). It is not clear which precise curtain is referred to. There were two, one protecting the holy place (which only the priests could enter), the other protecting the Most Holy Place (the Holy of Holies, accessible only to the high priest). The language of the Gospels does not by itself enable us to decide which of the two was meant, but when the writer to the Hebrews avails himself of similar symbolism (Heb. 9:7–8, 12) it is clear that what he is referring to is the Holy of Holies. Under the Levitical arrangements, the curtain signified that the Most Holy Place was so sacred that even the high priest could enter it only once a year, on the Day of Atonement (Yom Kippur). Now, however, following the sacrifice of Christ, the curtain is torn, the way is open, and every believer can enter the Holy of Holies by the 'new and living way' that he has opened for us through his flesh. And not only has he, our great high priest, gone through the veil, he has stayed in; and unlike the Levitical high priest, he has sat down, his work finished once and for ever, at the right hand of the Majesty on high (Heb. 1:3). The corollary of this is the priesthood of all believers. Each of us is entitled to approach the throne with confidence (Heb. 4:16) and when we approach it, the Son of God sits there before us, our friend at court, casting the lustre of his obedience and sacrifice over all who come in his name.

The earthquake

The third incident, the earthquake, is recorded only by Matthew: 'The earth shook, the rocks split and the tombs broke open. The bodies of many holy people [saints] who had died were raised to life' (Matt. 27:51–52). There can be no doubt that Matthew records the story as a historical event, and as such it is completely consonant with the biblical world-view. God has complete control over his creation: the darkness which had covered the land from the sixth to the ninth hour is witness to that, as is the Old Testament account of the sun standing still (Josh. 10:13) and, indeed, Jesus' own action in stilling the storm on the Sea of Galilee (Mark 4:35–41). Later, in the book of Acts, an earthquake will be one of a chain of divinely ordered events leading to the conversion of the Philippian jailer (Acts 16:26). Here, in Matthew's account of the crucifixion, the earthquake, like the earlier darkness, signals the extraordinary nature of what is happening at Calvary. The cross will have veritably seismic consequences not only for the human race, but for the whole cosmos.

The splitting of the rocks is a natural consequence of the earthquake, and the opening of the tombs a natural consequence of the splitting of the rocks, but there is some uncertainty as to the precise sequence of events. Did those who rose from the tombs appear in Jerusalem immediately, or was their appearance deferred till after Jesus' resurrection? The latter is more likely, and totally consistent with the text. But the uncertainty does not affect the essential symbolism. Christ, by dying, has conquered death, and now, as the crucified Messiah, possesses the keys of death and Hades (Rev. 1:18). Here, in the immediate aftermath of Jesus' death, is a foretaste of what will happen at the end: 'a time is coming when all who are in their graves will hear his voice and come out' (John 5:28–29).

The rent veil points to Jesus as the way; the open tombs point to him as the life.

Resurrection

The day ends with the burial of Jesus (Mark 15:42–47): the last word, surely, and the end of Jesus' story. But none of the Gospels ends with the cross. God has yet another word to speak: 'He has risen! He is not here. See the place where they laid him' (Mark 16:6).

From a literary point of view the most striking feature of the resurrection narrative is the prominence it gives to the women: Mary Magdalene, Salome and Mary, the mother of James the younger (Mark 16:1). It is hard to imagine any creator of myth or legend choosing these as the first witnesses to the risen Jesus. The prevailing culture was highly patriarchal, even to the extent that the testimony of a woman was inadmissible in a Jewish court of law. In the case of Mary Magdalene her credibility was further prejudiced by her medical history. She was one of those whom Jesus had cured of evil spirits (Luke 8:2), yet it was to her that the risen Jesus spoke his first word, and that first word was 'woman' (*gynē*): 'Woman, why are you crying?' (John 20:13). Nothing but the fact that this is how it actually happened can explain the choice of such witnesses; the supreme instance, perhaps, of the foolishness of God (1 Cor. 1:25). They would literally have been laughed out of court.

Yet the narrative exudes authenticity. The women had noted where Jesus was laid (Mark 15:47) and the very devotion that had taken them to Jerusalem in the first place now impelled them to perform one last office, the anointing of his body. The sentiment was scarcely rational: Joseph and Nicodemus had already lavished myrrh and aloes on Jesus' body (John 19:39), though the women may not have known this. Besides, any anointing assumed that Jesus' death was just like any other death, ignoring his own clear prediction that he would rise within three days.

But it would be churlish to criticise them. Like the woman who poured perfume over Jesus' head (Mark 14:3), they did what they could. They had to control their impatience till the sabbath was past, but as soon as that moment came they headed into town to buy the spices. Then there was a further delay. They cannot go to the tomb in the darkness, partly because they shrink from handling a dead body in pitch blackness, and partly because it would be difficult to carry out the anointing without light. But as soon as the sun rises off they go. And then they remember the stone. Who will roll it away? They have no idea, but they press on regardless. Something will turn up. When they get there, the stone has already been rolled away, but as they enter the tomb they see a terrifying sight: a figure in white, seated. He tries to calm their fears, pointing to the place where the body of Jesus had lain. There is nothing there. 'He's not here! He's risen!' They flee, terror-struck; and with that word Mark ends his Gospel.

It is, surely, the most remarkable ending in the history of literature: *ephobounto gar*, 'for they were afraid'. Enigmatic though it is, it strikes a keynote. In the resurrection we are in the presence of the uncanny; of the irreducibly holy; of that for which we can offer no explanation. Instinct flees.

But for our present purpose, focused as we are on the cross, what matters is that here we have the ultimate affirmation of the divine sonship of Jesus. To see its full significance, however, we need to keep our eyes firmly on what went before. Not only was Jesus crucified, he was crucified as a blasphemer, and the whole point of his execution, as far as the Jewish authorities were concerned, was to discredit him finally and for ever. His messianic claims were buried with him.

But if so, they also rose with him. The pre-Easter claim of 'the blasphemer' was 'visibly and unambiguously confirmed by the God of Israel': the very God he had allegedly blasphemed.[25] Now he is, 'My Lord and my God!' (John 20:28).

What does all this mean for our understanding of the cross? Fundamentally, that we approach the task of interpretation from the high vantage-point of the resurrection. The one between the two thieves is God's beloved Son. But this creates its own anomaly. What is *he* doing there?

---

25. Wolfhart Pannenberg, *Jesus: God and Man* (London: SCM Press, 1968), p. 67.

3. THE DIVINE PARADOX: THE CRUCIFIED SON

As we stand back to reflect on the finished story of the passion, two facts strike us immediately.

First, Christ suffered the penalty due to sin. This is not a mere theory. Even less does such a statement by itself make the sufferings of Christ more horrific than they really were. The sufferings are a fact, and no theory can either add to them or subtract from them. But in terms of the biblical world-view the penal nature of his suffering is also a fact. Christ died, and as far as the human species is concerned, death is penal. The clearest statement of this is in Romans 6:23, 'the wages of sin is death', but it is a recurring theme, indeed an axiom, throughout Scripture. When God first revealed his will to the human race and warned Adam and Eve not to eat the fruit of the tree of the knowledge of good and evil, he issued a clear warning: 'when you eat from it, you will certainly die' (Gen. 2:17). This is the background to Paul's treatment of the parallel between the first Adam and the Last Adam in Romans 5:12–21. Death entered the world through sin (v. 12);[1] the many died through the trespass of the one (v. 15); death reigned by the trespass of one man (v. 17); and sin reigned in death (v. 21).

---

1. That is, as far as the human species is concerned. Assuming that the fossil record gives an authentic picture of species which existed before the creation of man, death was clearly a fact in the animal and plant kingdoms from the very beginning.

This is a matter on which the Christian canon is unambiguous. Death is the curse pronounced on sin. It follows from this that the question whether Christ's sufferings were penal immediately becomes a factual, not a theological, one. Did he receive the wages of sin? The answer has to be a categorical 'Yes!'

The second thing that strikes us is that in the overall context of the Gospel narratives, the sufferings of Christ were utterly anomalous; so much so that in themselves they almost defy explanation.

There are in fact three anomalies. The first derives from the sinlessness of Christ. Here again the biblical witness is unambiguous. He was human, and he was tempted, but he was without sin (Heb. 4:15). Paul describes him as one who 'had no sin' (2 Cor. 5:21), and he himself lays down the challenge, 'Can any of you prove me guilty of sin?' (John 8:46). Why then, if innocent, does this man receive the wages of sin? How can the curse fall where it is not deserved?

The second anomaly is that this man, suffering on the cross the wages of sin, is the Son of God:

> Who is he on yonder tree
> Dies in grief and agony?
> 'Tis the Lord, O wondrous story!
> 'Tis the Lord, the King of glory![2]

What is *he* doing here, hanging between two felons, his life-blood ebbing away? How can the eternal Logos, who in the beginning was with God, and was God – how can he now be reaping the bitter harvest of sin?

But there is a third, and even deeper, anomaly: the involvement of God the Father. As we have already seen, this is the burden of such passages as John 3:16 and Romans 8:32; and Isaiah had already foretold that the Lord would bruise his Servant and make his life a guilt-offering (Isa. 53:10). Nor was this merely a matter of eternal divine foreordination, though it was certainly that: he died by God's 'deliberate plan and foreknowledge' (Acts 2:23). There was also a much more direct involvement on the part of the Father, fully justifying the language used by many of our greatest hymnwriters as they reflect on him 'who did not spare his own Son, but gave him up for us all'.

Not everyone, however, has seen the part played by God the Father through the lenses of such adoration. On the contrary, it is on this point that recent critics of the Christian doctrine of atonement have been most virulent. Chalke and Mann gave the criticism its headline, charging evangelicals with portraying

---

2. From 'Who is he in yonder stall', Benjamin Handy, 1833–67.

the cross as 'a form of cosmic child abuse',[3] but similar criticism has also come in more serious vein via the wider feminist critique of patriarchy and its associated abuse of women and children. Joanne Carlson Brown and Rebecca Parker, for example, claim that 'Christian theology with atonement at the center still encourages martyrdom and victimization'; lament that 'divine child abuse is paraded as sacrifice'; and complain that 'to argue that salvation can only come through the cross is to make God a divine sadist and a divine child abuser'.[4]

For all the extreme, headline-grabbing, nature of the language, however, there is nothing particularly modern in such criticisms. As long ago as the twelfth century, Peter Abelard laid down the challenge: 'How did the death of his innocent Son so please God the Father that through it he should be reconciled to us?' And he went on:

> Indeed, how cruel and wicked it seems that anyone should demand the blood of an innocent person as the price for anything, or that it should in any way please him that an innocent man should be slain – still less that God should consider the death of his Son so agreeable that by it he should be reconciled to the whole world![5]

A real problem

Yet such criticisms, whether from the twelfth or the twenty-first centuries, perform one invaluable service: they remind us that there is a real problem at the heart of the story of the cross. We cannot walk blithely by it as if there were nothing disturbing here. There is; and if we are not initially shocked and repelled by it, we shall never understand it. It has to be a 'scandal' before it can become good news. Why is the Son of God hanging on that tree? Does God know? And if he does, why does he permit it? And why does he even leave himself open to the suspicion of being responsible for it? There is no way we can observe what is going on here and simply conclude, what a wonderful

---

3. Stephen Chalke and Alan Mann, *The Lost Message of Jesus* (Grand Rapids: Zondervan, 2003), p. 182.

4. Joanne Carlson Brown and Rebecca Parker, 'For God So Loved the World', in Joanne Carlson Brown and Carole R. Bohn (eds.), *Christianity, Patriarchy and Abuse* (New York: The Pilgrim Press, 1989), pp. 3, 2, 23.

5. For an introduction to Abelard, see Eugene R. Fairweather, *A Scholastic Miscellany; Anselm to Ockham*, Library of Christian Classics (London: SCM Press, 1956), pp. 276–299. The quotations are from p. 283.

demonstration of love! Love to whom? Love to the Son, crushed by it? Or love
to us, seeking our own love in return? How could we love someone who for no
compelling reason sacrificed his own Son?

We need a doctrine of the cross which faces up realistically to the enormity
of the Father's involvement at Calvary. Why did God do this – *have* to do this
– to his Son?

The first response to the criticisms of Brown, Parker and others must be
to concede at once the justice of the feminist protest against patriarchy. From
time immemorial, men have dominated, subjugated, oppressed and exploited
women; and Christian men have not been guiltless. Too often the idea of male
'headship' (Eph. 5:23) has been taken as warrant for husbands to claim unchal-
lengeable authority over their wives and children; sometimes appeal has even
been made to 'order' and subordination in the Trinity (the Father first, the Son
second, the Spirit third) as warrant for a similar order in gender relations.[6] Yet,
far from being well grounded in the scriptures, such inequality is a clear violation
of the order God established at creation, when the woman, no less than the
man, was made in the image of God and given a full share in the mandates to
subdue the earth and to rule, serve and protect the ecosystem (Gen. 1:28; 2:15).
Patriarchy also violates the pattern set by Jesus. As we have already seen, the
first word spoken by the risen Christ was 'woman', and the first thing he said
was, 'Why are you crying?' (John 20:15). Is this symbolic: a reflection of the
Lord's compassion for the weeping women of the world? Throughout his
ministry, Jesus moved easily among women and uniformly treated them with
the utmost respect. For example, he engaged the woman of Samaria in a
profound theological conversation (John 4:7–26); allowed Mary of Bethany
to sit at his feet, the position usually taken by the (male) students of a rabbi;
and, most remarkably of all, chose women as the first human heralds of his
resurrection.

---

6. According to Wayne Grudem, for example, while the Son and the Holy Spirit
   are equal in deity to the Father, they are subordinate in their roles, and this
   subordination is to be reflected in human relationships, particularly in gender
   relations: 'Just as God the Father has authority over the Son, though the two are
   equal in deity, so in a marriage, the husband has authority over the wife, though
   they are equal in personhood.' (*Systematic Theology: An Introduction to Biblical Doctrine*
   [Leicester: IVP, 1994], pp. 249, 459). *Prima facie*, at least, it is hard to reconcile such
   role-subordination with the language of the Athanasian Creed (25, 26): 'And in this
   trinity none is before, or after; none is greater, or less. But the whole three persons
   are co-eternal and co-equal.'

But if there is nothing in the example of Jesus to justify patriarchal oppression or child abuse, is it conceivable that it might find some justification in the story of the cross? This would be the moral influence theory of the atonement in reverse: the *im*moral influence of the cross. But it beggars belief that believers have ever taken the story of Calvary as authority for abusing a child or its mother, any more than they have taken the story of Abraham sacrificing Isaac (Gen. 22:1–19) as warrant for child sacrifice. It is precisely those most likely to glory in the cross who would have shuddered to adopt a sovereign, once-for-all priestly act of transcendent deity as the model for human parenting.

Jesus did indeed suffer under a patriarchal system of justice. All the leading agents in his condemnation, from Pilate to Judas Iscariot, were men. In the process, human justice (patriarchal justice) was exposed as a system which operated through treachery, perjury, cruelty and corruption. It was satanic: an instance of the one who had the 'power of death' (Heb. 2:14) exercising his power through a patriarchal judicial system stamped with his own image. But it was the very injustice of the judicial condemnation which destroyed the foundations of Satan's kingdom. Only by an unjust sentence could Christ have died, and without his death there could have been no redemption. But at the same time, the judgment passed on Jesus is also a judgment passed on Pontius Pilate; and as such it places every human justice system in the dock.

Child abuse?

But what of the more specific claim that the cross is an example of 'child abuse' (the adjective 'cosmic' is quite redundant here, since it was not the cosmos, but God the Father, who was allegedly guilty of abuse). The charge is completely inept, because it isolates the story of the crucifixion from the total New Testament witness to Jesus.

It ignores, for example, the fact that for most of his life Jesus enjoyed the love, protection and encouragement of his heavenly Father. This is why he was able to live a life free from anxiety, confident that he was never alone (John 8:16) but that God was always within earshot; and this is why, too, he could say it was his meat and drink to do the will of the one who had sent him (John 4:34). An abused and damaged child he was not.

Similarly, the charge wilfully ignores the obvious fact that at the time of the alleged 'abuse' Jesus was not a child, but a mature adult, able to make his own free choices and willing to take responsibility for them. From this point of view, and even at its grimmest, the cross no more amounts to child abuse than did the action of the British government in dropping grown men and women behind enemy lines as agents of the Special Operations Executive during the Second World War. Like them, Jesus was a volunteer. Once in the world, he had freely chosen the path that led to Calvary (Phil. 2:8), and, equally freely, he had resolved to lay down his life for his friends (John 15:13). In accordance with this, he made no attempt to escape when the arresting party approached, even though he had often evaded his enemies before. He says simply, 'Shall I not drink the cup the Father has given me?' (John 18:11).

Even more glaringly, the child-abuse charge ignores the clear New Testament witness to the unique identity of Jesus. Not only was he not a child; he was not a mere human. He was God: the eternal Logos, the divine Son, the Lord before whom every knee will one day bow (Phil. 2:10). This is no helpless victim. This is the Father's equal. This is one who in the most profound sense is one with God; one in whom God judges himself, one in whom God condemns himself, one in whom God lets himself be abused. The critics cannot be allowed the luxury of a selective use of the New Testament. It is the very same scriptures which portray the cross as an act of God the Father which also portray the sufferer as God the Son, and the resulting doctrine cannot be wrenched from its setting in the Christian doctrine of the Trinity. The 'abused child' is 'very God of very God'. It is divine blood that is shed at Calvary (Acts 20:28) as God surrenders himself to the worst that man can do and bears the whole cost of saving the world.

Yet Jesus is never, not even for a moment, man's helpless victim. He is indomitable in his Spirit-filled humanity; and when he completes his mission by giving up his Spirit, God, the allegedly 'abusive' Father, exalts him to the highest place, commands every knee to bow and orders the entire universe to confess him Lord of all (Phil. 2:9–11).

The Father's involvement

But what can we say as to the precise nature of the Father's action at Calvary? The New Testament answer is breathtaking. He acted in the role of priest. Just as Jesus 'gave' his life a ransom for many (Mark 10:45) so God the Father 'gave' his one and only Son; just as Christ 'delivered up' himself as a fragrant offering (Eph. 5:2) so God the Father 'delivered up' his own Son (Rom. 8:32). Clearly, then, corresponding to the priesthood of the self-giving Son there is a priesthood of God the Father. From this point of view, Golgotha becomes his temple, where, far from abusing a child or sadistically inflicting cruelty, he is engaged in the most solemn business that earth can witness. He is offering a sacrifice. The cross is his altar, and his own Son the sacrifice.

The evidence that Jesus and his apostles understood the cross in terms of sacrifice is overwhelming. There is something deeper here, however, than the struggle of bewildered disciples to find concepts by which to explain the tragedy which had overtaken their master. It was not human ingenuity that discovered in the Old Testament sacrifices an interpretative framework for the cross. On the contrary, God himself had provided that framework. In the order of knowing, the Levitical sacrifices came before the sacrifice of Calvary; but in the order of being, the sacrifice of Christ came first. He was the Lamb ordained before the foundation of the world, and the Levitical system was but his shadow. We need to be careful here. Christ was not a priest only metaphorically. He was the true priest, and his sacrifice the real sacrifice. It was the Aaronic priesthood that was figurative, and its sacrifices that were metaphorical. Just as Jesus was 'the Root of David' (Rev. 5:5), so he was the root of the Passover, the sin offering and the scapegoat, all of which were divinely configured to prefigure him. The understanding of Jesus' death as a sacrifice is not a human convention, but a divine revelation.

Even the sacrificial rituals which featured so prominently in non-Jewish religions were pointing in the same direction. Every Gentile city had its temple, its priests and its sacrifices, and these clearly sprang from that 'seed of religion' which, as Calvin suggested, God has planted in every human heart.[7] The human species never loses its fear of the judgment of God (Rom. 1:32) and the blood which flowed in pagan temples was tribute to that. When the apostles used sacrificial terminology in preaching the gospel they knew they were using concepts which Corinthians and Ephesians would instantly understand. They might think it ridiculous that a crucified Jew should be proclaimed as the atoning sacrifice for the sins of the world, but they knew, instantly, what the concept meant.

We have already noticed that at the Last Supper Jesus represented himself both as the Passover lamb and as the covenant sacrifice ('this is my blood of the covenant', Mark 14:24). The same sacrificial connotation is implied in Jesus' reference to the bread and wine as symbolizing his 'body' and 'blood', the two component parts of the bodies of sacrificial animals. But long before the Last Supper, John the Baptist had already pointed to Jesus as 'the Lamb of God, who takes away the sin of the world!' (John 1:29). John himself, as the son of a priest, would have been familiar with sacrificial ideas and fully aware of the daily, weekly, monthly and annual rituals involving the slaughter of sacrificial lambs. Questions have been asked as to how John could have arrived so early at such an understanding of Jesus, especially as the idea of a suffering Messiah

---

7. *Institutes*, I:IV, 1.

was no part of Jewish expectation. Even Jesus' disciples were taken aback when he predicted his own sufferings and death (Mark 8:32–33). But John, Jesus' cousin, may have gathered this insight from conversations with Jesus himself, and it is clear that from the very beginning Jesus anticipated that his end would be violent (Mark 2:20). It is also entirely possible that John, like the Ethiopian chancellor, had wondered to whom Isaiah was referring when he spoke of the Servant being 'led like a lamb to the slaughter' (Acts 8:32–35; Isa. 53:7); and through such musings he may well have come to a much deeper understanding than was prevalent among his contemporaries. But the main consideration, surely, is that John was a prophet (indeed, the greatest among the prophets, Matt. 11:11), and as such enjoyed, like Peter later, an insight which only divine revelation could have given him.

Attempts to link the phrase, 'the Lamb of God', to specific Old Testament texts have been unconvincing, not because there are no relevant texts but because we cannot be sure that any one of them was present to John's mind as he spoke. Isaiah, as we have seen, refers to the Servant being led like a lamb to the slaughter, but although this clearly highlights his sacrificial suffering (and his meekness) it does little to explain in what sense Jesus was the lamb 'of God'. What is clear, taking account of the completed canon, is that Jesus was the lamb *foreordained* by God: 'foreknown', as Peter points out, before the foundation of the world (1 Pet. 1:20, ESV). From this point of view, this particular lamb was central and foundational to the divine plan from all eternity. Other sacrifices, both pagan and Levitical, are but shadows of his, and reflect but dimly that atoning reality which God had proposed from all eternity to enact on the cross of Calvary. The Lamb of God is the *one* lamb: the real, substantive, once-for-all sacrifice for sin.

Linked to this is the fact that Jesus is the lamb *provided* by God, and this takes us back to the words spoken by Abraham to Isaac as they went up together to Mount Moriah. 'Where is the lamb for the burnt-offering?' asked Isaac (Gen. 22:7). 'God himself will provide the lamb, my son,' replied the patriarch, and when the trial of his faith and commitment were over, he named the place, *Yahweh yireh*, 'The LORD Will Provide' (Gen. 22:14). This takes us close to the heart of the paradox of Calvary. God requires the lamb; God provides it; and God offers it. But he provides it not from outside of himself, but from within: from within offended deity. He spares not his own Son (Rom. 8:32). The Son of God becomes the Lamb of God.

The Baptist describes him as 'bearing away' the sin of the world: putting a distance between the world and its sin in a manner reminiscent of the scapegoat, which on the Day of Atonement carried all the sins of the people to a solitary place in the distant desert (Lev. 16:22). This is the clear import of the verb *aireō* in John 1:29, but in order to be carried *away* the burden must first be *carried*. This is why in the Septuagint version of Isaiah 53:4 the verb is not *airein* but simply *pherein*: 'he carries our sins'. Although this is an imprecise translation of the Hebrew overall (what the Servant carries, literally, is not our 'sins' but our 'infirmities'), the idea of bearing or carrying sin is prominent in the Old Testament, where it clearly means bearing the guilt of sin, answering for it or suffering its consequences. Leviticus 5:1, for example, lays down that if a witness refuses to testify 'he shall bear his iniquity' (ESV: NIV, 'will be held responsible'). Similarly, anyone who commits incest will bear their iniquity (Lev. 20:19–20). In this light, the words of the Baptist in John 1:29 can only mean that Christ bears away the sin of the world by taking responsibility for it, suffering for it and, eventually, dying for it. He is, uniquely and archetypically, the sin-bearing Lamb.

Jesus also appears as the Lamb in 1 Peter 1:19, where redemption is attributed to 'the precious blood of Christ, a lamb without blemish or defect'. The language is clearly sacrificial, recalling the Levitical stipulation that every gift or burnt-offering presented to Yahweh had to be without defect (Lev. 22:19), and there was a similar instruction with respect to the Passover lamb (Exod. 12:5). As with so many of the seminal theological statements of the New Testament, Peter's concern here is primarily ethical, not doctrinal: what he wants to drive home is the importance of living our lives in this world as pilgrims characterized by reverent fear of our heavenly Father. But the way he reinforces the lesson is by reminding us of the cost of redemption: not silver and gold, but the precious blood of this unique sacrifice.

A similar link between the Lamb and blood appears in Revelation 5:6, where we find the shocking image of the slaughtered lamb standing in the centre of the throne. In this passage, the word for 'lamb' is not the usual *amnos*, but the diminutive *arnion*, which John regularly uses in the Apocalypse. Though the distinction between the two words was somewhat eroded by this time, it may still contain here a hint of 'a little lamb', to heighten the contrast between what John actually saw and what the elder had led him to expect. He was expecting to see a lion, the 'Lion of the tribe of Judah' (Rev. 5:5), but when he looked, what he saw was a little lamb; and though the Lamb stands, erect and majestic, there are unmistakeable signs that he has been sacrificed.

John had seen him on the cross; now he sees him on the throne. The victim reigns, and instead of a chorus of derision there is now a great symphony of adoration (Rev. 5:9–14). And at the heart of the chorus, a glorious proclamation that it was the *blood* of the Lamb that secured redemption:

> You are worthy to take the scroll
>   and to open its seals,

because you were slain
> and with your blood you purchased for God
> persons from every tribe and language and people and nation.
(Rev. 5:9)

John had already made this very point in his opening doxology, 'To him who loves us and has freed (lit., 'loosed') us from our sins by his blood' (Rev. 1:5). In Ephesians 1:7 Paul likewise declares that we have redemption 'through his blood'; in Romans 3:25 he describes Christ Jesus as an expiatory sacrifice (*hilastērion*) 'through his blood'; and in Ephesians 2:13, he declares that we have been 'brought near' by the blood of Christ. In Ephesians 5:2, he uses generic sacrificial terminology: constrained by his love, Christ gave himself up for us as 'a fragrant offering and sacrifice to God'. The word 'offering' (*prosphora*) is a comprehensive term for any gift brought to God, but the accompanying word, *thysia*, refers to a 'bloody oblation', an animal which had been slaughtered (from the verb, *thyein*, to kill) and placed on the altar (*thysiastērion*).

Such examples could be multiplied, but this emphasis on blood has proved repugnant to many sectors of modern theology, ill at ease with what they see as a primitive, sub-ethical concept of religion. Even in the nineteenth century the New Testament scholar B. F. Westcott offered a sanitized version, arguing that blood, as used in this context, pointed not to death but to life:[8] life released and made available to others, who appropriate it through faith. This provoked James Denney to pronounce that, 'a more groundless fancy never haunted and troubled any part of Scripture',[9] but others were glad to follow Westcott's lead, and his idea has proved remarkably durable.[10]

---

8. Brooke Foss Westcott, *The Epistle to the Hebrews: The Greek Text with Notes and Essays* (London: Macmillan, 1889), pp. 293–295.

9. James Denney, *The Death of Christ*, ed. R. V. G. Tasker (London: Tyndale Press, 1951 [1902]), p. 149.

10. See, for example, C. H. Dodd, *The Epistle of Paul to the Romans* (London: Collins [Fontana], 1959), p. 72; and, more recently, Lorraine Cavanagh, *Making Sense of God's Love: Atonement and Redemption* (London: SPCK, 2011), p. 38. The same point of view is reflected in the article on *haima* ('blood') in *TDNT* (vol. 1, pp. 172–176): 'The early Christian representation of the blood of Christ is simply the metaphorical garment clothing the thought of the self-offering, the obedience to God, which Christ demonstrated in the crucifixion.' For an evangelical response see A. M. Stibbs, *The Meaning of the Word 'Blood' in Scripture* (London: Tyndale Press, 1947), and Leon Morris, *The Apostolic Preaching of the Cross* (2nd ed., London: Tyndale Press, 1960), pp. 108–124.

We must be careful not to ignore the truth contained in this position. Christ did indeed surrender the whole of his life to God, and he was clear about this from the first: 'I have come down from heaven not to do my will but to do the will of him who sent me' (John 6:38). His whole existence was one of obedience, and this obedience was central to its atoning significance. John Murray even argues that 'obedience' is the most inclusive rubric related to the atonement, and that all other categories such as sacrifice and redemption may be comprehended under it: 'The Scripture regards the work of Christ as one of obedience and uses this term, or the concept that it designates, with sufficient frequency to warrant the conclusion that obedience is generic and therefore embracive enough to be viewed as the unifying or integrative principle.'[11]

This is certainly the perspective from which Paul views the work of Christ in Romans 5:12–19, where the *disobedience* of the first Adam is expiated by the *obedience* of the Last. We cannot, however, separate the obedience of Christ from his sacrifice, nor his sacrifice from his dying. As we are reminded in Philippians 2:8, he obeyed even to the extent of dying, which clearly implies that the obedience required of Jesus consisted of more than living a self-denying, self-limiting and self-sacrificing life. He had to lay down his life. He had to die; this was a command he had received from the Father (John 10:17). However important, then, the saving significance of the life of Christ, it is clear that he came into the world not only to dedicate, but to 'pour out', his life. His obedience had to culminate in the supreme sacrifice: the literal, physical shedding of his blood. He had come not only to be the priest, but to be the sacrifice.

The references to his blood are clear evidence of that. There can be little doubt that, away from ritual and sacrifice, blood in the Old Testament (as in most other cultures) pointed to a violent death. When, for example, Macbeth cried,

> Will all great Neptune's ocean wash this blood
> Clean from my hands?
> (*Macbeth*, Act 2:2)

he was clearly referring to the guilt he bears for the death of Duncan. Similarly, when the blood of Abel cried out to the Lord from the ground, the clear implication is that his death cried out to be avenged (Gen. 4:10); and when God decreed, 'Whoever sheds the blood of man, by man shall his blood be shed'

---

11. John Murray, *Redemption Accomplished and Applied* (Grand Rapids: Eerdmans, 1955), p. 19.

(Gen. 9:6), the reference, plainly, is to homicide and its corollary, the death-sentence. The same principle underlies Numbers 35:33, 'Bloodshed [ESV: 'blood'] pollutes the land, and atonement cannot be made for the land on which blood has been shed, except by the blood of him who shed it.' It would be absurd to suggest in such an instance that atonement would be made by a life dedicated to service.

Support for Westcott's understanding of blood is sometimes derived from Leviticus 17:11, 'the life of the flesh is in the blood' (NRSV). This, it is argued, links blood to life, not to death. But in this same context the blood that makes atonement is not blood as such, but blood sprinkled against the altar: the blood, in other words, of a slaughtered animal, deprived of its life. This is the very point made in Hebrews 9:22: 'without the *shedding* of blood there is no forgiveness'.

This is particularly noteworthy since Hebrews is the only New Testament book which specifically refers to Christ as a priest, and in doing so it specifically links his priesthood to blood and sacrifice. The writer draws heavily on the Levitical arrangements, clearly regarding them as prefiguring the work of Christ, but at the same time he underlines clear contrasts between the Aaronic priest-hood and that of Christ. For one thing, whereas the Aaronic order had to repeat its rituals, day after day, year after year, Christ's sacrifice availed once for all, making his people perfect for ever. For another, while the Aaronic high priest entered only the earthly, man-made sanctuary (a mere copy of the true one), Christ entered heaven itself (Heb. 9:24). And while the Levitical offerings could secure only an outward, temporary, ceremonial cleanness, and only a ritual purity (Heb. 9:13), Christ has effected a real purification (Heb. 1:3) and secured an eternal redemption and a perfect holiness (Heb. 9:12).

But all these contrasts rest on an even more fundamental one: the blood they brought, respectively, into the Most Holy Place. The one went in bearing blood that was not his own, but the blood of a dumb animal. The other entered 'by his own blood' (Heb. 9:12); and here the writer makes the link between sacrifice and death absolutely clear: just as man is destined 'to *die* once . . . so Christ was *sacrificed* once to take away the sins of many' (Heb. 9:28). To die and to be sacrificed are synonymous; or, as Leon Morris puts it, 'sacrifice is inherently the destruction of the victim'.[12]

In reality, then, Westcott's theory as to the meaning of 'blood' is, as Denney recognized, no more than a misguided attempt to deflect criticism from the New Testament's stress on the death of Christ. The apostles, by contrast, leave

---

12. Morris, *The Apostolic Preaching of the Cross*, p. 116.

us in no doubt that it was by dying that Christ redeemed us. This is why the Gospels give such prominence to the story of the passion, and in doing so they reflect the importance assigned to his dying by Jesus himself. As we have seen, he had deliberately stressed that the grain of wheat could bear fruit only if it died (John 12:24); and following Peter's confession at Caesarea Philippi, he had made plain, to the acute distress of the disciples, that his death was an inescapable part of his mission, and that behind it there lay a divine necessity: 'the Son of Man *must* suffer many things . . . and *must* be killed' (Mark 8:31).

It was in accordance with this that in instituting the Lord's Supper Christ specifically placed his death at the very heart of this central Christian rite. Not only did the sacrament highlight, in its core symbolism, the shedding of his blood, it was to be an enduring commemoration and proclamation of his death (1 Cor. 11:25–26); and it was for this death, so proclaimed, that the breaking of bread was to be a recurring moment of eucharist.

From a human point of view this emphasis on the cross is baffling. Every prudential consideration suggested that these first Christian preachers should divert attention from it as much as possible. To Jewish ears, the idea of a crucified Messiah was a contradiction in terms. To Gentiles, the claim that the salvation of the world had come through a crucified Jewish criminal was an absurdity. To both Jew and Gentile, the suggestion that death, particularly death on a cross, could bring eternal life, was blasphemous idiocy; had the early church had a professional director of communications, he would have said, categorically, 'We don't do the cross! Stay on-message, and focus on his wonderful ethical teaching.'

Yet it was the cross they 'did'. This was the wisdom of God! This was the power of God! This, precisely this, was what redeemed the world. When Paul went to Corinth, famous neither for monotheism nor for morality nor for a tormented conscience, this was the first thing he preached: 'I delivered to you as of first importance what I also received: that Christ died for our sins' (1 Cor. 15:3, ESV). There was the *fact*: 'Christ died'. And there was the doctrine: 'for our sins'. This was his 'word', the *logos* of the cross; and from this sense of priorities, Paul never deviated. In his second letter to the Corinthians, he tells them that the very heart of Christ's love lies in the fact that he *died* for all (2 Cor. 5:14). He tells the Romans that Christ *died* for the ungodly (Rom. 5:6), that we were reconciled to God through the *death* of his Son (Rom. 5:10), and that the strong brother must not destroy the weak brother for whom Christ *died* (Rom. 14:15). He tells the Colossians that God made 'peace through Christ's blood, shed on the cross' (Col. 1:20), and he tells the Thessalonians that Christ *died* for us so that we should live together with him (1 Thess. 5:10). Peter is equally categorical: Christ, he says, *died* for sins once for all, to bring us to God (1 Pet. 3:18).

Objections may be brought against such a doctrine on the grounds that it is immoral or that it is absurd or that it is primitive. But it is hard to deny that it is not only apostolic, but also absolutely fundamental to apostolic preaching, and because it is apostolic it is binding on the Christian church. There remains scope, of course, for discussion of its meaning. But there can be no scope for proposals to remove it from the heart of the gospel and replace it with something else. More than any other single article of the creed, 'crucified under Pontius Pilate' is the heart of Christianity.

Why?

But what was the point and purpose of this self-sacrifice of God the Son, so closely coordinated by God the Father? The apostolic answer is unambiguous: the death of Christ was piacular. It was an atoning sacrifice for sin, and fundamental to this was the fact that the sacrifice was offered not to man, but to God. Its intention, therefore, was not to impress humans, but to impress God. This was already apparent in the institution of the Passover. The blood sprinkled on the doorposts and lintels of the Israelites was not there to impress the Egyptians. It was there to attract the attention of God so that the angel of judgment would pass the marked households by (Exod. 12:13). The same was true of the later Levitical sacrifices. They were specifically linked to sin: to sins of ignorance and inadvertence in the case of individuals and their sin offerings (Lev. 4:1–12); to 'sins in holy things' in the case of the nation as a whole (covered by the rituals of Yom Kippur, Lev. 16:3–34). This is why the offerer was required to lay both hands on the head of his offering: by doing so, as the ritual of Yom Kippur specifically mentions, he was putting his sins on the head of the sacrificial victim; and that same ritual also stipulated that prior to sending the scapegoat off into the wilderness the high priest was 'to confess over it all the wickedness and rebellion of the Israelites – all their sins' (Lev. 16:21). It was precisely these sins, so confessed, that the live goat carried away into the desert, distancing the people from their sins, and the outcome was set forth unambiguously in the refrain, 'and he/they will be forgiven'. We find it, for example, in connection with the sin offering: 'In this way the priest will make atonement for the community, and they will be forgiven' (Lev. 4:20). The same phraseology occurs in Numbers 15:25, this time in connection with the ritual prescribed when the whole community sinned unintentionally: 'The priest is to make atonement for the whole Israelite community, and they will be forgiven.'

It was this concept, with all its vulnerability to criticism by the 'modern mind', which the apostles, guided by the Spirit of the risen Christ, adopted as the framework for their 'word of the cross'; and it has remained the church's 'word of the cross' ever since. It is sometimes claimed that in contrast to its official dogmas on the Trinity and the person of Christ the church never adopted any formal doctrine of the atonement.[13] Yet the absence of a formal deliverance (by, for example, an ecumenical council) should not blind us to the fact that there has been agreement on the core elements of this doctrine down the Christian centuries and across all traditions. There has been unanimity that we owe our salvation to the death of Christ; that that death was an oblation and a sacrifice; and that this sacrifice was piacular, atoning for sin, making peace with God and securing forgiveness. Indeed, the reason that no council was ever convened to settle the doctrine of the atonement was that these positions (unlike, for example, the deity of Christ) were never challenged in the early church. The great doctors of the church simply took it for granted. We see this in, for example, Athanasius (c. 296–373), the greatest of the Greek Fathers. His work *The Incarnation of the Word of God* contains our earliest discussion of the atonement, and its focus on the sacrificial death of Christ is unmistakeable: 'It was by surrendering to death the body which He had taken, as an offering and sacrifice free from every stain, that He forthwith abolished death for His human brethren by the offering of the equivalent.'[14] He also makes clear that he saw the death of Christ as *vicarious* sacrifice:

> Thus, taking a body like our own, because all our bodies were liable to the corruption of death, He surrendered His body to death instead of all, and offered it to the Father. This he did out of sheer love for us, so that in His death all might die, and the law of death thereby be abolished because, having fulfilled in his body that for which it was appointed, it was thereafter voided of its power for men.[15]

The Latin Fathers wrote in similar vein. Augustine is typical: 'The death of the sinner springing from the necessity of condemnation is deservedly abolished by the death of the Righteous One springing from the free choice of His compassion'.[16] 'The bonds of many sins in many deaths,' he writes later, 'were loosed,

---

13. See, for example, Horace Bushnell, *The Vicarious Sacrifice* (London: Strahan and Co., 1871), p. xiv: 'No doctrine of the atonement or reconciling work of Christ, has ever yet been developed, that can be said to have received the consent of the Christian world.'

14. *The Incarnation of the Word of God*, tr. A Religious of C.S.M.V. (London: Geoffrey Bles, 1944), 35.

15. Ibid., 34.

16. Augustine, *On the Holy Trinity*, IV.2 (4) (NPNF, First Series, vol. III), p. 71.

through the one death of the One which no sin had preceded. Which death, though not due, the Lord therefore rendered for us, that the death which was due might work us no hurt.'[17] And Augustine, like Athanasius, understands the death in terms of sacrifice: 'Whereas by His death the one most real sacrifice was offered up for us, whatever fault there was whence principalities and powers held us fast as of right to pay its penalty, He cleansed, abolished, extinguished.'[18]

This same note continues to be sounded by both Anselm (c. 1033–1109) and Aquinas (1224–74), the two most influential figures in western mediaeval theology. Anselm's *Cur Deus Homo?* ('Why Did God Become Man?') set the agenda for all later discussions of the atonement, and there can be no mistaking his emphasis on the death of Christ as absolutely central to our redemption.[19] Not only does he lay down that 'man could not be reconciled to God except by a man-God who was capable of dying',[20] but he stresses that it was for the very purpose of dying that the Son of God became man, and even goes so far as to speak of him as 'this man, who could not have existed if it were not for the fact that he was going to die'.[21]

Aquinas, still the dominant influence in Roman Catholic theology (and compulsory reading for generations of Protestant divines after the Reformation), sounded a similar note, declaring that, 'Christ's death is the cause of our salvation'.[22] Then, having laid down that 'it is the same thing to speak of Christ's death as of his Passion', he speaks of this passion as 'the proper cause of the forgiveness of sins'.[23] And he, too, invokes the category of sacrifice: 'All the ancient sacrifices were figures of that true sacrifice which the dying Christ offered for us.'[24] Then, referring to the 'dignity of the life which was laid down

---

17. Ibid., IV.13 (17).

18. Ibid., IV.13 (17).

19. The most accessible edition of *Cur Deus Homo?* is in *Anselm of Canterbury: The Major Works*, ed. Brian Davies and G. R. Evans (Oxford: Oxford University Press, 1998). Quotations are generally from this edition, specifying book and chapter. See further discussion in ch. 8, pp. 173–176.

20. Anselm, *Cur Deus Homo?*, 2:21.

21. Ibid., 2:16.

22. Thomas Aquinas, *Summa Theologiae*, Pt III Q. 50 Art. 6. Quotations are from *St Thomas Aquinas Summa Theologica*, 5 vols., tr. Fathers of the English Dominican Province (Notre Dame: Ave Maria Press, 1981). Aquinas's discussion of the atonement can be found in vol. IV, pp. 2258–2302.

23. *Summa Theologica*, Pt III Q. 49 Art. 1.

24. Ibid., Pt III Q. 47 Art. 2.

in atonement, for it was the life of One who was God and man', he concludes, 'therefore Christ's Passion was not only a sufficient but a superabundant atonement for the sins of the human race'.[25] And finally, it was an atonement precisely because it was penal: 'It is a fitting way to satisfy for another to submit oneself to the penalty deserved by that other. And so Christ resolved to die, that by dying he might atone for us, according to 1 Pet. iii.18: *Christ also died once for our sins.*'[26]

Such quotations make plain that not only were the elements of what is often dismissed as merely a 'conservative evangelical' doctrine already present in the Fathers of the early church, East and West, but also that they had already been presented in systematic form by Thomas Aquinas. The early Fathers may not always have been clear as to the precise way in which the cross atoned: for example, they sometimes vexed themselves over the question, 'to whom was the ransom paid, God or the devil?' But they were absolutely clear that the redemptive power of Christ lay precisely in his death, the one great sacrifice for the sin of the world. Any attempt, therefore, to shift this focus (to, for example, the transforming and moralizing power of Jesus) is a departure from the teaching of the greatest doctors of the church. More important, it is a defiance of New Testament teaching. This is recognized even by such a writer as R. C. Moberly, who was no friend of what he called 'a logical theory of atonement, rigid, hard, and technical',[27] yet warmly endorsed the position that 'no conception of the work of Christ, or of the hope of Christians, is really compatible with the New Testament, which would sweep aside the fact, or minimise the transcendent significance, of the death on Calvary, regarded as the unique atoning sacrifice for the sins of mankind'.[28]

That is a judgment in which all Christians can rest.

---

25. Ibid., Pt III Q. 48 Art. 2.

26. Ibid., Pt III Q. 50 Art. 1.

27. R. C. Moberly, *Atonement and Personality* (London: John Murray, 1901), p. 386.

28. Ibid., p. 389.

PART 2

THE WORD OF THE CROSS

4. SUBSTITUTION: THE MAN FOR OTHERS

The very clarity of the New Testament emphasis on the cross presents us with a serious challenge. How could the life, let alone the death, of one man in a far-off country two thousand years ago be the salvation of the human race? How could his blood benefit me?

Part of the answer is that while the crucified one was a man, he was no mere man. He was the Son of God, acting and suffering in cooperation with the Father and the Holy Spirit. This is the primary answer to 'the scandal of particularity'. The death of this one 'man' has universal and inclusive significance because in him the Creator acts and the Creator suffers. By its very nature such an event, with the triune God at its heart, is bound to have cosmic significance. Anything less would have been out of proportion to the divine energy and the divine pain concentrated at the cross of Calvary.

But there is a second factor over and above the divine identity of the sufferer: the special relationship between Christ and the human race. It is encapsulated in two prepositions: he was 'with' us, and he was 'for' us.

Christ *with* us

First, Christ was with us. The angel had announced him as such, 'Immanuel (which means "God with us")' (Matt. 1:23). The Apostle John made the same point. Not only had the Word become flesh: he had dwelt among us (John 1:14), sharing not only our nature but our history and our experience. It is this 'with us' and this 'among us' that is fleshed out in the Gospel narratives of the life of Jesus. He stood where we stand, sharing our feeling of creaturely dependence, knowing that in God he lived and moved and had his being. Even at the profoundest spiritual level he was dependent on the encouragement of his heavenly Father and on the ceaseless ministry of the Holy Spirit. He shared, too, our sense of moral obligation, and felt the force of 'ought': 'I have a baptism to undergo, and how distressed I am until it is completed!' (Luke 12:50). He shared our joys: the joys of friendship, of family life, and of an environment where the birds of the air and the flowers of the field told the glory of earth's maker and the care of a heavenly Father. But he shared, too, our darker emotions: sorrow, consternation, and fear, and even the wish that God's will might be different, lest he be unable to cope (Mark 14:32–36).

Above all, he shared with us the misery of our human condition: human existence as determined by the fall. He knew poverty, homelessness, contempt, loneliness, rejection, death in its cruellest form and, at last, the loss of all sense of the presence of God. He lived amid squalor, violence and injustice. He heard the cursing, the blasphemy and the threats. He was tormented by the needs of the widow, the orphan and the leper. He felt for the tax-collector. He feared for his people. He wept for the world.

It is from within this humanity that he acts for us, intervening and entreating. He knows how we feel and what we need, and his experience of life at the edge has taught him pity for all sorts and conditions of human beings. This is why he is a compassionate high priest (Heb. 2:17), and this is why, when he offers himself, it is as one who has been tempted and tested like ourselves in every way (Heb. 4:15). His is a human obedience, and his is a human sacrifice, brought to God by the race that sinned, and from within that very race.

But solidarity is not itself atonement, only its prerequisite. It is an indispensable quality in a high priest, but it does not dispense with the need for sacrifice; nor will it serve as a sacrifice. The Old Testament offerer confessed sin over the head of the victim, and may well have done so with profound feelings of awe and reverence, but the lamb still had to be slain. Even if Jesus' solidarity with us had extended to the point where he had full personal experience of human sin, the resulting confession, no matter how well informed, and no matter how deeply felt, would have been no atonement. Without the shedding of blood there was to be no remission.

In reality, Jesus had no personal understanding of human sin. He knew no sin (2 Cor. 5:21). He was tempted; more so, indeed, than any person. But temptation, sometimes subtle, sometimes violent, never broke or seduced him. He may indeed have felt the shame of the sins of those he loved, but even if repentance could have served as an adequate atonement Jesus could never have offered it. As we have already seen, Jesus often identified with the sentiments of the psalmists, but one psalm he never quotes is the fifty-first. He could never have offered the sacrifice of a broken and contrite heart (Ps. 51:17) because at the heart of such contrition lies the personal possessive pronoun 'my': '*my* transgressions . . . *my* iniquity . . . *my* sin' (Ps. 51:1–3). Jesus, having never sinned, could never have spoken such a 'my'. He could give his people the gift of repentance, but he could never repent *with* them; and even if he could, such repentance would never have dreamed of presenting itself as an atonement. Repentance knows that sin must be expiated, as well as confessed.

Christ *for* us

Christ *with* us, then, cannot be enough. The Christian doctrine of atonement requires Christ *for* us, a relationship to which the New Testament bears abundant witness. The *for* itself, however, points to two closely related but nevertheless distinct concepts: Christ our representative and Christ our substitute.

First, Christ was our representative, acting on our behalf and charged with securing and protecting our interests. This is clearly implied in, for example, his work as advocate. John highlights this in 1 John 2:1: 'We have an advocate with the Father, Jesus Christ the righteous' (ESV).[1] (The technical meaning, 'lawyer', 'attorney' may be rare in pre-Christian and extra-Christian writings, but the Latin Fathers regularly translated *paraklētos* as *advocatus*. That will not by any means suit all New Testament occurrences of the word, but it does suit perfectly here.) This clearly presupposes that we are in deep trouble, and the context explains why: 'if anybody sins'. Sin puts us in a position where we need an attorney.

The idea of representation is also present in the portrayal of Christ as inter-cessor. Already in the Gospel of Luke (Luke 22:31–32) we find Jesus praying for Peter: 'I have prayed for you, Simon, that your faith may not fail.' The intercession of Jesus is also prominent in John 17:9–26, where Jesus prays both for the Twelve (v. 9) and for those who will come to faith through their ministry (vv. 20–26). This intercession clearly derives authority from Jesus' identity as the divine Son, but it draws its full force from his completed work (John 17:4).

---

1. Similarly the 2011 NIV; the older NIV obscures the idea by paraphrasing *paraklētos* as 'one who speaks to the Father in our defence'.

The full meaning of this becomes clear only in the great cry of John 19:30, 'It is finished!' The advocacy is based on Jesus' self-sacrifice and death.

The specific language of intercession is first applied to Christ in Romans 8:34: 'Who then is the one who condemns? No one. Christ Jesus who died – more than that, who was raised to life – is at the right hand of God and is also interceding for us.' The general idea behind the verb (*entynchanō*) is that of petitioning someone on behalf of someone else. Christ's intercession, as Paul describes it here, is 'for us': those whom God has chosen and justified (Rom. 8:33). It was hardly necessary for him to spell out *to* whom the intercession is directed. The intercessor is at God's right hand, anticipating John's reference to the advocate 'with' the Father (1 John 2:1). It is, of course, no concern of the intercession to make God love us. He has already delivered up his Son for us (Rom. 8:32) and there could be no greater mark of his love. Yet the intercession has a distinctly forensic ring. There are voices (Rom. 8:33) bringing charges against those whom God has justified and seeking a damning verdict against them, and there are forces seeking to separate them from the love of God (Rom. 8:35). Christ's pleading is clearly a pleading in our defence, and his very presence at God's right hand a living insistence that God's love must not let us go.

The other passage which refers specifically to the intercession of Christ is Hebrews 7:25: 'He is able to save completely those who come to God through him, because he always lives to intercede for them.' Here intercession is directly associated with Jesus' priesthood. Indeed, it is the fact of his priesthood, and particularly the contrast between it and the Levitical priesthood, which prompts the thought of his living for ever. The Aaronic priests were prevented by death from continuing in office. Jesus, on the other hand, is alive for evermore, which means that his voice on behalf of his people never falls silent. But the intercession is also linked to his sacrifice. He has no need to offer daily, weekly and monthly sacrifices, because he has offered one great definitive sacrifice: himself (Heb. 7:27). It is this sacrifice which speaks; the eloquence of his intercession lies in his blood. The perfect priest has offered the perfect sacrifice.

Considering the importance of Christ's priesthood in later Christian theology it is remarkable that the letter to the Hebrews is the only New Testament document which describes him as such. It is clearly implied, however, whenever he is spoken of as 'offering' himself or 'giving' himself. This was clearly priestly work, and it is here, in his priestly work, that Christ supremely acts as our representative. In terms of an age-old distinction, while the prophet represents God before men, the priest represents men before God, acting not on his own behalf, but on behalf of his people. This was pre-eminently true of Christ. In life and in death, in obedience and sacrifice, he served others. This is the great underlying theme of Philippians 2:5–11. Christ Jesus looked not to his own interests, but to the interests of others. But it had already been the theme of the Servant Song in Isaiah 53. It was the Servant who was despised and rejected and subjected to suffering, but it is *we* who are healed, *we* who are justified, *we* whose sins are carried away and *we* who come to enjoy *shalom*. In the New Testament this becomes a dominant theme. Christ represents us. He is the one who acts, but he acts for our benefit, not his own. It is we who are redeemed, reconciled to God and justified. He intercedes, and *we* are delivered from the wrath to come, freed from the dominion of the darkness (Col. 1:13) and given full rights as God's children (Gal. 4:5).

Substitution

But the biblical 'for', linking Christ to his people, involves more than representation. It also, and supremely, involves *substitution*.

This has been the voice of Christian devotion down the centuries: 'In my place condemned he stood.'[2] But it has also been the consistent voice of the great doctors of the church. The strongest statement is found in a famous passage in Luther's 1535 *Lectures on Galatians*. He is commenting on Galatians 3:13, 'Christ redeemed us from the curse of the law by becoming a curse for us' and he writes:

> Thus the whole emphasis is on the phrase 'for us.' For Christ is innocent so far as His own Person is concerned; and therefore He should not have been hanged from the tree. But because, according to the Law, every thief should have been hanged, therefore, according to the Law of Moses, Christ Himself should have been hanged; for he bore the person of a sinner and a thief – and not of one but of all sinners and thieves. For we are sinners and thieves, and therefore we are worthy of death and eternal damnation. But Christ took all our sins upon Himself, and for them He died on the cross. Therefore it was appropriate for Him to become a thief and, as Isaiah says (53:12), to be 'numbered among the thieves' . . . He is not acting in His own Person now. Now he is not the Son of God, born of the Virgin. But he is a sinner, who has and bears the sin of Paul, the former blasphemer, persecutor, and assaulter; of Peter, who denied Christ; of David, who was an adulterer and a murderer . . . In short, He has and bears all the sins of all men in His body – not in the sense that He has committed them, but in the sense that He took these sins, committed by us, upon His own body, in order to make satisfaction for them with His own blood.[3]

---

2. 'Man of Sorrows! what a name', Philipp Paul Bliss, 1838–76.

3. *Luther's Works*, vol. 26, p. 277.

But the idea of substitution was no invention of Luther's. It is already found in the fourth century in Athanasius, who wrote, 'Thus taking a body, like our own, because all our bodies were liable to the corruption of death, He surrendered His body to death *instead of all*, and offered it to the Father.'[4] Aquinas, as we have seen, speaks the same language.[5] It was from within this tradition that Calvin insisted so strenuously on the substitutionary nature of Christ's death:

> To take away our condemnation, it was not enough for him to suffer any kind of death: to make satisfaction for our redemption a form of death had to be chosen in which he might free us both by transferring our condemnation to himself and by taking our guilt [Lat. *piaculum*] upon himself ... This is our acquittal: the guilt that held us liable for punishment has been transferred to the head of the Son of God (Is. 53:12). We must, above all, remember this substitution [Lat. *compensatio*], lest we tremble and remain anxious throughout life – as if God's righteous vengeance, which the Son of God has taken upon himself, still hung over us.[6]

Karl Barth warmly endorsed Luther's remarks on Galatians 3:13. 'In substance,' he wrote, 'Luther's drastic commentary on this exchange is quite right';[7] and this endorsement extended even to what might be seen as the Reformer's extreme statement that Christ became 'the greatest thief, murderer, adulterer, robber, desecrator, blasphemer, etc., there has ever been anywhere in the world'.[8] But Barth himself also devoted one of the finest sections of his *Dogmatics* to the question of the precise meaning of 'for us', and while (as ever) there is a risk of reading him though our own lenses, there can be little doubt that he viewed Christ as standing in our place.[9] He formulates his material under the title, 'The Judge Judged In Our Place' and insists that, 'even the

---

4. Athanasius, *Incarnation of the Word of God*, p. 34. Italics mine.

5. Aquinas, *Summa Theologica*, Pt III Q 50 Art 1.

6. *Institutes*, II:XVI, 5.

7. Karl Barth, *Church Dogmatics*, 4 vols., eds. G. W. Bromiley and T. F. Torrance (Edinburgh: T&T Clark, 1956–75), IV:I, p. 238.

8. *Luther's Works*, vol. 26, p. 277.

9. IV:I, pp. 211–283. One reason for caution is that Barth appears to have a peculiar understanding of sacrifice, taking it to point primarily to the death of the 'old man'. God wills and demands that this man 'should go up in flames and smoke'. See especially pp. 274–283.

strongest "with us" is not enough to describe what Jesus Christ is in relation to us'.[10] The 'decisive statement,' he writes, must be that 'what took place is that the Son of God fulfilled the righteous judgement on us men by Himself taking our place as man and in our place undergoing the judgement under which we had passed'.[11] Then, in a brief note on *anti*, *hyper* and *peri*, the three Greek prepositions which convey the sense of 'for', he argues that, 'these prepositions speak of a place which ought to be ours, that we ought to have taken this place, that we have been taken from it, that it is occupied by another, [and] that this other acts in this place as only He can, in our cause and interest'.[12]

There follows a series of epigrammatic statements in which Barth reiterates the idea of substitution: 'Jesus Christ was and is for us in that He took the place of us sinners'; 'He makes their evil case His Own'; 'He has made Himself a sinner for us'; he 'let himself be put in the wrong'; 'the passion of Jesus Christ is the judgement of God in which the Judge himself was the judged'; 'He willed to take our place as sinners and did, in fact, take our place'.[13]

Clearly, then, the idea that Christ died in our place is no eccentric minority view in the history of Christian proclamation, far less an extreme one. It has been central to the church's message from the beginning, and cherished by all who gloried in the cross of Christ. But is it cherished merely as something which has been passed on from Christian heart to Christian heart, or is it, beyond that, warranted by divine revelation as part of that 'word of the cross' which the apostles received from the Lord and which they in turn delivered to us through the pages of the New Testament?

The most fundamental argument in favour of substitution is that it is implicit in the very fact that Christ's death was a sacrifice. This immediately takes us beyond the idea of mere representation. A priest is a representative, acting on behalf of his people and, in the supreme act of his office, offering a sacrifice on their behalf. But Christ does not merely offer the sacrifice; he becomes the sacrifice. He is not simply one who dies with the rest of us or pleads that we be spared the death sentence. He is the one who dies in order that we be spared this death. He drinks the cup so that we should not drink it; is cursed so that we should not be cursed; is forsaken so that we should not be forsaken; is condemned so that we should not be condemned. He is not only priest but

---

10. *Church Dogmatics*, p. 229.

11. Ibid., p. 222.

12. Ibid., p. 230.

13. Ibid., pp. 235, 236, 238 (×2), 254, 258.

victim; not only offerer but offering, doing for us what needed to be done but which we could not do, and which, once done, we need never do for ourselves.

To change the perspective: the advocate not only sympathizes with his client and not only pleads for him, but takes his place in the dock. He becomes the accused. He becomes the condemned and guilty one. He is led out to execution not only with his client, but in his place. The client goes free. The advocate is crucified, receiving the wages of his client's sin.

Christ died for our sins

But the idea of substitution is also implicit in the way the scriptures connect Christ's death with sin. From the biblical perspective, as we have seen, all human death is the retribution due to sin, and to this the death of Christ was no exception. He, too, died because of sin. What is remarkable, however, is that the sin he died for was not his own. He died, says Paul, for *our* sins (1 Cor. 15:3). He repeats the point in Galatians 1:4, where he speaks of Christ as the one 'who gave himself for *our* sins'. And Peter strikes the same note in 1 Peter 2:24: 'He himself bore *our* sins in his body on the tree'. Yet it was nothing new. Isaiah had already sounded it:

> *He* was pierced for *our* transgressions,
>   *he* was crushed for *our* iniquities;
> the punishment that brought *us* peace was upon *him*,
>   and by *his* wounds *we* are healed.
> We all, like sheep, have gone astray,
>   each of us has turned to our own way;
> and the LORD has laid on *him*
>   the iniquity of *us* all . . .
> for the transgression of *my* people he was punished.
> (Isa. 53:5–6, 8)

The statement that Christ died for *our* sins is also found in English versions of Romans 4:25: 'He was delivered over to death for our sins and was raised to life for our justification.' In this passage, however, the Greek preposition translated 'for' is *dia*. Used with the genitive case, it means 'through' or 'by means of'. Used with the accusative, as it is here, it means 'on account of'. Clearly, then, what Paul is saying in Romans 4:25 is that Christ was delivered to death 'on account of our sins', or, as Cranfield expresses it, Christ's atoning death was necessitated by our sins.[14] Here, once again, there is an echo of Isaiah 53, where the Septuagint uses *dia* in exactly the same way: 'he was pierced *on account of our transgressions*, he was bruised *on account of our iniquities*' (Isa. 53:5). The link with sin could scarcely be clearer, yet the sin was not his, but ours. He bore the sin of the many.

In Romans 8:3, Paul uses yet another preposition, *peri*, to define the relation between Christ and sin: Christ was sent not only 'in the likeness of sinful flesh', but 'for' sin (*peri hamartias*). The key point here is that this was the phrase commonly used in the Septuagint to denote the sin offering: a reflection of the fact that the same words (*ḥaṭṭā'â* and *ḥaṭṭā't*) are used in Hebrew for both 'sin' and 'sin offering'. Christ is explicitly compared to the sin offering in Hebrews 13:11–12:

> The high priest carries the blood of animals into the Most Holy Place as a sin offering, but the bodies are burned outside the camp. And so Jesus also suffered outside the city gate to make the people holy through his own blood.

The ritual is prescribed in Leviticus 4:1–21, and one consistent element is that whatever the sin which made such an offering necessary, in each case the offerer had to lay his hands on the head of the victim prior to its being slain. The natural explanation for this is that it symbolized the transference of the sin and the guilt to the sacrifice; and it was as such, as the sin-bearer, that the animal was slain. In the case of Romans 8:3 we are specifically told that when Christ came 'for sin' (*peri hamartias*) God condemned sin *in his flesh*. Earlier, in John 6:51, Jesus himself had spoken of giving his flesh for the life of the world. Peter, too, uses similar language: 'he himself bore our sins in his body on the cross' (1 Pet. 2:24). The implication is clear: the flesh or body of Christ became the locus of atonement. Here the condemnation fell. Here the curse fell; and as always it fell 'for sin'. What made it unique was that it was not his own sins, but ours, that he carried in his body. It was the condemnation which we, not he, deserved, that he endured.

Christ dying for *us*

Not only did Christ die for sin, however. He also died *for sinners*. He died *for us*. This is the clear message of key New Testament passages, and in almost every

---

14. C. E. B. Cranfield, *The Epistle to the Romans*, vol. 1, International Critical Commentary (2 vols., Edinburgh: T&T Clark, 1975), p. 252.

case the language and context make plain that the expressions mean not merely that he died on our behalf or for our benefit, but that he died in our place. He died as our substitute.

One of the clearest expressions comes from the lips of Jesus himself: 'even the Son of Man did not come to be served, but to serve, and to give his life a ransom for many' (Mark 10:45). As so often, the occasion for this seminal Christological statement is a low-level dispute about basic ethical attitudes: which of the disciples would be greatest when the kingdom came? Jesus resolves (or dissolves) the dispute by redefining greatness. In *his* kingdom greatness consists not of lording it over others, but of serving them; and he reinforces the point by stating bluntly the purpose of his own mission. He has come to serve, and the precise service he has come to render is to lay down his life as a ransom for many. The preposition used here is not *hyper*, which has the same wide range of meaning as the English *for*, but the much more specific *anti*, which in the vast majority of instances has the meaning 'instead of'.[15] There is a clear example of this in Luke 11:11, 'What father among you, if his son asks for a fish, will instead of a fish give him a serpent?' (ESV). In Mark 10:45 this basic meaning is reinforced by the link with *lytron* (ransom). As Friedrich Büchsel points out in his article on *anti*, the thought is not simply that Jesus *gives* himself for many, but that he gives himself a *ransom* for many: 'For the *polloi* have not only forfeited a favourite possession but their very lives, themselves; and what Jesus gives them is His very life, Himself. What he does on their behalf is simply to take their place.'[16] He is the ransom-price which makes possible the great exchange. He dies; the many live. He is handed over; the slaves of sin go free, no longer to receive its wages or experience its curse.

There is a clear echo of Mark 10:45 in 1 Timothy 2:6, which speaks of Christ Jesus 'who gave himself a ransom for all'. The preposition here is *hyper*, which is less specific than *anti*, but in this instance the word for 'ransom' is no longer simply *lytron* but the compound, *antilytron*. This is the only occurrence of this word in the New Testament and its use here suggests that Paul wished not merely to echo the words of Jesus, but to underline the substitutionary nature of his death. He gave his life as a *substitutionary-ransom*.

The preposition *anti* is not used in any further instance to define the relation of Christ to sinners. The preposition *hyper* prevails. Yet this does not detract in

---

15. 'By far the commonest use of *anti* is the simple "instead of"'. James Hope Moulton and George Milligan, *The Vocabulary of the Greek Testament Illustrated from the Papyri and other Non-Literary Sources* (London: Hodder and Stoughton, 1952).

16. *TDNT*, vol. 1, pp. 372–373.

any way from the emphasis on substitution expressed so clearly by Jesus himself. In almost every case the context makes plain that he was acting not merely on behalf of sinners, but in their place.

This is clear in, for example, Paul's exposition of the idea of reconciliation in 2 Corinthians 5:18–21. He begins by emphasizing that it was God himself who took the initiative: 'All this is from God, who reconciled us to himself'. But what is remarkable is the precise nature of the initiative which God took. Rather than proceeding directly from loving us to forgiving our sins, God went 'through Christ': he 'reconciled us to himself through Christ' (v. 18). And what he did through Christ was this: 'he made him who had [knew] no sin to be sin for us' (v. 21). This points to a remarkable identification between Christ and sin. The Apostle John speaks of Christ being 'made flesh' (John 1:14); Paul, even bolder, speaks of him being 'made sin'. This cannot mean that he was made sinful. The passage itself forbids it: he *knew* no sin. Nor, in terms of precise translation, can we adopt the rendering that God made him a 'sin offering'. The chiasmic structure of the sentence requires an antithesis: we who knew no righteousness become *righteousness* because he who knew no sin became *sin*. Yet, in effect, a sin offering is what he became. He was sacrificed because he had contracted sin and thus became liable to its penalty. And he suffered that penalty not simply in solidarity with us, to share its pain *with* us, but to secure an indemnity for us. He became the surety who would pay our debts in our place, and the result is spelt out clearly in verse 18 of this very chapter: our trespasses are not reckoned to us. They are no longer debited to our account, because they have been debited to his. Our sin became his sin. His righteousness became our righteousness.

Paul had spoken to similar effect in his earlier letter to the Galatians. In Galatians 2:20, for example, he had written in the most personal terms, describing Christ as 'the Son of God, who loved me and gave himself for me'. Here again the import of *hyper* has to be inferred from its context. Paul is not saying merely that the Son of God spoke up for him or intervened on his behalf. He is saying that he *delivered up* himself for him (that Greek verb, *paradidōmi*, again). The language is priestly and sacrificial, and provides yet another echo of the words of Jesus in Mark 10:45: 'he gave himself as a ransom for me'.

The language of Galatians 3:13 is even more striking: 'Christ redeemed us from the curse of the law by becoming a curse for us'. Here again, 'for' is *hyper*; and here again the context makes plain that no mere idea of solidarity or vaguely well-intentioned intervention will suffice. The precise nature of the intervention is made plain, and it clearly involved Christ taking our place. The Law declared us 'cursed' (Gal. 3:10). Christ took that curse upon himself and redeemed us from it. He paid the price that set us free, and that price far surpassed any service that any advocate, attorney, priest or barrister could perform for those they represent. He took the curse due to the sin of the whole world upon himself. He ascended the cross. He descended into hell. He became the one condemned by the judiciary, mocked by the multitude, forsaken by his Father, laid low by death. This is the last word in the great trilogy. He was made flesh; he was made sin; he was made a curse. Why? Because he took our place. With what effect? The blessing of Abraham comes upon the accursed (Gal. 3:14).

Later, in the letter to the Ephesians, written from prison, Paul's mind is still focused on this same vicarious suffering of Christ, even when (once again) his object is to give basic moral guidance. 'Husbands,' he says, 'love your wives, just as Christ loved the church and gave himself up *for* her' (Eph. 5:25). This echoes language he had used earlier in the same chapter (v. 2) where he urges them to imitate God, 'and live a life of love, just as Christ loved us and gave himself up for us a fragrant offering and sacrifice to God'. Here again the non-specific *hyper* must take its meaning from the context. What did Christ do for us? Did he merely intervene in some general way to protect our interests? Clearly, it was more than that, far more. He was not merely with us, to share, but in our place, so that in him we received the just recompense for our sins. It cannot be put more memorably or more succinctly than in the words of old-fashioned frontier evangelism: 'He die; me no die.'

Must every human being answer for their own sin?

Two further considerations need to be borne in mind.

First, if Christ was not our substitute, bearing our guilt and paying our dues, then every human being must carry his or her own sin. Much modern theology seems happy to accept this conclusion. Guilt, it is assumed, is non-transferable. But if this is so, redemption is impossible. If 'my sin' (Ps. 51:3) remains forever my sin, I must personally carry it to the throne of judgment, and if so, I am done for. The wrath, that impersonal law of retribution which C. H. Dodd wished to substitute for the personal anger of a holy and righteous God,[17] will get me.

It was this that Luther grasped so clearly and expressed so brilliantly in his comments on Galatians 3:13:

> Because he bears the sins of the world, His innocence is pressed down with the sins and the guilt of the entire world. Whatever sins I, you, and all of us have committed,

---

17. See, for example, C. H. Dodd, *Romans*, pp. 47–50.

or may commit in the future, they are as much Christ's own as if He Himself had committed them. In short, our sins must be Christ's own sin, or we shall perish eternally.[18]

He continues in the same vein:

> If the sins of the entire world are on that one man, Jesus Christ, then they are not on the world. But if they are not on Him, then they are still on the world ... if He is innocent and does not carry our sins, then we carry them and shall die and be damned in them.[19]

Secondly, without substitution the death of Jesus Christ, the Son of God, becomes unintelligible. Why does the sword of justice fall here, on this man, by God's hand, at the cross of Calvary?

But the moment we ask this, we face a more fundamental question: is there a sword of justice at all? The biblical concept of justice, we are told, differs radically from the old classical, forensic concept of justice, summarized in the principle, *suum cuique* ('to each their own'), a principle which clearly implied that the wrongdoer would receive what was due to him. The Hebrew concept, by contrast, was relational and covenantal, rather than forensic, and was synonymous in practice with the faithfulness of God. It stressed not that God punishes wrongs, but that he puts wrongs right.

It is far from clear, however, that the Old Testament notion of justice or righteousness differed radically from the classical. Righteousness was not a specifically Hebrew concept, nor was knowledge of it confined to those who enjoyed the light of special divine revelation. It was familiar to the Gentiles, and like the related concepts of truth and virtue, it engaged the attention of classical philosophers. Granted, they did not link it closely to the idea of a divine covenant, but then neither did the original Hebrew usage. The first biblical occurrence of the idea of righteousness is in Genesis 6:9, where Noah is described as 'a righteous man'. This is before we find any reference to the covenant. He was righteous by the moral standards of his contemporaries; 'blameless among the people of his time'. In later Greek and Roman thought this came to be more precisely focused in the principle that the righteous man respects the rights of others and gives everyone his due. It is hard to see any conflict between this and the biblical idea of righteousness. Every human being

---

18. *Luther's Works*, vol. 26, p. 278.
19. Ibid., p. 280.

has rights: some simply by being human, others by virtue of some promise, contract or covenant. Every righteous person will concede these rights.

In relations between God and the human race (or individual) these rights are defined by covenant; or, which is the same thing, by the promises God has given; or, which is still the same thing, by the law. God has left us in no doubt as to what will secure his favour and what will provoke his displeasure. This is where the idea of righteousness meshes with that of the divine faithfulness. God's faithfulness means that he will keep his word. In particular, he will keep his promises to his people. He will execute justice for them, and act to save them.

But God's faithfulness also means that he will punish wrong, and this is reflected in the fact that every human society, and every human individual, believes in retributive righteousness. Made in God's image, we never lose our conviction that some forms of conduct deserve punishment (Rom. 1:32). This is why every state has its justice system, designed to punish those who violate the rights of their fellow citizens. Starting from the principle that 'the safety of the people is the first law' we recognize that if evil is left unchecked human life will quickly become impossible. This is why God has ordained the 'powers that be' (Rom. 13:1, KJV), charged them with striking terror into the hearts of criminals and invested them with 'the power of the sword' (in modern terms, the power to arrest, detain and imprison). Without such arrangements, we could never lead 'peaceful and quiet lives' (1 Tim. 2:2): a point made neatly by Nicholas Wolterstorff, when he writes, 'A crucial part of shalom is justice; you can't have shalom without justice.'[20]

We can of course ask, 'whose justice?', and then proceed to argue that there are no agreed universal standards. What is a crime in one society (for example, incitement to religious hatred) may not be a crime in another. But that is not the point. The point is that amid all the variables every society agrees that crime must be punished, rights protected and evil deterred. Besides, there is no evidence that the more 'civilized' a society becomes, the less store it sets by retribution. International law now seeks out war criminals as never before; and in modern, so-called permissive, Britain the criminal justice system extends not only to rapists, terrorists, murderers and child-abusers, but to illegal parking, corporate homicide and breaches of environmental protection legislation; and beyond these to racial abuse, gender discrimination and violation of gay rights.

Society is clearly convinced, then, that it has the right to execute justice and exact retribution. Many theologians, however, allow God no such right. He has

---

20. Nicholas Wolterstorff, *Hearing the Call: Liturgy, Justice and World* (Grand Rapids: Eerdmans, 2011), p. 424.

no business, they say, with retribution. 'Dieu me pardonnera; c'est son métier' ('God will forgive me; that's his job'), said the expatriate German poet, Heinrich Heine on his deathbed. From such a perspective, God is expected to forgive unconditionally, welcoming the returning prodigal with open arms and asking no questions. To all sins, whether against himself or against humans, he simply (and as a matter of course) turns the other cheek.

Are we then to deny God what we arrogate to ourselves? Is there no higher court than our human high courts and supreme courts; no tribunal to which, with dying breath, the oppressed can appeal, and where abusive patriarchs, cruel tyrants and corrupt judges will finally be called to account?

If so, then our human systems of justice have no validity. Only as instruments of ultimate justice and only by authorization of the Supreme Judge can our petty jurisdictions claim the right to put people in handcuffs, place them in the dock and commit them to prison. Only the most solemn divine warrant can make it right for one person to deprive another of his freedom. 'If God is not a judge,' wrote the nineteenth-century Scottish theologian, Hugh Martin,

> it is impossible to account for the existence of that noble and solemn office on earth at all. God might as well create the faculties of sight and hearing in men, without Himself being possessed of ability to see and hear, as He could put it into men's hearts to maintain judgement in human government if he were not a lawgiver and judge himself.[21]

Whatever can be said in favour of a non-retributive deity who reacts to sin and crime with otiose indifference and takes no action beyond telling the abused victims to turn the other cheek, this is not the God of the Hebrew-Christian scriptures. In the Pentateuch he gave Israel a detailed penal code. In the first four chapters of the prophecy of Amos he announced imminent retribution on Israel's neighbours, on Israel herself, and on Judah. And in Romans 13, as we have seen, he not only gave a clear mandate to secular government, but laid down clear guidelines for its operation. It exists to express *his* anger, not that of humankind; to deter the lawless and to protect the innocent. So long as it adheres to this mandate, government has validity. When it abandons it, it has none.

But God's punishment of the wrongdoer is not confined to those judgments which he has delegated to human judicatories. There is a judgment after death (Heb. 9:27), and far from being a sub-Christian judgment, applying draconian standards and meeting out draconian punishments, it will be a judgment

---

21. Hugh Martin, *The Atonement: In Its Relations to the Covenant, the Priesthood, the Intercession of Our Lord* (repr. Greenville: Reformed Academic Press, 1997 [1870]) p. 180.

delegated to the Lamb, that very Son of God who is the incarnation of the divine love and who bore our sins on the cross of Calvary. All of us must, indeed, appear before the judgment seat of Christ (2 Cor. 5:10), and on that day, at this supreme tribunal, against whose findings there can be no appeal, there will be neither partiality nor indifference. The Lamb, the Son of Man, will divide the sheep from the goats; and the latter will feel the full force of divine retribution: 'Depart from me, you who are cursed, into the eternal fire prepared for the devil and his angels' (Matt. 25:41).

Why, then, does God ask us to forgive unconditionally (Matt. 18:22)? Why does he command us not to resist an evil person? And why does he ask *us* to turn the other cheek (Matt. 5:39) when he himself intends, at the end, to visit sin with condign punishment?

We are bound, of course, to take these precepts with total seriousness. They are the boundary-markers which distinguish the disciples of Jesus Christ from the world around them. But at the same time we must recognize their limitations. They do not apply in all circumstances and in all capacities. When the harm is limited to ourselves, and the damage confined to my own cheek or my own reputation, then we offer no resistance. But in other capacities there is an unconditional obligation to resist. God does not ask parents to turn a blind eye to defiance from their children, or judges to acquit the guilty or rulers to ignore the lying scales of the fraudulent merchant, the criminal negligence of the jerry-builder or the violence of the abusive husband. Nor did he command Martin Niemöller and Dietrich Bonhoeffer to offer no resistance when Hitler set out to exterminate Jews and gypsies.

God, the Supreme Judge, is not pledged to non-resistance in the face of evil. He is pledged to do what is right (Gen. 18:25), and he has made the terms of his relationship with the human race unmistakeably plain: 'for those who are self-seeking and who reject the truth and follow evil, there will be wrath and anger' (Rom. 2:8–9). This judgment will extend to every breach of human rights. But God, too, has his rights, otherwise, since he alone has the power to enforce them, the whole concept of rights collapses. No human court can tolerate rejection of its jurisdiction or contempt for its procedures. Similarly, the Judge of all the earth can brook no rejection or usurpation of his jurisdiction. Those who set themselves up as the final arbiters of their own behaviour, whether towards God or towards people, are safe only in an atheistic universe.

It is absolutely right, then, that the sword of justice should fall on the criminal and that the agent of the divine wrath should punish the wrongdoer. There can be no amnesty for rapists and drug-pushers. But how can the sword of justice fall here, at Golgotha? Pilate may be corrupt, but is God also corrupt or blind, that he should condemn sin here, where there is no sin? How can the curse of the law fall where the law has not been broken? Should the soul that has not sinned, die? Surely, to quote Martin again, 'The universe were one vast hell of suspense and horror, if God's wrath could alight elsewhere than where it is *deserved*.'[22]

From this point of view it is the cross itself that requires a theodicy. How can God justify what he did at Calvary? What gave him the right to sacrifice his own Son? Only the doctrine of vicarious punishment can provide an answer. The sword falls at the precise point where justice located the sin of the world: in Jesus' own body, on the tree. The sword falls here because it is right that it should fall here; and it is right because 'in my place condemned he stood'.[23] Otherwise the cross is a black hole; an irrational evil; the act of a capricious or malevolent deity. Indeed, as Donald Baillie remarks, 'the crucifixion might well seem to be the final *reductio ad absurdum* of the belief that the world is governed by a gracious providence'.[24]

But if we take to heart the union between Christ and his people, then the cross itself is redeemed. It has its own *logos* (1 Cor. 1:18). Through this union with his people (his brothers and sisters, his friends, his bride, his children) he contracts their sin and assumes responsibility for their debts. The cross then becomes the locus where their sin receives its just recompense and their debts are paid.

But is it not immoral that the innocent should suffer in the place of the guilty?

No human law, admittedly, makes provision for the vicarious punishment of the wrongdoer, but we must take the biblical doctrine as a whole, and that means paying attention to the special features of Christ's substitution. The most important of these is that Christ takes our place voluntarily, and behind this lies the fact, already noted, that he came into the world in accordance with a plan of salvation agreed from eternity between the Father, the Son and the Holy Spirit. Christ, as the divine Son, was a full party to this agreement, not as an inferior or junior, but as an equal. He did not become mediator by a sovereign divine decree, or by the imperious command of a divine superior. Instead, prompted by love for the world he assumed, voluntarily, the role of mediator; and prompted by the same love the Father agrees to send him and the Holy Spirit to anoint him. It is by this covenant that Christ is united to his people. With his own loving consent he becomes their head, their representative, their surety and their substitute; and by entering into this union he undertakes not

---

22. Martin, *Atonement*, p. 146 (italics his).

23. 'Man of Sorrows'.

24. Donald M. Baillie, *God Was In Christ: An Essay on Incarnation and Atonement* (London: Faber and Faber, 1948), p. 184.

only to act on their behalf but to contract their debts and to assume their liabilities. From this point of view, the road to Calvary began in eternity, when the divine Son volunteered, 'Here am I! Send me!' There was surely nothing immoral here. The Son of God had a right to love this way, and the triune God had a right to save this way. Who could forbid the Eternal Son becoming surety for his people? And who could forbid him, having become their surety, to love them to the extreme of accepting their doom in their place?

But it is important, too, that the substitute was a divine person. Jesus was not some third party dragged reluctantly into a quarrel which was none of his business. He was the offended party, and he had the right to demand satisfaction from the other. Instead, by becoming man he qualified himself to become that other, and in the name of that other to atone for the offence. The Son of God became the last Adam. This conserves the principle that the atonement must be made in the nature that sinned: Jesus offered human obedience.

Yet, from the other and higher point of view his ministry was a transaction between the persons of the blessed Trinity. The Son finished the work the Father gave him to do; and then Father glorified the Son. Joel Green and Mark Baker in their work *Recovering the Scandal of the Cross* portray this as an intolerable paradox: 'one member of the Trinity punishing another member of the Trinity'.[25] This precise wording is, of course, not found anywhere in Scripture, nor, so far as I know, in the publications of any proponent of the doctrine of penal substitution. But some such paradoxes are unavoidable if we are to hold fast by the doctrine that it was the eternal Son who died on the cross. God was forsaken by God. God was delivered up by God. Nor does this undermine the fact that the Father and the Son are one, and act as one. This is the covenant between them: the Father shall deliver up, and the Son shall offer himself. But even *in extremis*, even on the cross, the Son is still the 'beloved Son'.

Nor does the New Testament hesitate to remind us that that here, in the divine identity of the victim, lies the glory of the sacrifice of Christ. This is precious blood (1 Pet. 1:19), not only because it is that of an unblemished lamb, but because it is the blood of God (Acts 20:28). This is the secret of its power to expiate and redeem: he is *himself* the atonement for our sin (1 John 2:2), not his sufferings merely, or his obedience merely, but himself. It is the blood of the Son of God (of the divine humanity) which is given, so willingly, for the sin of the world. Anything less, and Calvary would never redeem us. It could only *impress* us, leaving us clinging to the fragile hope that the semi-anguished

---

25. Joel B. Green and Mark D. Baker, *Recovering the Scandal of the Cross: Atonement in New Testament and Contemporary Contexts* (Bletchley: Paternoster, 2000), p. 147.

cries of our own repentance would serve as an adequate atonement, a sentiment no true penitent could ever entertain.

But does this not mean, as Green and Baker also suggest, that the cross changes nothing but a legal ruling, and that 'an individual could be saved through penal substitution without experiencing a fundamental re-orientation of his or her life'?[26]

From an evangelical perspective there is, of course, an unintentional grain of truth in this accusation. A fundamental reorientation of our lives is not a precondition of our being accepted by God. We are justified by faith, and what faith puts its trust in is not any reorientation of our lives, but the blood of Christ. We are justified freely by his grace through the redemption that is in Christ Jesus (Rom. 3:24). At that point, we are still 'ungodly' (Rom. 4:5), and as such in no position to negotiate peace with God.

But at another level this remark overlooks the fact that penal substitution was never proposed as a complete doctrine of salvation. It was but one element in a much more comprehensive doctrine which took account of our need not only of atonement, but also of renewal and transformation. These may be distinguished, but they are inseparable, and each has its own distinctive preposition. Christ died *for* us, but to enjoy the *shalom* he secured for us, it is also necessary that we come to be *in* him; and if we are in him there is an inevitable reorientation of our lives, as Paul reminds us in Galatians 2:19: 'I no longer live, but Christ lives in me'. His old life 'in the flesh' is now behind him. Instead, he is a 'new man', but he is a new man only 'in Christ'. This is the only place where we can experience atonement and reconciliation, but we cannot be in that place without also experiencing renewal and transformation. Union with Christ brings a double blessing, sanctification as well as justification. It is impossible to have the one without the other. The union that instantly puts us in the right with God also ensures that the life of his Son flows through our veins, working its miracle of transformation till at last we are completely Christ-like.

To change direction slightly: the agent, the one who reorientates us, is the Holy Spirit, and the great guarantee that there can be no 'salvation' without reorientation is that we cannot be united to Christ without also being united to the Spirit. When Christ comes in, the Spirit comes in. But the Spirit cannot come in until there is peace through the blood of the cross, and this link between atonement and the gift of the Spirit is made brilliantly clear in Galatians 3:13–14. The immediate objective of Christ's being made a curse for us was that we might be redeemed from the curse of the law. But beyond that lay another, final

---

26. Green and Baker, *Scandal of the Cross*, p. 149.

objective: that we might receive the promise of the Spirit through faith. This is
what the cross achieved: *shalom* in the first instance, but beyond that the
life-changing, reorientating ministry of the Holy Spirit.

But does all this focus on the cross, and particularly the idea of redemption
through vicarious sacrifice, not glorify human suffering? This is certainly not a
charge that can be brought against the story of the passion as told in the Gospels.
Far from satisfying any macabre interest in the procedures of execution, the
narrative confines itself to the bare details. For further information (for example,
to produce such a film as *The Passion of the Christ*) researchers have to look far
beyond the Gospels. In no way do the evangelists themselves milk the story
either to maximize the horror or to indulge sentimentality. Yet enough is said
to strip suffering of all its glamour. The site of the execution is a sordid, ugly
place, and the whole story is shrouded in intrigue, corruption and injustice. Far
from glamorizing violence, the cross is an exposé of it: a reminder that it stalks
not only the sordid underworld but the corridors of human power and the
courts of human justice. The human perpetrators (Judas, Pilate, the religious
authorities, the mob) are all painted in the darkest colours, barbarously slaying
the innocent. Yet they do not stand alone, as if human violence were confined
to politicians, judges, mindless mobs and ecclesiastics. They are representative
of an earth that is filled with violence (Gen. 6:11), a violence that cries out for
retribution and atonement.

But the men of violence are not the only agents at Calvary. God is here, too:
God, above all, who 'did not spare his own Son' (Rom. 8:32). By choosing to
save the world through the cruelty of the cross, is he not glorifying violence?

If that were the case, however, what God would be glorifying would be
violence against himself, because it is he, in the person of his Son, who hangs
there. If the cross encourages anything, it is not violence against wives and
children, but deicide: an assault on deity itself. Besides, if the logic behind this
objection were sound, then violence (especially violence against women and
children) would be especially prevalent among believers in vicarious atonement.
While it would be vain to claim that patriarchal abuse never occurs among
evangelicals, there is not a shred of evidence that their doctrine of the cross
encourages abnormally high levels of such an evil.

But let's look more deeply, remembering that the Crucified One is there as
the divine substitute for sinners. What is being glorified here is not malicious
or arbitrary violence but justice: that justice of which our human judicatories
are but a shadow, and in which alone they can find their validity. God forgives
sin, but he never condones it. He made that plain when, after the exodus, he
gave Israel its criminal code; and he made it plain when he sanctioned the use
of the sword by the governing authorities (Rom. 13:4). The only violence God

condones is the violence of due legal process. Thus, in the divine economy Christ died under judicial sentence; and he died only because he assumed the guilt of all the violence man had ever perpetrated. Substitution is not the problem. It is the solution. Christ suffered as the great debtor to law and to God; and in doing so he showed the power, wisdom and dedication of the divine love which was willing both to face the wrath of man and to bear in itself the whole cost of our redemption. The violence of the cross, like so much that masquerades as human justice, was barbaric and lawless, but it was a violence of which God chose to be the victim. He went towards it, and while at the most fundamental level he chose it as the instrument of his atonement, the means by which God's Lamb would be offered up, it was also the means by which God learned to understand, at the deepest level, the pain of the oppressed, the bereaved and the unutterably lonely. It was not merely physical. His descent into hell meant, as Joseph Ratzinger pointed out, that he went to a place which love could never reach.[27] That is where God learned to empathize. The Chief Shepherd walked in the valley of death.

But even if the apostolic doctrine of the cross does not glorify violence as such, does it not glorify meek acquiescence in violence? This is a charge often made by feminists. Elizabeth Bettenhausen, for example, writes, 'Christian theology has often imposed upon women a norm of imitative self-sacrifice based on the crucifixion of Jesus of Nazareth. Powerlessness is equated with faithfulness'.[28]

There is a degree of inconsistency here. The only alternative to meeting violence with meekness is to meet it with violence, or at least with a show of force, yet Dr Bettenhausen also declares (on the very same page) that, 'no violence . . . is ever divine will'.[29] But the inconsistency should not blind us to the truth that lies at the core of her protest. Christian men have too often championed a concept of 'biblical manhood and womanhood' which not only justified the behaviour of domineering patriarchs, but bred expectations that a woman would always sacrifice her own interests to those of her husband and children. He would forge ahead; she would practise *kenosis*. He would be the successful husband; she would be the supportive wife. In extreme instances this might even include keeping silent about sexual abuse and staying in a marriage despite being a battered spouse.

But to suggest that an abusive patriarchy can claim sanction from the story of the self-sacrifice of Jesus borders on the perverse. The New Testament

---

27. Ratzinger, *Introduction to Christianity*, p. 300.
28. From her foreword to Brown and Bohn, p. xii.
29. Ibid.

invokes the cross as the paradigm of *male* self-sacrifice: 'Husbands, love your wives, just as Christ loved the church and gave himself up for her' (Eph. 5:25); far from declaring that the role of the wife is to make sure, at whatever cost to herself, that her husband becomes all that he can be, it lays down that the husband is to ensure that she becomes all that she can be. This, surely, is what Paul meant when he spoke of 'nourishing and cherishing' (Eph. 5:29, ESV). Christ did not sacrifice himself in order that his church become a quivering wreck. He died to make her glorious and radiant (Eph. 5:27). No man, then, can stand at the cross of Calvary and feel inspired to live as a selfish, domineering patriarch. Nor can he find in the headship of Christ as exemplified at Calvary (Eph. 5:23) any warrant to treat a woman as his slave. In Christ, there is neither male nor female (Gal. 3:28); and Jesus certainly never intended the command to turn the other cheek to apply only to his female followers.

Nor did he ever lay down that those who glory in the cross (Gal. 6:14) must stand aside from the struggle for women's rights. On the contrary, we have every warrant to absolve a woman from the obligation to stay in an abusive relationship (1 Cor. 7:15); and a duty to fight for the rights of women as Paul fought for the rights of Gentiles and William Wilberforce for the rights of slaves. In neither instance did a belief in vicarious atonement breed meek acquiescence in violence.

God resisting evil

Finally, precisely as an act of atonement the cross is an atonement for violence itself. But more is happening here than Christ meekly bearing the guilt of our human crimes. Far from demonstrating God's meek acquiescence in violence, the cross shows him at war with it, and determined to destroy it. This is why one of the key themes of the atonement (to be explored in ch. 11) is victory. At Golgotha, God executed justice. At Golgotha, Christ conquered death, disarmed the evil powers, and destroyed Satan's empire. That victory has still to receive its final, public acclamation, but in the meantime, sure of victory, we here are at war with the spiritual forces that seek to destroy us; vocal, as was Christ, in defence of the marginalized and the powerless; and opposed to all that threatens to reduce our civilization to a new dark age.

And in all this, we draw inspiration from the one who came into this world not only to suffer, but to fight the devil on his own ground.

5. EXPIATION: COVERING OUR SIN

The grandeur of the cross, as the New Testament conceives it, lies in the fact that here the Son of God offered himself in the place of sinners. But what did the cross, so understood, achieve? The answer is rich and varied. The cross achieved expiation, propitiation, reconciliation, justification, redemption, forgiveness and victory; and even this list is not exhaustive.

Many have seen this variety of terms as a problem in itself, arguing that it shows that the New Testament contains no unified concept of the atonement, but only one that is at best fragmentary, and at worst, incoherent. But does the variety of terms do any more than remind us that no single concept is adequate to bring out the full meaning of the cross? Mere multiplicity of terms can hardly be a problem. For example, God has many titles and sustains many different relations to the world (lord, king, judge, shepherd, father, for instance), but this is surely not a symptom of incoherence, even though some of the concepts (such as 'father' and 'judge') seem to us scarcely compatible.

A similar range of titles and functions is applied to Christ. He is the Logos, God, the Son of God, the Lord and the Son of Man; he is the Messiah, the Mediator and the Saviour; and he is prophet, priest and king. None of these, alone or all together, exhaust the significance of Jesus, yet they give a unified and coherent picture of his glory.

The same is true of the concepts applied to the atonement. No single one tells the whole truth, nor do all of them together (at least as understood by us) exhaust the meaning of the cross. Yet neither do they merely present the many-sidedness of Calvary. The various concepts are interrelated and inter-dependent, and together they give a thrilling and coherent picture of what the cross achieved. Christ died for our salvation, and this salvation included all the aspects denoted by the New Testament vocabulary of the cross.

Only metaphors?

But not only is there a great variety of terms and concepts. The terms them-selves, we are told, are mere metaphors and ill-adapted for the construction of theological doctrines, particularly for the construction of such dogmas as penal substitution. Metaphors cannot be taken literally, and may often have only a tenuous connection with reality and actuality.

It is by no means clear, however, what is meant by describing biblical language on the atonement (or indeed theological language in general) as metaphorical. It may be, as C. S. Lewis suggested, that all language about non-physical things is metaphorical.[1] It is certainly true that many biblical words, like words in general, suggest pictures, particularly in their etymology. For example, if we speak of something as 'edifying', we are invoking the idea of building a house ('edifice'), but that does not mean that the edifying practice does not bring some real positive benefit, just as each brick brings the house nearer completion. Similarly, the word 'expiate' as used by biblical writers derives from the Hebrew verb, *kipper*, which means 'to cover' and referred in its original usage to covering one physical object with another. Clearly, this is not what the cross achieves. But does this mean that there is no 'real' covering of sin, or that the specialized word, 'expiate', derived from cover, points to something purely figurative, leaving the sin still exposed provocatively before God?

It is also true that atonement talk is analogical. The theologian has no option but to 'speak as a man' (Rom. 3:5, KJV), and while aware of using 'childish prattle' is also aware that there are continuities between God's actions and ours (as there are continuities between animal actions and his own). For example, God 'formed' Adam from the dust of the ground (Gen. 2:7) and the specific verb used (*yāṣar*) is the one normally used to describe the work of the potter. This clearly suggests an analogy between the work of God and the work of the potter, but does this mean that God is creator only metaphorically? Similarly God's anger is analogous

---

    1. C. S. Lewis, *They Asked for a Paper: Papers and Addresses* (London: Geoffrey Bles, 1962), p. 161.

to ours, but does this make it merely metaphorical? If so, is his love also only metaphorical?

The truth, surely, is that our creativity, anger and love are but pale shadows of his. We are images of him, not he an image of us. Had the world never existed, God would still have been love, and had the human race never existed God would still have been angry with Lucifer and his cohorts.

In the same way, there are analogies between our human relations with each other and God's relations with us. Sometimes, for example, there is a breakdown in human relationships. In the same way sin has brought a breakdown in relationships between ourselves and God; instead of peace there is enmity and alienation. Are these mere metaphors? If so, reconciliation, too, is but a metaphor, and the peace established by the cross merely figurative.

The problem becomes even more serious when we ask (as we already have) whether Christ is a priest only metaphorically, offering but a metaphorical sacrifice. If so, who is the real, non-metaphorical priest, and where is the real sacrifice? Besides, if his priesthood is metaphorical we have to ask whether his divine sonship is also purely figurative: a mere shadow of ours, and not quite the real thing. Such reasoning puts the truth (even partial truth) entirely beyond our grasp. But the reality, surely, is that human priesthood and human sacrifices and human sonship are but pale shadows of the divine. It is our human priesthood that is metaphorical, not his. To say this is simply to reflect the priority of the invisible over the visible and of the eternal over the temporal. This is why the fact that Christ has no successors is not a detraction from his priesthood, but an enhancement of it; and why the fact that though *begotten* he is not *originated* enhances his sonship rather than detracts from it. No human language can be applied to the divine without exposing its own limitations.

Suppose we were to replace 'metaphor' with another figure of speech, the simile. There is little functional difference between them, the main thing being that simile, as distinct from metaphor, compares things by use of the word 'like'. E. L. Mascall illustrates what this might mean if applied to the atonement: 'thus the saving work of Christ is something like winning a battle, something like curing a disease, something like releasing a prisoner, something like repatriating an exile'.[2] As Mascall acknowledges, the saving work of Christ is not *exactly* like any one of these, but he suggests that they are far more serviceable if brought together into a coherent pattern, where each modifies and illuminates the other. But even so, all we acquire is 'a less inadequate understanding of the

---

2. E. L. Mascall, *Whatever Happened to the Human Mind: Essays in Christian Orthodoxy* (London: SPCK, 1980), p. 124.

Saviour's work than we should have if we used only one of them or refrained from using any of them at all'.[3]

But has God left us with nothing better than a 'less inadequate' understanding of the achievement of his Son? Have we nothing but elusive shadows and images? There may indeed be metaphors and similes for the divine anger and for the divine love (in the case of the latter, for example, a mother's devotion to her child, Isa. 49:15), but the anger and the love are not metaphors but realities. Similarly, there may be metaphors for expiation and propitiation, but expiation and propitiation are not metaphors. They are real, meaningful statements of the difference the cross has made to relations between God and humanity.

'Models'

Side by side with the predilection for the word 'metaphor' there has now arisen a predilection for another: 'model'. Green and Baker, for example, entitle chapter 5 of their book *Recovering the Scandal of the Cross*, 'Models of the Atonement'. This use of 'models' in a theological context goes back at least as far as Ian T. Ramsey's *Religious Language*, first published in 1957.[4] Ramsey instanced 'cause', 'wisdom' and 'goodness' as models we apply to the deity: things we are familiar with in daily life and which give us pictures that help us understand God, with whom we are not familiar. By 1977 the word was being used freely by the authors of *The Myth of God Incarnate*, but with little consistency.[5] At its simplest, it meant merely 'example', as when Jesus was referred to (though not necessarily endorsed) as the model of true humanity. At other times it referred to the 'mythological' models by which Christian believers describe religious realities which are indefinable by human language. Among these are the models of God as father and God as person, and among these, too, are various models by which Christians attempted to define their understanding of Jesus: the 'inspirational' model, for example, and the 'incarnational'. Each such model is bound to be 'poetic truth' or 'mythological truth' rather than 'literal fact'.[6] On the other hand, the truth of God's 'self-giving love' must, apparently, be retained, even though,

3. Mascall, *Whatever Happened to the Human Mind?*, p. 124.
4. Ian T. Ramsey, *Religious Language: An Empirical Placing of Theological Phrases* (London: SCM, 1957).
5. John Hick (ed.), *The Myth of God Incarnate* (London: SCM Press, 1977).
6. Ibid., p. 34.

according to Ramsey, 'love' is applied to God only as a picture derived from familiar human experience. Consistency would seem to require that love, too, be taken as no more than a mythological model. But, then, perhaps consistency itself is also a mere model.

By 1976, G. W. H. Lampe in his Bampton Lectures was also applying the word 'model' to Christology, though only to argue that the incarnation of a pre-existent divine being is not the only 'model' that can meet the requirements of the Christian idea of a Saviour.[7] It was this that provoked Mascall to protest that it was not helpful to speak of the Trinity and the incarnation as 'models': 'For, if Christianity is true, the essence of our religion is a personal relation between us and God, and between us and Jesus; and I do not find it easy to have a personal relation with a model . . . for the understanding of the nature and function of Christian doctrine, "model" is a very unsatisfactory model indeed.'[8]

It is easy enough to see how the word 'model' as used in art (an artist's model, for example) can be applied to some aspects of Christianity. Christ is, among other things, the model whom we ought to imitate as we live our Christian lives; and, more profoundly, Christ is the model that God keeps his eye on as he transforms and renews us till we at last we are completely conformed to the image of his Son (Rom. 8:29). We can also, with due caution, use the word 'model' in the sense that Ian T. Ramsey used it, moving from familiar daily experiences to a better understanding of spiritual realities. Our personal experience of reconciliation, for example, can provide a model for the restoration of good relations (šālôm) between ourselves and God.

But beyond such applications, the usefulness of the word 'model' is severely limited, particularly in connection with the atonement. We cannot use it as engineers do, for example, to create a scale-model of some projected work in order to give the client an idea of what it will eventually look like; or even, indeed, to assure themselves that their plan will work. So-called models of the atonement come *after* the cross, and far from offering visual images of it are but non-visual explanations of *what* happened, *why* and *with what consequences*. Theories of the atonement are not models of the crucifixion, only attempts to understand it. Yet, even then, what is achieved is not such an understanding as geneticists can offer of the DNA molecule by creating a visible structure or diagram which clearly illustrates its double-helix formation.

---

7. G. W. H. Lampe, *God As Spirit: The Bampton Lectures, 1976* (Oxford: Clarendon Press, 1977), p. 14.

8. Mascall, *Whatever Happened to the Human Mind?*, p. 125.

It is no more possible to create a visible model of the atonement than it is to create a visible model of God himself (in whose heart the atonement takes place).

But then neither can we create a mathematical model of the atonement, as Einstein was able to do for the relation between mass and energy with his famous formula, $E=mc^2$. Mathematics applies only to what is measurable, and is no more applicable to the atonement than it is to love. For the same reason, digitalized computer models are equally out of the question.

Back, then, to basics. Any viable theology of the cross has to be rooted not in human invention or imagination, but in divine revelation; and what revelation gives us is not a set of models from which we are to make a selection or which we are merely to use as a starting-point for our own creative reflection, but a definitive and canonical word of the cross. In accordance with this, what such magisterial theologians as Anselm, Aquinas, Luther, Calvin and Hodge thought they were setting forth was not 'models' but a coherent doctrine which reflected, they believed, God's own understanding of what was transacted at Calvary; an understanding which was encapsulated in a series of God-given keywords, such as expiation, propitiation and reconciliation. The fact that these concepts are divinely given means that we can neither ignore nor replace them. On the other hand, we cannot simply repeat them parrot-fashion. They give us the building-blocks of a doctrine, not the doctrine itself. What we have to do is explain, expound and correlate them in order to make them intelligible (though never palatable) to the world of our day.

Culture-bound?

But are these concepts not culture-bound? Notions such as sacrifice and pro-pitiation may have been perfectly intelligible in the world of the first century; today they are not only alien but, when unpacked, profoundly offensive. Is there not a need, then, for a set of new models and metaphors?

There is a fascinating ambivalence in comments of this sort. On the one hand, we are challenged to proclaim the atonement in terms which connect with people's reality, using language and metaphors that draw on the shared experience of our own particular time and place.[9] On the other, we are warned against the danger of removing the scandal of the cross by imposing upon it the framework of a particular culture. Hence the need to *recover* the scandal

---

9. Green and Baker, *Recovering the Scandal of the Cross*, p. 146.

of the cross, leaving us in some perplexity as to whether, for example, the problem with the idea of penal substitution is that it *is* scandalous (that is, offensive to modern humans) or that it *removes* the scandal. Charles Hodge, for instance, is accused of trying to remove the scandal by accommodating the doctrine of the atonement to the idea of criminal justice which prevailed in the eastern United States in the mid-nineteenth century.[10]

Which is it to be? We need to be clear where the scandal of the cross lies: not primarily in such concepts as expiation and propitiation, but in the *prima facie* absurdity that a crucified first-century Jewish criminal is the Saviour of the world, and that his cross was the actual instrument of that salvation. Side by side with that lies another scandal: the assumption that all human beings, from Francis of Assisi to Joseph Stalin, are sinners in need of salvation in the first place. And, as if all this were not enough, the further scandalous idea that God is not all-indulgent love, but is dreadfully provoked by sin and needs to be pacified.

Christian theology dare not make itself palatable by eliminating any of these elements from its message. The challenge, instead, is to make them intelligible and accessible. But this, after all, is no more than the basic task of hermeneutics, to transport the message from one language, age and culture to another. This is not a challenge confined to Christian theologians. It also faces those trying to sell Western democracy to an Islamic society and those struggling to promote birth-control on the Indian subcontinent.

On the other hand, we should not exaggerate the alien nature of the key concepts of the atonement. The notion of sacrifice, for example, is by no means foreign to the contemporary mind (though we must always be careful not to confuse 'contemporary' with 'Western'). Even the practice of ritual animal sacrifice still persists in, for example, Africa's traditional religions and some schools of Hinduism. It is also a feature of the annual Muslim Festival of Eid ul-Adha (commemorating the sacrifice of Ishmael/Ismul); and in the United States the right of adherents of Santeria to practise ritual sacrifice has been recognized by the Supreme Court. But even where ritual animal sacrifice is no longer practised, the core idea still survives in everyday speech. Parents still make sacrifices for their children; members of the armed forces still make the 'supreme sacrifice'; and individuals still deliberately 'sacrifice themselves' to save the lives of friends and colleagues.

Such 'sacrifices' are not offered as acts of atonement. Nevertheless, they are reminders that the idea of one human making sacrifices for another, and even

---

10. Ibid., pp. 146–150.

laying down her life for others, is by no means foreign to modern culture. We may share Wilfred Owen's cynicism with regard to what he called, 'The old Lie', *dulce et decorum est pro patria mori* ('It is sweet and seemly to lay down one's life for one's country'),[11] but we have no difficulty understanding it; and by the same token we have no difficulty understanding St Paul's exultant exclamation, 'the Son of God loved me and gave himself for me' (Gal. 2:20).

Other key concepts of the atonement are likewise still current. Millions of Roman Catholics still attend a Mass in which the body of Christ is offered as a 'propitiatory' sacrifice, just as they regularly offer 'satisfaction' in respect of the sins confessed in the sacrament of penance. The idea of reconciliation is even more familiar, not only in marriage counselling, for example, but also in international relations, where conflicting nations strive to achieve peace through negotiation. Even in industrial relations (and increasingly in civil court cases) arbitration aims at 'bringing the two parties together': precisely the idea behind the word 'atonement' (at-one-ment).

In the same way, we are only too familiar with stories of people being taken hostage and being liberated (redeemed) only on payment of a ransom. Even the idea of a 'debt to justice' is still current: people released from prison commonly refer to themselves as having 'paid their debt to society'.

These examples are evidence enough that the key concepts of the New Testament doctrine of the atonement are by no means as outmoded and unintelligible as many modern theologians would have us believe. On the contrary, they are deeply rooted in enduring features of human relationships. At the same time, however, we have to come to terms with the fact that coherence and logic are never enough to persuade human beings of the truth of the Christian gospel. It takes little to convince us that God, as love, is not overly troubled by our sins and can easily ignore them. It takes much more to convince us that we are seriously sinful, that not even love can ignore this, that there can be no forgiveness unless that sin is atoned for, and that the only possible atonement is the self-sacrifice of the Son of God; a sacrifice offered not on a golden crucifix, but on a crude and barbarous scaffold. Here, humanity mocks, rather than adores, and our revulsion is aggravated by the modern confusion between the religious and the aesthetic. What we expect to find when we penetrate to the heart of a great world faith is a magnificent cathedral, glorious music, visual splendour and cathartic eloquence. When Pompey and his soldiers entered the Holy of Holies in AD 63 they were scandalized to find no image there: not a 'god' in sight. The scandal of Christianity is even greater. Its

---

11. In the poem 'Dulce Et Decorum Est', 1917.

EXPIATION: COVERING OUR SIN

holy of holies is a cross where its Saviour hangs, bloodied and beaten, between two thieves.

There is beauty here, of course, but not such beauty as the natural eye can see. As the Apostle Paul reminds us, the preaching of the cross is offensive folly to 'the person without the Spirit' (1 Cor. 2:14). Nor is this some new, modern problem, as if only those who live in a high-tech society are offended by the cross. After all, it was first-century people who crucified Jesus in the first place. Clearly, they were offended by *himself* before they were offended by his cross. Besides, the message of the Suffering Servant was already offensive to the Jews of Isaiah's day, and Paul faced the same problem in his own. As Hengel points out, 'for Paul and his contemporaries the cross of Jesus was not a didactic, symbolic or speculative element but a very specific and highly offensive matter which imposed a burden on the earliest missionary preaching'.[12] So offensive was it, indeed, that to believe in it was seen as a sign of madness.[13] This is no excuse for not preaching the gospel with all the skill, wisdom, passion and logical force we can muster. But more is needed than mere human persuasiveness. No one can see the truth of the kingdom unless, in the words of Jesus, he is born again, or unless, in the words of Paul, the gospel comes 'not simply with words, but also with power, with the Holy Spirit and with deep conviction' (1 Thess. 1:5). In the last analysis, only God can show us the beauty of his Son and the glory of his cross. Otherwise, we shall remain forever members of the chorus of derision.

Our task, then, is not to make an assessment of the prevailing 'sociology of knowledge' and then craft a message in keeping with the preconceptions and plausibility-structures of the age. Our task is much simpler. As preachers and theologians we are mere heralds, and as such the challenge facing us is not to ask what moderns are willing to believe, but what God has commanded us to say. If we are content to adhere to the apostolic faith, the answer is unambiguous: 'Go and preach Christ crucified.' But he also added a rider, that we should do it 'with Spirit-taught words' (1 Cor. 2:13).

We have been left in no doubt what these words are: expiation, propitiation, reconciliation, redemption and victory. But what, precisely, do these words mean?

---

12. Martin Hengel, *Crucifixion*, p. 18.
13. Cf. Justin Martyr, *First Apology* I, 13:4: 'For they proclaim our madness to consist in this, that we give to a crucified man a place second to the unchangeable and eternal God' (ANF, vol. 1).

The atonement and sin: *expiation*

The concept of expiation has suffered from being presented as an unwelcome 'liberal' alternative to propitiation. The background to this is C. H. Dodd's research into the meaning of the Greek verb *hilaskesthai* and its cognate noun, *hilasmos*. Dodd not only argued that this word-group never connoted 'propitiation' but claimed, further, that the whole idea of propitiating an angry deity was sub-Christian. The word 'propitiation' should therefore be banished from Bible translations and replaced with the word 'expiation'.[14] The result was a swing of the evangelical pendulum to the opposite extreme. The word 'expiation' is now in bad grace and those who propose it as an appropriate translation in key New Testament passages are liable to find their orthodoxy under the microscope.

Such polarization is entirely unnecessary. 'Expiation' highlights the effect of the atonement on sin, whereas 'propitiation' highlights its effect on God. Sin is expiated, God is propitiated and, as Büchsel points out,[15] these cannot be separated. God can be propitiated only if sin is expiated; and sin is expiated only in order that God may be propitiated.

The clearest New Testament expression of the idea of expiation is in Hebrews 2:17, but unfortunately this is obscured in the most widely used English versions. The key point of the verse is that Jesus was made like his people in every way so that he might be a faithful and compassionate high priest. The question is, 'What did he achieve in his capacity as high priest?' According to the KJV, it was 'to make *reconciliation* for the sins of the people'. However, the underlying Greek word, *hilaskesthai*, never means 'reconciliation', in either biblical or secular Greek; besides, of all the New Testament writers, Paul is the only one to speak of reconciliation, a concept which has its own dedicated vocabulary (*katallagē* and its cognates). The NIV renders the passage, to 'make atonement for the sins of the people', which conveniently avoids having to choose between expiation and propitiation, but looks very much like an evasion. There is no biblical word corresponding to atonement, an entirely Anglo-Saxon compound meaning *at-one-ment* (as we have already seen). The ESV, by contrast, bites the bullet and boldly renders, 'to make propitiation for the sins of the people'.

It is hard to avoid the impression that dogmatic considerations are unduly influencing recent evangelical translations, as if the word 'expiation' were to be

---

14. See especially C. H. Dodd, *The Bible and the Greeks* (London: Hodder and Stoughton, 1935), pp. 82–95.

15. *TDNT*, III, p. 316.

EXPIATION: COVERING OUR SIN

avoided at all costs and the word 'propitiation' to be introduced wherever possible (ESV also uses propitiation in every other instance of the *hilaskesthai* word-group: Rom. 3.25; 1 John 2:2; 1 John 4:10). As already suggested, the prejudice is entirely unnecessary, but, quite apart from that, the grammar of Hebrews 2:17 makes plain that the natural translation would be, 'to expiate the sins of the people'. The object of the verb is not God, but 'the sins'; and sins cannot be propitiated. They can only be expiated. Admittedly, this is an unusual construction. Apart from this passage the verb is seldom, if ever, used with sin as the object in either biblical or secular Greek. But that is how it is used here, and we must respect that. The only alternative is to invoke some recondite grammar, such as, for example, that here the accusative is an 'accusative of reference', opening the door to the rendering, 'made propitiation with reference to the sins of the people'. But if the obvious grammatical relations give a perfectly intelligible (though perhaps unwelcome) sense, why invoke other, more esoteric rules? Even if it be argued that *hilaskesthai* always hints at propitiation it never does so in the absence of expiation. It is the expiation that propitiates, and here, in translations of Hebrews 2:17 the idea of expiation should be explicit. Christ *expiated* the sins of the people.

This is in line with other phrases used by the writer to the Hebrews to describe the effects of Christ's sacrifice. It purged away sin (Heb. 1:3); it did away with sin (Heb. 9:26); it secured the forgiveness of sin (lit. its *aphesis* or dismissal, Heb. 9.22); it 'took away' sin (Heb. 10:4). The wider usage of scripture is similar. In John 1:29, for example, the Baptist describes Jesus as 'the Lamb of God, who takes away the sin of the world'. The same spatial imagery, highlighting the idea of removal, occurs in the ritual of Yom Kippur, where the scapegoat carries into the wilderness all the iniquities of Israel. Only by this act of expiation is God propitiated.

The link between *hilaskesthai* and sin continues in the three other New Testament occurrences of this concept: Romans 3:25, 1 John 2:2 and 1 John 4:10. In the first of these, Paul declares that God presented Christ as a *hilastērion* by his blood through faith. There has been much scholarly debate on the details, but the key issue for our purposes is the meaning of *hilastērion*. At one level, the question is a grammatical one: is it a noun or an adjective (in form, it could be either)? If it is an adjective it means that God presented Christ as one having the quality of being 'expiatory'. If it is a noun it means that Christ was presented as an expiation. But there is another possibility. The word *hilastērion* may have a very specific meaning. Throughout the LXX (e.g., Exod. 25:17 and 37:6; cf. Heb. 9:5) it translates the Hebrew *kappōret*, the solid gold lid of the Ark of the Covenant, traditionally referred to as 'the mercy seat' in English versions. Under this cover were the two tablets on which God had inscribed the Decalogue, and on it, on Yom Kippur, was sprinkled the blood of the sin offering when the high priest entered the Holy of Holies (Lev. 16:15) to make atonement for the sins of the people. It was clearly a point of supreme significance in the religion of Israel. George Smeaton even went so far as to call it 'the centre-point of the entire Old Testament economy'.[16] The only other occurrence of the word in the New Testament is in Hebrews 9:5, where the writer speaks of 'the cherubim of the Glory, overshadowing the *hilastērion*'. This clearly refers to the mercy seat (NIV, 'atonement covering').

There is no reason to depart from this meaning in Romans 3:25. Quite apart from being linguistically accurate it is also profoundly suggestive. The mercy seat was not merely a lid. It was a cover, and as such (a *kappōret*) it was closely linked to the verb *kipper* (to expiate) and to the noun *kōper* (an expiation). Calvin, not given to excessive use of Levitical symbolism, describes the restricted literal understanding of the mercy seat as 'a tame explanation', and declares (commenting on Exod. 25:17), 'I doubt not but that Moses alludes in this word to a metaphorical meaning, for the law requires a covering to cancel our transgressions'.[17] He adheres to this interpretation in his commentary on Romans 3:25, though somewhat more cautiously: 'There is, I think, an allusion in the word *hilastērion*, as I have said, to the ancient mercy seat, for he informs us that in Christ there was exhibited in reality that which was given figuratively to the Jews.'[18]

It was here, at the mercy seat, that Yahweh met with his people; and it was here that he spoke to them (Exod. 25:22). We can be sure that it was by no accident, but by divine design, that the meeting point was the place where the tablets of the (broken) law were covered by the blood-sprinkled lid. This was the most sacred point in the cultic institutions of Israel, the most holy point

---

16. George Smeaton, *The Doctrine of the Atonement According to the Apostles* (repr., Peabody: Hendrickson, 1988 [1870]), p. 137.

17. John Calvin, *Commentary on the Last Four Books of Moses arranged in the Form of a Harmony*, vol. 2 (Edinburgh: Calvin Translation Society, 1853), p. 156.

18. John Calvin, *The Epistles of Paul the Apostle to the Romans and to the Thessalonians*, tr. Ross Mackenzie, ed. D. W. Torrance and T. F. Torrance (Grand Rapids: Eerdmans, 1995), p. 75. Geerhardus Vos also takes *hilastērion* to refer to the mercy seat. See *Redemptive History and Biblical Interpretation: The Shorter Writings of Geerhardus Vos*, ed. Richard B. Gaffin (Phillipsburg: Presbyterian and Reformed, 1980), p. 375. John Murray, however, takes a contrary view: 'there is good reason for believing that in this case it means "propitiatory offering"' (*The Epistle to the Romans: The English Text with Introduction, Exposition and Notes*, vol. 1 [Grand Rapids: Eerdmans, 1959], p. 117.

within the Most Holy Place, not because of its physical function as a lid, or because of its visual splendour as a sheet of pure gold 112 centimetres in length and sixty-eight centimetres in breadth, but because it was the place of symbolic atonement and a pointer to the real atonement to be accomplished on the great Yom Kippur at Calvary.

Calvin is confident that when Paul uses the word *hilastērion* in Romans 3:25 he is referring to 'this metaphor' (the mercy seat), 'because God was propitiated towards believers by the covering of the law'.[19] The Roman Catholic commentator, Joseph A. Fitzmyer agrees:

> *hilastērion* is better understood against the background of the LXX usage of the Day of Atonement rite, so it would depict Christ as the new 'mercy seat', presented or displayed by the Father as a means of expiating and wiping away the sins of humanity, indeed as the place of the presence of God, of his revelation, and of his expiatory power.[20]

Here, if anywhere, is an authoritative 'model' of the atonement. Christ not only provides, but *is,* the 'atonement cover' which obscures our sins from the sight of God, expiating our guilt by his blood. This is metaphor, of course, and seriously anthropomorphic: God cannot but see. But it is by no means an unusual metaphor. In Psalm 25:7, for example, David prays, 'Do not remember the sins of my youth'; and in Psalm 79:8 Asaph pleads, 'Do not hold against us the sins of past generations'. The prophets, too, strike the same note. In Isaiah 43:25 God declares that he will remember our sins 'no more'. Most striking of all is Micah 7:19, which portrays God as hurling all our sins into the depths of the sea.

Clearly, God does not forget, any more than he suffers from impaired vision. But the sacrifice of Christ has so covered our sins that they are operationally invisible. Our guilt is no longer a provocation to God.

Once we accept the idea of Christ as the 'atonement cover' we can begin to draw other conclusions from Romans 3:25 and its context. Perhaps the most important of these is that the expiatory power of Christ lies in his blood. He is a *hilastērion* 'in' or 'by' his blood. This is slightly complicated by the question whether the phrase 'in his blood' is to be taken with 'faith' or with *hilastērion.* The former is preferred by the older (1984) edition of the NIV, which reads,

---

19. Calvin, *Harmony of the Pentateuch*, vol. 2, p. 156.

20. Joseph A. Fitzmyer, *Romans: A New Translation with Introduction and Commentary*, Anchor Bible, vol. 33 (London: Geoffrey Chapman, 1993), p. 350.

'God presented [him] as a sacrifice of atonement, through faith in his blood'. The newer (2011) NIV, however, takes the latter option, as does the ESV, which reads 'whom God put forth as a propitiation by his blood, to be received by faith'. Though this verges on paraphrase, it avoids the idea that our faith is itself a constituent element in the expiation/propitiation. Our faith trusts in the expiation, but it is not part of it, even though we have to insist that the *hilastērion* avails nothing unless we put our trust in it. It is by his blood, in and by itself, that Christ expiates sin and by doing so secures forgiveness and all the other blessings of the covenant (Matt. 26:28).

It is sometimes objected that this leaves us with the incongruous image of Christ as both the 'atonement cover' and the blood sprinkled upon it. But in terms of their significance and efficacy the two cannot be separated. The 'atonement cover' was nothing without the blood but, conversely, the blood itself would have been unavailing had it been sprinkled anywhere else. The overall image is no more challenging than that of Jesus entering the Most Holy Place carrying his own blood (Heb. 9:12) or the earlier typology of the Day of Atonement, where Christ is both the slain goat of the sin offering and the living goat who carries the people's sin into the wilderness. The underlying emphasis is absolutely clear: it is as a sacrifice that Christ atones. We have expiation by his blood.

We should also note the stress in Romans 3:25 on the initiative of God the Father: it was he who presented his Son as a *hilastērion*. It has proved almost impossible to dissociate the evangelical doctrine of the atonement from the caricature that it portrays God as an implacable, vengeful deity for whose goodwill Christ had to pay a heavy price. This is clearly not the picture Paul presents here. Instead, it is precisely God himself who brings forward the sacrifice which expiates our sin. Evangelicalism has always had a firm grasp of this and John Murray spoke for the whole tradition when he wrote, 'It is quite alien to biblical thought to overlook the agency of God the Father in the provisions of redemption and it is perversion to represent the Father as won over to the exercise of grace and mercy by the intervention of Christ's pro-pitiatory accomplishment.'[21]

But why did God have to intervene and what was it that made the sacrifice of Christ necessary? The answer lies back in Romans 3:23: 'all have sinned and fall short of the glory of God'. Here again the link between *hilaskesthai* and sin is clear, and it is highlighted further in Romans 8:3, which declares that the precise thing that happened at Calvary was that there God condemned *sin*. It received its doom in the flesh of his own Son. That doom was also its expiation.

---

21. Murray, *Romans*, vol. 1, p. 117.

But why did there have to be a mercy seat in the first place? Why the need for a sacrifice, and for blood? To demonstrate God's righteousness, says Paul. This is complicated by the fact that in this section of Romans (Rom. 3:21–26) the apostle uses the word righteousness (Gk *dikaiosynē*) in two different senses. In the earlier verses (21 and 22) it clearly refers to the righteousness which God confers on us in the grace of justification and which we receive through faith. This is the righteousness of which Paul speaks in Philippians 3:9, describing it not simply as the righteousness *of* God, but as a righteousness *from* God; not a divine attribute before which the apostle fell in adoration, but a gift which he coveted. The righteousness to which he refers in Romans 3:25, however, is the divine attribute of righteousness; not something God gives or which we may seek, but a quality which God demonstrates in presenting Christ as a *hilastērion*. The 1984 NIV reflects the difference between the two concepts (though they are expressed by the same word in the original) by using the translation 'justice' in verse 25.[22]

One implication of Paul's language here is that what God did at Calvary was in the public domain, in marked contrast to what happened on the Old Testament Day of Atonement. When the high priest entered the Holy of Holies he was all alone and entirely out of public view in a place where no man living had ever been but himself. He alone saw the mercy seat and he alone was witness to the sprinkling of the blood. At Calvary, all was different. Here the sacrifice was 'presented' and 'lifted up' (John 12:32), and so public that even the daily commuters to Jerusalem could see it. In the centuries that followed, all eyes have had access to it through the Gospels. Yet even in them there is a degree of hiddenness. While we have clear access to the outward, physical sufferings of Jesus, the veil into the sufferings of his soul is lifted only partially. We struggle to say anything about the meaning of his forsakenness, and we know even less about the pain of God his Father.

But back again to the core question: what was demonstrated? God's righteousness! At the same time, of course, the cross also proclaimed God's love (Rom. 5:8), but righteousness must not be collapsed into love. It was because God is righteous that sin required expiation; it was because he is love that he provided it. What is in view here in Romans 3 is God exacting retribution and publicly condemning sin in his capacity as Judge of all the earth, a judge who must do right (Gen. 18:25). No external force or law compels God to condemn sin. Even to say that he condemns it because it is right to do so is not enough.

---

22. The new NIV, however, does not maintain the distinction, but renders v. 25, 'to demonstrate his righteousness'.

From a Christian point of view, the foundation of ethics lies in what God *is*. He is good, and it is because he is good that he commands what is right. But precisely because he is good he recoils from all inhumanity and all lawlessness. What he is in the very core of his being means that he cannot condone it or walk by on the other side. By very necessity of his nature he abhors it. There can be no peaceful coexistence between God and un-expiated sin, any more than there can be a truce between God and the devil.

There are two aspects to the demonstration of divine justice referred to in Romans 3:25. First, there is a retrospective aspect. By the time Christ was presented as the *hilastērion*, God had already been forgiving sins for thousands of years, and it looked very much as if in forgiving them he had been condoning them, leaving them unpunished. What right had he to do so? It is not a question we in the twenty-first century commonly ask in respect of God's judicial processes, but we ask it frequently enough with regard to our own. The acquittal of the guilty, and the imposition of what we see as over-lenient sentences on those convicted of serious crimes, still causes public outrage. If we saw things from God's point of view we would, to say the least, be equally puzzled by the divine leniency. But here, in Romans 3:25 Paul explains it. God's forgiveness of the sins of Adam and Noah and Abraham and Jacob and David was justified by the fact that their sins would one day be expiated at the *hilastērion*, by the blood of Christ Jesus.

But there is also a demonstration of God's rectitude in what Paul calls 'the now time' (Rom. 3:26). When God justifies those who have faith in Jesus he is actually pronouncing the wicked righteous (Rom. 4:5), or justifying the ungodly, as it is rendered in the KJV. Is this not a perversion of justice? No! God has already demonstrated his justice by presenting Christ as the expiation for our sins. Our guilt is covered and washed away, and God is therefore just in justifying sinners in the present age. His remitting of sins is no arbitrary indulgence, but an absolutely right response to the blood of Christ. Paul reinforces this by linking expiation and justification to a third concept, redemption (Rom. 3:24). We are forgiven not simply as sinners but as sinners who have been redeemed by the expiatory blood of Christ.

These links must not be broken. The blood expiates; the expiation redeems; and the redemption justifies.

1 John 2:2

The concept of expiation also occurs (twice) in the first letter of John. The form John uses is *hilasmos*, and here again the versions struggle to find an appropriate translation. Recent versions such as the NIV and the NRSV opt for 'atoning sacrifice'. The KJV, followed by the ESV, chooses 'propitiation'; and this, the 'appeasing' or 'placating' of God, will clearly be the ultimate outcome of the sacrifice of Christ. But the immediate reference in both 1 John 2:2 and 1 John 4:10 is to expiation: the *hilasmos* is 'for our sins'. It covers them.

This link with sin is particularly clear in the context of 1 John 2:2. The first verse provides the setting: 'if anybody does sin'. John's immediate concern is to reassure believers (he addresses them as his 'dear children'), and the reason for his concern is that false teaching has clearly been spreading with regard to the question of Christians sinning. John himself makes plain the high expectations he holds with regard to Christian conduct: 'I write this to you so that you will not sin' (1 John 2:1). The full implication of this becomes clear in 3:9: 'Those who have been born of God do not sin, because God's seed abides in them' (NRSV). Indeed, 'they cannot sin, because they have been born of God'. It looks very much as if some false teachers were pushing an antinomian point of view and conveying the impression that sin in believers was no great matter. John wishes to counter this, but he is aware at the same time that other false teachers were taking the opposite line. They were claiming to be 'without sin', a position John dismisses as self-deception (1 John 1:6–8).

There is a clear tension between these two positions. If we cannot sin, how can it be self-deception to claim to be without sin? The tension cannot be resolved, as it is in the NIV, by appealing to the fact that John uses the present tense of the verb 'to sin', stressing that this is a 'present continuous' tense and then offering the translation, 'No one who is born of God *will continue to sin*' or '*cannot go on sinning*' (1 John 3:9, italics mine). This is too great a weight for such a subtle distinction; and in any case if we say that we do not keep on sinning we are still deceiving ourselves.

John himself does not address the tension between *cannot* sin and *do* sin. The one pointer he offers is in 1 John 3:4, 'sin is lawlessness'. The Greek word here is *anomia*, the root of our English 'anomaly'. Sin is not only both defiance and evasion of the law of God. It is inherently absurd and beyond logical understanding. How could Lucifer, a prince of light, sin? How could Adam, the image of God, sin? And above all, how can a Christian believer sin, when she draws every breath and takes every step as someone renewed by grace, indwelt by the Holy Spirit and united to Christ? It is absurd, and we must learn to view it with abhorrence and revulsion.

But we do sin; and when it happens, what are we to do? This is where the *hilasmos* comes in. Believers cannot sin, 'but if anyone does sin, we have an advocate with the Father, Jesus Christ the righteous' (1 John 2:1, ESV).

The word 'advocate' translates the Greek *paraklētos*, literally 'someone called in'. Its meaning ranges from 'helper' to 'exhorter' to 'encourager' to 'advocate', and it is this last courtroom sense that is required here. We are in serious trouble, charged with sin, unable to deny it and in danger of the displeasure and anger of God. We need an advocate; and we have one, 'Jesus Christ the righteous'. From other sources (for example, 1 John 4:14) we know that the advocate is the Son of the Father before whom he pleads, but what is emphasized here is not his sonship but his character and reputation. He is not in court to plead the personal innocence of his clients. Their guilt is taken for granted. If he himself were not righteous he could not practise at this bar; he would be in the dock, himself accused and in need of an advocate. But he *is* righteous, and he possesses that status as one who shares the same nature and has faced the same temptations as those he pleads for. He identifies with them, and brings to his advocacy not only the authority of his divine identity and of the high regard in which he is held in the court in which he appears, but also his reputation as one who holds the law in the highest respect, who never deviated from it in his own life, and who will ask for no deviation from it in the course of his pleading. His plea (*paraklēsis*), like himself, will be righteous.

This pleading, John tells us, is addressed to 'the Father' (*pros ton patera*), and we must bear in mind here that he is Father not only to the advocate but to the 'dear children' he represents, as is made plain in 1 John 3:1. Christ does not plead with God to become their Father, nor is his advocacy aimed at securing his goodwill. He is already Father, and he already loves them (as becomes even clearer in 1 John 4:10), and the advocacy is addressed not to a reluctant deity but to one who delights to pardon and bless.

Yet as advocate he must have a case, and he does. He can point to the *hilasmos*, the expiation. His case is not that they have not sinned, but that their sins have been expiated; and not only so, but that he himself is the expiation. How? In this particular passage, John makes no reference to blood, but he has already spoken of it plainly in 1:7: 'the blood of Jesus, his Son, purifies us from all sin'. Here, once again, it is clear that the direct effect of the sacrifice of Christ was to expiate sin. It washed it away (*katharizei*). This is the essential prelude to propitiation; and this is why the fact that God is 'faithful and just' (1 John 1:9) makes us confident that he will forgive our sins. He owes it to the *hilasmos*.

And Christ himself is the *hilasmos*. This implies, of course, that he is a complete, all-sufficient expiation, requiring no supplement and no repetition. The sinner need bring nothing in his hand. But it also means that when it comes to the atonement there is an essential link between the person and the work of Christ. Not only is God's Son our advocate, he is himself our atonement.

Care is needed here, however. John is not suggesting that the very constitution of the person of Christ is itself a covering for our sin, as if the coming together of deity and humanity in the mystery of the incarnation were itself sufficient to reconcile God and man. It manifestly was not. Christ had to do more than become incarnate. He had to die, because life could come only through death and remission of sins only through blood. What John wants to keep before us is the uniqueness of this particular *hilasmos*. The blood shed here is the blood of the Son of God. In Acts 20:28 Paul is even more daring. God has purchased his church with his own blood. This is what covers our sins. And this is the advocate's case: 'I took these sins and made them mine. I put my name on them, shed my blood for them and carried them away. The little ones have nothing to answer.'

It would be crass to portray this in commercial terms and to speak, for example, as if blood of infinite value covered sins of finite value. John does not go in that direction. He is content to remind us that, in his Eternal Son, God has borne the whole cost of atoning for our sins. He has taken the strain of advocacy and borne the pain of expiation. He gave his life for the sin of the world. No other offering is required.

But what is fact here, and what is metaphorical? The use of courtroom imagery has clear precedents in the Old Testament. Isaiah, for example, begins his prophecy with what Alec Motyer calls 'a courtroom drama', in which the heavens and the earth are called as witnesses when Israel is arraigned and her guilt exposed (Isa. 1:2–9).[23] The same imagery occurs in Micah 6 where, once again, God summons Israel and calls creation as witnesses: 'Stand up, plead my case before the mountains; let the hills hear what you have to say' (Mic. 6:1).

Clearly, the language of such passages is drawn from human analogies, but this does not make the procedures they point to merely metaphorical. God is not a father and a judge in the same sense as he is a rock. He is a real judge and a real father. Indeed, as we have to keep reminding ourselves, it is *our* judging and *our* parenting which are metaphorical: poor shadows and images of the divine. By the same token, while the expiatory sacrifices of the Old Testament (and to some extent the corresponding pagan rituals) were but types and shadows, the sacrifice of Christ was their fulfilment and substance, achieving a real expiation. Similarly, while human courts had, and still have, their advocates and attorneys, this does not reduce the advocacy of Christ to something merely figurative. He is a real advocate, defending real sinners and presenting a real case. In every instance the divine reality transcends the human analogy, but this becomes a problem only if we forget that the human is the analogy to the divine, not the divine to the human. Judicial norms are as much part of the fabric

23. Alec Motyer, *The Prophecy of Isaiah* (Leicester: IVP, 1993), p. 42.

of the universe as physical laws.[24] God has delegated the administration and adjudication of these norms to our human justice systems, but the highest court on earth can make only a provisional judgment. The supreme court, to which all human judicatories are subject and by which they will be judged, is in heaven. Here real breaches of real law will be judged by God the Judge of all; and it is at the bar of this court that Christ, the Advocate Supreme, appears to present a real case for real sinners.

For the whole world?

John is not content, however, to proclaim that Christ is the expiation for our sins. He adds a further significant detail: 'and not for ours only but also for the sins of the whole world' (1 John 2:2, ESV). This echoes the language of John 1:29, which spoke of Jesus as 'the Lamb of God, who takes away the sin of the world'.

In the light of such statements do we have to believe in universal redemption: the doctrine that Christ died to expiate the sin of every human being and to obtain redemption for every sinner? This question is not addressed directly by the New Testament itself, nor was it debated at the time of the Reformation, but it became a serious issue for the Reformed churches when a party of Dutch theologians (the Remonstrants) submitted what came to be known as 'The Five Arminian Articles' to the Estates of the Netherlands in 1610. Article II specifically quotes 1 John 2:2 and lays down that Christ 'died for all men and for every man', obtaining redemption and the forgiveness of sins for them all.[25] This view has profoundly influenced evangelicalism. John Wesley, for example, embraced it passionately, boldly declaring that, 'Christ died, not only for those who are saved, but for those who perish'.[26] More recently, Donald Bloesch has referred to every human being as 'a blood-bought soul'.[27]

---

24. On this, see further Thomas F. Torrance, *Juridical Law and Physical Law* (Edinburgh: Scottish Academic Press, 1982).

25. See Philip Schaff, *The Evangelical Protestant Creeds*, vol. 3 of *The Creeds of Christendom with a History and Critical Notes*, 3 vols. (New York: Harper, 1882), p. 546. Cf. Roger E. Olson, *Arminian Theology: Myths and Realities* (Downers Grove: IVP Academic, 2006), p. 221: 'Christ's death was for everyone even if only actually applied to those who believe.'

26. John Wesley, *Sermons on Several Occasions,* 5 vols. (London: Wesleyan Conference Office, 1876), vol. 3, p. 428.

27. Donald G. Bloesch, *Jesus Christ: Saviour and Lord* (Carlisle: Paternoster Press, 1997), p. 168.

The doctrine of universal redemption was countered by the Synod of Dort (1618–19), which was convened specifically to answer the Remonstrants and which included representatives from almost all the other Reformed churches (including the Church of England).[28] Dort laid down what has come to be known as the doctrine of limited or definite atonement: Christ effectually redeemed those, and those only, who from eternity were chosen to salvation.[29] This remains the official position of those churches which still subscribe to later reformed creeds such as the Westminster Confession. Its definitive statement in English is John Owen's treatise *The Death of Death in the Death of Christ.*[30]

Alongside these two positions there arose a third which purported to adopt a mediating position, seeking to graft the doctrine of universal redemption on to the doctrine of unconditional election. The result is what came to be known as hypothetical universalism: the doctrine that Christ died in one sense for all (including the reprobate) and in another sense for the elect. It was no easy matter, however, to define the difference. What was generally offered was some variation on the theme that Christ died 'with absolute intention for the elect, with conditional intention for the reprobate, provided they believe'. The name usually associated with this position is Moïse Amyraut (Lat., Amyraldus), a divine of the seventeenth-century French Reformed Church.[31] This is why it is often referred

---

28. The official position of the Church of England is expressed in Article XXXI of the *Articles of Religion* (1562): 'The offering of Christ once made is that perfect redemption, propitiation, and satisfaction, for all the sins of the whole world, both original and actual.' It is by no means certain, however, that this is a formal endorsement of universal redemption, since it antedates Arminius and its intention seems to have been to assert (over against the Roman Catholic view of the Mass as a recurring propitiatory sacrifice) the uniqueness and finality of Calvary. This is why the Article adds, 'there is none other satisfaction for sin, but that alone'.

29. *The Canons of the Synod of Dort*, II:VIII. See Schaff, *The Evangelical Protestant Creeds*, p. 587.

30. *The Works of John Owen*, 24 vols., ed. William H. Goold (repr., London: Banner of Truth Trust, 1967 [Edinburgh, 1850–53]), vol. X, pp. 140–428. An earlier reprint, *The Death of Death in the Death of Christ* (London: Banner of Truth, 1959), contains an excellent introductory essay by J. I. Packer (pp. 1–25). See further, B. B. Warfield, *The Plan of Salvation* (rev. ed., Grand Rapids: Eerdmans, n.d.); and David Gibson and Jonathan Gibson (eds.), *From Heaven He Came and Sought Her: Definite Atonement in Biblical, Historical, Theological and Pastoral Perspective* (Wheaton: Crossway, 2014).

31. Amyraut's seminal work was his *Brief Traitté de la Predestination et de ses Principales Dépendances* (1634). He was cited to explain and defend his views at the French National Synod of Alençon in 1637.

to as Amyraldianism, but even before Amyraut hypothetical universalism was already being advocated by Bishop James Davenant, the leading Anglican representative at the Synod of Dort,[32] and Davenant was followed by a distinguished cohort of British theologians, including not only Richard Baxter[33] but some highly vocal members of the Westminster Assembly (most notably Edmund Calamy); and modern Britain still has its Amyraldian Association.[34]

On this, more than almost any other theological question, it is crucially important to define the precise point at issue. Theologians in the tradition of Dort felt the force of such passages as 1 John 2:2 and sought to listen to them. They never denied, for example, what they called the intrinsic sufficiency of the sacrifice of Christ. In and of itself it was sufficient to redeem the whole world and, indeed, many worlds besides; and had it been God's intention to save each and every member of the human race, and bring every sinner home to glory, no greater sacrifice (and no other sacrifice) would have been required but the one offered on the cross of Calvary.

Nor did these divines ever deny that Christ was to be preached fully and freely to every human being, and not only preached, but preached with passion and urgency, pressing home the importance of instant compliance with the offer of salvation. Dort itself was adamant on this, insisting that the promise of the gospel, together with the command to repent and believe, 'ought to be declared and published to all nations, and to all persons promiscuously and without distinction'.[35] The argument that only a doctrine of universal redemption can sustain Christian mission is nullified by the fact that men who were firm believers in definite atonement (Charles Spurgeon, for example) were perfervid evangelists and others (like Alexander Duff and William Chalmers Burns) were prepared to work as ground-breaking missionaries in some of the most hostile spiritual environments on earth. They went out not because they believed in universal

---

32. For Davenant's mature views, see his *Dissertation on the Death of Christ as to its Extent and Special Benefits*. This is the title of the English translation (1831) by Josiah Allport of the original Latin edition published in 1650 (Davenant had died in 1641). This translation was appended by Allport to his 1832 translation of Davenant's *Exposition of the Epistle of St. Paul to the Colossians* (1627), but it was omitted from the Banner of Truth reprint of the commentary published in 2005. The *Dissertation* was republished separately by Quinta Press (Oswestry) in 2006.

33. Richard Baxter, *Universal Redemption of Mankind by the Lord Jesus Christ* (London: 1694).

34. See Alan C. Clifford (ed.), *Christ for the World: Papers Delivered at the 2006 Conference of the Amyraldian Association* (Charenton Reformed Publishing: Norwich, 2007).

35. *Canons of Dort*, II:V.

redemption, or because they had resolved in their own minds the tension between unconditional election and universal proclamation, but because they heard the divine commission to preach the gospel to every creature (Mark 16:15) and happily accepted John Preston's paraphrase, 'Go and tell every man without exception that there is good news for him'.[36] Christ was a saviour for the whole world, the only Saviour, and the whole world was to be urged to avail itself of his services. His cross was the one mercy seat: to it all might come, and to it alone might they come. And when confronted by this invitation the sinner has no right to enquire into eternity past to determine whether or not they are elected, any more than they have a right to project themselves to the day of judgment to check whether they are a sheep or a goat. All that matters is the present moment in which God through the preacher confronts us with the wonder of his love.

Reformed theologians tended to be more reserved, however, when it came to expressing God's *love* for the world, and more reluctant to say to Everyman, 'God loves you'. Yet, if God loves the world, and if we are part of the world, we have the right, surely, to include ourselves in the love of God, personally and individually? The reluctance to preach this (and even to believe it) stems from a confusion, as if faith came before the love of God and we must therefore limit the statement, 'God loves you', to believers. The reality is that God's love comes before our faith and is, indeed, its object. It is what we believe in. It was from this perspective that Calvin defined faith as 'a firm and certain knowledge of God's benevolence toward us'.[37] Conversely, unbelief is the contemptuous rejection of God's love.

We must distinguish, however, between the statement 'God loves you', and the statement, 'You are saved'. It is not the business of the evangelist as such to tell people that they are saved, but it is his business to tell them that they are loved and that if they accept that love and put their trust in it they will be saved.

The precise question

What, then, is the precise question raised by the doctrine of universal redemption? The Remonstrants themselves set it firmly in the context of the divine

---

36. John Preston, *The Breast-plate of Faith and Love* (London: 1634), p. 8. Preston and his contemporaries were not aware, of course, of doubts over the authenticity of Mark 16:9–20.

37. *Institutes*, III:II, 7.

decree: by an eternal, unchangeable purpose God had determined to save out of the fallen human race those who would believe in his Son, and in pursuance of this decree Christ by his death obtained redemption and forgiveness for all people. The question, in other words, is about the divine intention: did God in giving his Son, and did his Son in giving himself, intend by his death to redeem each and every human being? We may have profound reservations over the question and even regret that it was ever asked. But it *was* asked, and when those who first asked it (the Remonstrants) answered it in terms of universal redemption they challenged the Reformed churches to respond. Dort had no alternative but to oppose them and to affirm the counter-doctrine that Christ intended to redeem only his elect.

On the face of things, this is a direct antithesis, leading to the widespread misconception that while Arminianism teaches that Christ redeemed all people, Calvinism teaches that he redeemed only the elect. *Prima facie*, the latter offers a much narrower vision than the former. But all is not as it seems. The Remonstrants did not argue that God decreed to *save* all men: he decreed to save only those who would believe in Christ, and when they laid down that Christ obtained forgiveness for all people they immediately uttered the caveat that no one actually enjoys this forgiveness except the believer.[38] This is an instant reminder that the doctrine of universal redemption is not a doctrine of universal salvation. In fact, it makes no difference to the eventual number of the redeemed. According to the Remonstrants all believers are saved; according to Dort all the elect are saved. But in the last analysis (as Dort saw it) the two constituencies are exactly identical, since all the elect (and only the elect) become believers.

The Arminian perspective (and this is what controls almost all modern evangelism) has all the appeal of apparent simplicity: 'Only believe!' It is easy to convince ourselves that with appropriate persuasion, good organization and modern means of communication millions may be induced to take this 'simple step'. But what if we are spiritually dead (Eph. 2:1), and if believing is utterly beyond our capacity? Has God made provision to enable all people and every person to exercise the faith without which the purchased redemption remains for ever beyond them? Only to a limited extent, said the Remonstrants: God offers cooperating grace to help them come to faith, but this grace can be resisted. People can say 'No!' to God, and God will not override that 'No'. The result is sombre in the extreme. Multitudes of the redeemed, for whom Christ obtained forgiveness, perish.

---

38. Article II of *The Five Arminian Articles*.

When Dort, however, spoke of Christ redeeming the elect, and the elect only, it entered no caveat. All those for whom Christ died are *effectually* redeemed. This highlights the real difference between Dort and Arminianism. It is not a question of the number of the redeemed. It is a question of the quality of the redemption; a question, eventually, of what the cross really achieved. The doctrine of definite atonement does not leave our redemption hanging on a 'decision for Christ', a decision which, by ourselves, we are utterly incapable of making. Instead, the cross itself secures the gift of faith (as it secures every other grace, including repentance and holiness and perseverance and glory) for all those whom God has ordained to eternal life. We have already seen this link in such passages as Galatians 3:13–14, where it is made plain that Christ died not only to redeem us from the curse of the law but to ensure that we receive the promised Spirit, and we see it again in Ephesians 5:25–27, which speaks of Christ giving himself for the church not merely to make her salvation vaguely possible, but to wash and cleanse her and transform her into something blameless and radiant.

Christ did not die merely to put preachers in a position where they could hopefully offer his salvation to all men. He died to ensure that an innumerable multitude would respond to that offer and enter into eternal life. Otherwise we face the dread possibility that he could have died in vain. This was a matter of real concern to Bishop Davenant, particularly since one Dutch Remonstrant (a gentleman by the name of Grevinchonius) went so far as to argue that the passion of Christ was like the throw of a dice, leaving it entirely possible that the offer of the gospel would not be taken up by a single individual: 'the redemption might be obtained for all, and yet applied to none'.[39] The only safeguard against this, as Davenant saw clearly, is the doctrine of election, according to which God has decreed from eternity to confer on his chosen what they could never have accomplished for themselves.[40] It was precisely to fulfil this decree, in all its definiteness and particularity, that Christ died.

What any doctrine of the extent of the atonement must provide is coherence within God's overall plan of salvation. There cannot, for example, be two un-coordinated divine decrees (as the Remonstrants suggested), one whereby God intended to *redeem* all people and another whereby he intended to *save* only those who believe in Christ. Nor can we conceive of God leaving it to chance (or to

---

39. Davenant, *Dissertation on the Death of Christ* (Quinta edn), p. 164.

40. This accords with Augustine's famous prayer, 'grant what you command, and command what you will'. See *Saint Augustine: Confessions*, tr. Henry Chadwick (Oxford: Oxford University Press, 1992), X:xxix.

the personal decision of people who are spiritually dead) whether or not any sinner will actually believe in Christ. Redemption from sin includes redemption from its power as well as from its guilt, and if the death of Christ actually saves (as distinct from rendering people merely salvable) it must secure not only forgiveness of sins but a change of heart. The blood of Christ made the church God's precious treasure (Acts 20:28). No way, therefore, is he going to run the risk of losing her. His giving of his Son (Rom. 8:32) cannot be separated from his absolute determination to confer on those he died for all that they need for life and godliness (2 Pet. 1:3).

Similarly, there must be coherence within the redemptive activity of the Trinity. Election is itself a trinitarian act involving the Father, the Son and the Holy Spirit, which means that the redeeming love of each is coextensive with the redeeming love of the others. It is inconceivable, therefore, that Christ would redeem all, but the Holy Spirit transform only some. It is precisely through Jesus Christ our Saviour that the Spirit has been poured upon us so abundantly (Titus 3:6). How could he bypass any sinner bought by the blood of the Son? Are we to accuse God of a lack of joined-up thinking?

By the same token there must be coherence between the work of the earthly, humiliated Christ and the work of the exalted, heavenly Christ. The post-resurrection Jesus is still redemption-active. It is he who gives eternal life (John 17:2) and he who opens hearts (Acts 16:14). Can we seriously believe that while his earthly work secured the redemption of each and every human being, his heavenly work is limited to only a fraction of those he redeemed?

And, equally, there must be coherence between the accomplishment of redemption and its application. According to the doctrine of definite atonement there is no disconformity between the one and the other. God applies his redemption to all for whom he accomplished it. Otherwise it would be to no avail. The Remonstrants themselves implicitly recognized this: without faith there could be no actual salvation. But then, without the new birth there can be no faith; and without the direct, intimate and invincible action of God there can be no new birth. An expiation of sin unconnected to spiritual renewal is no redemption. This is the fundamental problem with universal redemption. Multitudes of the redeemed are left to perish in the wilderness.

Finally, there must be coherence between the divine input to our salvation and our human experience of this salvation. Salvation clearly involves the human will, since everyone who hears the gospel is immediately faced with a choice: a choice which we alone can make, and a choice which is always free. But how can we make that choice when every inclination of our hearts is evil (Gen. 6:5)? We can make it, and come to Christ 'most freely', because we are made willing by his grace; a grace which even his elect can always resist, but which they can never overcome,[41] because it is the direct, personal action of the omnipotent God, rooted in his determination to save, and secured for us by the cross as an integral element in our salvation. The blood secured our 'decision for Christ' as surely as it secured the offer of salvation.

The nineteenth-century Scottish preacher-theologian, Thomas Chalmers, once expressed in no uncertain terms his regret that the question of the extent of the atonement had ever been raised,[42] and we may well share that regret, both because the arguments always savour of irreverent probing into the counsels of God, and because the doctrine of definite atonement (as Chalmers again remarked) 'perplexed the heralds of salvation', who sometimes found it hard to preach to all a salvation not intended for all.[43] But the issues involved here (once the doctrine of universal redemption rears its head) are not only, or even primarily, logical. They are of immense religious and spiritual moment.

One of these is the need to do justice to man's utter incapacity, left to himself, to respond to the gospel. To the Remonstrants, no less than to Abelard, we may say, 'you have not yet considered the gravity of sin'. A redemption that does not provide for overcoming our resistance to God's grace is no redemption at all.

But of even greater moment is the question of the glory of the cross itself. What is our debt to it? Did Christ merely render salvable those for whom he died, contenting himself with something like removing legal obstacles to their acceptance with God? Or did he aspire higher, and by his blood secure salvation in the complete and fullest sense, including renewal, preservation and glory?

It is this latter question that the doctrine of definitive atonement answers in the affirmative. When the redeemed stand before the throne, innumerable as the grains of sand on the seashore, they will know that they owe they owe their salvation from beginning to end to the blood of the lamb (Rev. 7:9–10).

1 John 4:10

In 1 John 4:10 John's concern is not to define the nature of the atonement, but to define the nature of love: 'This is love: not that we loved God, but that he

---

41. The Latin word *irrestibilis*, as used in the phrase 'irresistible grace', does not mean 'non-resistible' but 'invincible'.

42. Chalmers made this comment in the course of a class lecture on 'Particular Redemption'. See *Select Works of Thomas Chalmers,* ed. William Hanna (Edinburgh: Constable, 1856), p. 424.

43. Ibid., p. 425.

loved us and sent his Son as an atoning sacrifice for our sins.' Here, the insistence on the divine initiative is at its strongest. The expiatory sacrifice is not the
cause of the divine love, but its consequence and its expression. This is incomparable love and immeasurable love, God giving his Son as a sacrifice to cover
the sins of those who had treated him with rejection and contempt. It is a love
as old as God himself, and as free.

Yet in its impulse toward forgiveness it does not set aside the need for sin to
be expiated. Deep in the nature of God himself there is a necessity for a *hilasmos*.
But God not only requires it. He provides it; and he not only provides it, but
becomes it. The sacrifice is not only his own loved one, but one who is so loved
that he and the Father are one (John 10:30). In the One, therefore, the Three
come, said the ancient trinitarian doctrine of the *en-perichoresis*. But equally truly,
in the One the Three suffer. The Three are distinct agents at Calvary: the Father
giving, the Spirit upholding and the Son dying. But the Three are also One, not
only one in being, but one Being. In the Son, the one God tastes death and
expiates sin, not only by the blood of his own, but by his own blood (Acts
20:28). Love, the divine love, bears the whole cost of redemption: the Father's
love, which is also the love of the Three. The *hilasmos* is offered *by* God and
offered *to* God. This is the crowning *anomia*: the supreme paradox. But it is an
anomia 'forced' on God by that first, dreadful *anomia* in Eden, when humanity
rebelled against God and created a singularity which law as such could neither
explain nor redress, and to which even the divine love could offer no solution
except the self-sacrificing intervention of the Beloved Son. In the last analysis,
this intervention is a transaction between the persons of the eternal Trinity, and
it inevitably involves truths and perspectives far beyond our creaturely vision.
But whatever greater light we may one day enjoy, it will lead to no abandonment
of the concept of the *hilasmos*. On the contrary, it will throw Christ's sacrifice
into even greater relief and highlight the glory of Calvary as the place where
the blood of God's lamb expiated the sin of the world.

But how did Christ expiate sin? At the most obvious level he did so by dying
the very death that sin deserved. Behind this, of course, there lay that eternal
agreement between the three persons of the Trinity whereby the Eternal Son
became surety for sinners. This is not simply a case of the innocent taking the
place of the guilty. It is a case of God taking the place of the guilty, enduring
in himself his own condemnation of sin. When the cry went up for a *hilasmos*,
he gave himself, and he took our human nature precisely in order to put himself
in a position where he had blood to shed and a soul to pour out in death.

In Romans 5:19, however, Paul offers an additional and more comprehensive
perspective: 'For just as through the disobedience of the one man the many were
made sinners, so also through the obedience of the one man the many will be

made righteous.' Here the whole ministry of Jesus is subsumed under the category of obedience. This in no way dilutes the significance of the cross. Instead, it portrays the cross itself as the climax of his obedience, a point Paul makes explicitly in Philippians 2:8, where he describes Christ as becoming 'obedient to the point of death – even death on a cross' (NRSV). From this point of view, all that came before the cross, as well as the cross itself, was obedience: the obedience of the divine in the form of a servant. In the last analysis, it is this obedience and service, reaching its climax on the cross, that expiates the sin of the world. On the basis of this obedience God highly exalted his Servant; and in him he exalted the world whose sin he had borne and whose guilt his obedience had expiated. The righteousness of the last Adam covers the unrighteousness of the first.

6. PROPITIATION: AVERTING THE DIVINE ANGER

Expiation, as we have seen, is not an end in itself. It defines the effect of the atonement on sin. But what of the effect on God?

Stated in these terms, this instantly raises a problem. Can anything that happens outside of himself have an effect on God? Is he not the *unmoved* mover, eternally the same, neither moved to pity by human pain nor provoked to anger by human sin nor appeased by human sacrifice and service? And is his love not just what he is, in his very essence, and entirely independent of any influences and modifiers that humans can bring to bear?

The difficulty with this is the underlying assumption. The idea of God as the unmoved mover, affecting all things but himself affected by none, is not supported by God's self-disclosure in Scripture. At the very beginning of Genesis we find that he was sufficiently provoked by the sin of Adam and Eve to drive them out of Eden (Gen. 3:23); by the sinfulness of the cities of the plain to rain down fire and brimstone (Gen. 19:24); by the misery of his people in Egypt to come down and rescue them (Exod. 3:7–10); and, centuries later, sufficiently provoked by their apostasy to drive them into exile in Babylon. In all these situations God is portrayed as not merely proactive, but reactive.

This becomes even clearer if we look at the Bible's theology of prayer. It does not bring a merely reflexive benefit, simply making us feel better for having spread our concerns before the Lord. It is consistently portrayed as modifying God's own behaviour. For example, his intervention on behalf of his people in Egypt was due to the fact that he heard the crying of his people (Exod. 3:7). Similarly, when God threatened to destroy this very same people when they worshipped the golden calf, he was 'deflected' from his purpose only when Moses 'sought the favour of the LORD his God' (Exod. 32:11). The psalms are full of such moments. In Psalm 40:1–2, for example, the Lord heard David's cry and lifted him out of the mud and mire. We find the same thing again in Psalm 116:1, where the Lord heard the psalmist's cry for mercy. Psalm 130 strikes the same note: the cry from the depths (v. 1) leads to redemption and gratitude (vv. 7–8).

This same link between human intervention (prayer) and divine action is underlined in the New Testament. In Acts 12:5–7, for example, Peter's escape from prison is directly linked to the fact that 'the church was earnestly praying to God for him'. But even more significant is the weight attached to the intervention of Christ. We have already seen a key instance of this in 1 John 2:2, where Jesus is portrayed as our advocate before God. Romans 8:34 portrays him as interceding for us, as does Hebrews 7:25 ('he always lives to intercede for them'). The nature of this intervention on Jesus' part is clearly illustrated in John 17, where he prays not only for himself and the Twelve, but for the church down through the ages (John 17:20–26). But perhaps the most interesting intervention of all is in Luke 22:32, where Jesus assures Peter, 'I have prayed for you, Simon, that your faith may not fail.' The request is specific, mentioning Simon by name and focusing on a particular danger; and the verb, *edeēthēn*, is a strong one. In 2 Corinthians 5:20 Paul uses it to describe his own evangelistic passion: 'We implore on Christ's behalf: be reconciled to God.' With such urgency did Paul plead with sinners; and with such urgency did Jesus plead for Peter.

Which raises an interesting point: it is all too easy to argue from God's love that securing his blessing and favour is simply a matter of course, and that any idea of having to plead with him or persuade him is entirely misplaced. A brief word in his ear will suffice. But with what passion does Moses plead in Exodus 32:32: 'But now, please forgive their sin – but if not, then blot me out of the book you have written.' Daniel's great prayer on behalf of his exiled people is equally urgent: 'So I turned to the Lord God and pleaded with him in prayer and petition, in fasting, and in sackcloth and ashes' (Dan. 9:3). He clearly did not assume that all he had to do was to have a brief word with the divine love and all would instantly be well. Nor did Paul make any such assumption when he prayed for deliverance from his 'thorn in the flesh'. He besought the Lord not once, or twice, but three times (2 Cor. 12:8).

All this provides an important background to the atonement, indicating that God *is* affected by human intervention, mediation and prayer. But it also becomes clear that the fact of God's love does not mean that God's blessing comes easily and automatically. The priest comes with a sacrifice; the pleader in sackcloth and ashes; the supplicant with passionate persistence. All sought to influence, and sometimes even to modify, the divine behaviour. They pled for the favour of God.

It is within this framework of divine-human relations that we have to view the sacrifice of Jesus Christ. The Old Testament sacrifices were offered to God, and offered with a view to influencing his dealings with humanity. No doubt, the ritual also solemnized the offerer, but that was incidental to its main purpose. God's words with regard to the Passover are illuminating in this connection: 'and when I see the blood, I will pass over you' (Exod. 12:13). It was not the impression the blood made on the offerer or the onlooker that mattered. What mattered was that God would see it, and that as a consequence the destruction which would overtake the Egyptians would 'pass by' the blood-protected homes of the people of Israel. The import of the sin offering was the same. The sacrifice was to be presented before the Lord, slaughtered before the Lord and its blood sprinkled before the Lord; and its effect would be not that the offerers would then feel different, or better, but that the Lord would be moved to forgive their sins.

In the New Testament the same dynamics are evident. Any impression the sacrifice of Christ made on human beings (for example, demonstrating the divine love) was secondary. The primary movement was Godward. This is inherent in the very idea of an offering (*prosphora*) as something placed before the deity and sacrificed to him. But in some key passages it is made totally explicit. In Hebrews 9:14, for example, Christ is said to have 'offered himself unblemished *to God*' (italics mine). Exactly the same idea is expressed in Ephesians 5:2: Christ loved us and gave himself up for us 'as a fragrant offering and sacrifice *to God*' (italics mine). The sacrifice was offered to God in expiation of sin. It was he who smelt its fragrance.

But how does this relate to the immutability of God? Does the sacrifice of Christ change God (for example, from being angry to being well disposed to us)?

We must be careful not to define immutability in a way that obscures the fact that God's relationship with the world (and with men and women) is personal and interactive, not static. This is why God reveals himself in Scripture not by means of a series of propositions, but through narrative. This narrative begins with the creation story of Genesis, but it begins, not as the beginning of God's story, but as the beginning of the God-and-man story. This immediately raises the same sort of questions about divine changelessness as are raised by the story of the cross. Did creation change God? It certainly opened up for him a whole new set of relations. Before creation, there was God and nothing but God. He existed as the self-sufficient One, unique not only in that he alone was God but in that he alone *was*; and yet though he alone was, he was not alone, existing as an eternal solitary. The world was not created as a remedy for divine loneliness. On the contrary, he enjoyed consummate blessedness and satisfaction in the love between the Father, the Son and the Holy Spirit. There was no world to relate to, and no soul praying to him, yet there was perfect relatedness in the *with-ness* (John 1:1) which lay at the heart of the Trinity.

But creation dramatically ushers in a host of new relationships. There is a world for God to admire and take pleasure in (Gen. 1:31): a world to preserve and govern; a world over which he is Lord and Judge, and ultimately Redeemer. This new situation, something else existing outside of God and different from God, does not change what he is in himself, but it does mean a whole new set of relationships, totally consistent with the eternal relations between the persons of the Trinity, but also additional and different. Yet as he relates to this world which he has created, God remains the holy love which he always was.

Secondly, just as creation involves God in a whole new set of relationships, so does human sin. The moment that God creates the human species he experiences complete satisfaction. He has made a creature in his own image, and now the 'heavens and the earth' are 'very good' (Gen. 1:31). God is absolutely delighted. Added to the delight he had in his Son and in his Spirit there is now the delight he has in his creation, and particularly in this creature 'mankind'.

But then humankind sins. The image is ruined, the creation marred and the heavens and the earth no longer 'very good'. All is changed. Yet God remains holy love, and because he is holy love he is angry. Anger is not, strictly speaking, an attribute of God: not something he is in and of himself, but entirely relational. In the eternal relations of the divine persons there had been love and grace and holiness and righteousness and wisdom and power. But there had been no anger, because there was nothing outside of God, and therefore nothing to provoke it. It was aroused and provoked only by sin. Yet, although not like holiness an eternal quality of God's being, it arose by necessity from that holiness when sin presented its defiance and laid down its challenge. The anger was contingent, because sin was contingent, but it arose, of necessity, out of what God is. Anger is the calm, deliberate and proportionate way in which eternal and underlying holiness responds to sin. Because of what he is (morally immutable) he hates it, he condemns it and he opposes it as utterly repugnant and absolutely destructive. It is a new thing in God's world, but the holiness which is angered by it is no new thing.

But anger was not God's only reaction to sin. His love responded as well as his holiness, and it was this love that provided the *hilasmos*, expiating sin and propitiating God. Here, too, there is entire consistency. As holy love is angered by sin so holy love is propitiated by the atonement. Precisely because God was faithful and just, and despite the serpent's insinuation to the contrary, he fulfilled his word to Adam and Eve, 'you must not eat from the tree of the knowledge of good and evil, for when you eat of it you will certainly die' (Gen. 2:17); and precisely because he is faithful and just, he will forgive sin once it is expiated (1 John 1:9). In the one case God is moved to anger by sin. In the other, he is moved to forgiveness by the cross.

From this point of view, God's being propitious towards sinners is clearly an *effect* of Calvary. We must avoid the idea, however, that only *after* Calvary was God forgiving and propitious. It is clear from Romans 3:25 that the cross cast its effect before it, justifying God in forgiving sins he had forgiven millennia ago. The effect of the cross was eternal. Yet we must say this without detriment to the historical nature of the crucifixion. It took place precisely and once for all on Good Friday. Yet it is equally true that the Lamb was slain from the foundation of the world (Rev. 13:8), which means that the fragrance of the sacrifice was present to God before time began. The blood of Christ secured the forgiveness of Abraham as surely as it secured the forgiveness of Saul of Tarsus. God was propitiated in time, but he was propitious from all eternity. If it was true of Abraham that he 'saw my day' (John 8:56), it was even more true of God. He saw the blood before ever it was shed, and he passed by. God did not change on Good Friday.

Propitiation does not make God love us

It is against this background of a God whose relations with his creation are personal and interactive, and who is affected by events in time, that we must seek to understand the New Testament concept of propitiation. The basic connotation is clear enough. To propitiate means to deal with someone's anger. It happens when someone who is out of favour takes whatever steps are necessary to get back into favour. At its baldest (and, from a theological point of view, its most offensive) it means to placate or appease.

When we apply it to God, there are two things to be made plain at the outset. First of all, to *propitiate* is not to make God love us, or to turn his hatred into love. Propitiation relates to anger, not to hatred. God never hated the world or viewed it with malicious intention and ill-will. He loved it, from eternity, with a love uncaused, un-purchased and unconditional. This does not lead him to dispense with atonement; his nature requires it. But his love means that he himself provides the sacrifice he requires, and in the last analysis he *becomes* that sacrifice. He propitiates himself.

Yet that is not quite the whole truth. Christ offers himself not only as the Son of God but as the Last Adam, so that in him mankind atones for his own sin. There is 'one mediator between God and mankind, the *man* Christ Jesus' (1 Tim. 2:5, italics mine), and the atonement cost this man dear. But this man has no separate identity apart from the divine Son. The Last Adam *is* the Son of God, and it is this divine Son who bears the whole cost of atonement. The human race did not take the initiative, nor did it provide the lamb. God provided his own Lamb, and though the great ritual which takes place at Calvary involves a human sacrifice, the blood shed is God's own, and the whole transaction is one which takes place between the divine persons, the Father, the Son and the Holy Spirit. Mankind does not placate an angry deity, but God justifies his own remission of human sin.

To love is not necessarily to be propitious

Secondly, to love is not necessarily to be propitious. A human mother can be angry with her child: sometimes, indeed, the greater the love the greater the anger. Similarly, God can be angry with his own children. Paul reminds the saints at Ephesus, loved before the foundation of the world (Eph. 1:4), that they were once objects of wrath, just like others (Eph. 2:3). God never hated them; on the contrary he loved them. But though he loved them, he was not at peace with them, and though he had resolved from all eternity to adopt them, he had not yet done so. As a result they were still not members of his family, they had no sense of his love and they knew nothing of his promises. They were objects of God's love and of his displeasure at the same time. Nor does this possibility disappear altogether when we become Christians. Most of the Bible's references to God's anger point to his anger against his own people. As the writer to the Hebrews points out, he disciplines those he loves (Heb. 12:6, quoting Prov. 3:12). The same point is made in Revelation 3:19, 'Those whom I love I rebuke and discipline'.

There is a very fine statement on this in the Westminster Confession's chapter on justification, which lays down that although believers can never fall from the state of justification, yet they may by their sins 'fall under God's fatherly displeasure, and not have the light of his countenance restored unto them, until they humble themselves, confess their sins, beg pardon, and renew their faith and repentance'.[1] This clearly refers to backslidden believers. God never ceases

---

1. Westminster Confession, 11:5.

to love them, and he never ceases to regard them as righteous in his sight, yet until they return to him in penitence he withholds his favours. He loves them, but is displeased: another reminder that to love and to be propitious are not the same. God and the backslider have to 'make up'.

A paradigm shift

The traditional understanding of propitiation was that Christ covered (expiated) our sin by his obedience and sacrifice, and by so doing turned away the anger of God so that we, though deserving it, are no longer liable to it. In the twentieth century, however, there was a paradigm-shift, and the concept of propitiation came to be viewed with abhorrence, thanks mainly to the reiterated arguments of C. H. Dodd. On the face of things, Dodd's case is built on linguistic evidence, and particularly his examination of the verb *hilaskesthai* and its cognates. Dodd is impatient with the practice of rendering this word-group in terms of 'propitiation'. For example, commenting on Romans 3:25, he argues that the rendering 'propitiation' is misleading, 'for it suggests the placating of an angry God, and though this would be in accord with pagan usage, it is foreign to biblical usage'.[2] He is equally confident with regard to 1 John 2:2: 'The common rendering "propitiation" is illegitimate here as elsewhere'.[3]

These claims quickly created a virtual consensus in New Testament scholarship. Vincent Taylor even went so far as to remark, 'Dodd's researches have made it certain that there is no suggestion in *hilaskesthai* of appeasing an angry God'.[4] However, beneath Dodd's marshalling of the linguistic evidence there lay a more principial objection: 'wrath' was a pagan idea, inapplicable to the God of the Bible. It is hard to avoid the impression that the linguistic arguments were no more than rationalizations for a prejudice which had nothing to do with his linguistic researches.

Distinguished systematic theologians quickly aligned themselves with Dodd. Among them was Donald Baillie, though his position is compromised by his perception that propitiation means changing God's attitude from 'wrath and justice' to 'love and mercy'. This gives him a convenient man of straw to cut down: if you can show that love preceded the atonement (no very difficult task)

---

2. Dodd, *Romans*, p. 79.

3. Dodd, *The Bible and the Greeks*, p. 95.

4. Vincent Taylor, *The Atonement in New Testament Teaching* (3rd ed., London: Epworth Press, 1958), p. 124.

then you can triumphantly argue that, 'as regards the Johannine passages, it is clear that the word *hilasmos* does not mean anything like the appeasing of an angry God, for the *love* of God is the starting-point'.[5] Such a simplistic antithesis between anger and love represents an extremely shallow understanding of the cross. Kazoh Kitamori is much closer to the biblical perspective when he writes, 'the recognition of God's wrath is the beginning of wisdom' and then goes on to suggest that the very gospel of the cross is that, 'God loves the objects of his wrath and that he, in his love, embraces men alienated from him'.[6]

As with Dodd, so with Baillie: the denial of propitiation arises from a theological objection to the idea of divine anger, but Baillie is glad to bolster his case by appeal to 'Professor C. H. Dodd, who has made a careful study of the word [*hilasmos*]' and who 'assures us the rendering "propitiation" is misleading, being in accord with pagan usage but foreign to Biblical usage'. Baillie then concludes: 'His wrath must not be regarded as something which has to be "propitiated" and so changed into love and mercy, but rather as being identical with the consuming fire of inexorable divine love in relation to our sins.'[7] But what can this mean? That 'wrath' is identical with love? Was it (for example) the consuming fire of his love for ancient Roman civilization that led God to respond to their idolatry by giving them over to a 'depraved mind' (Rom. 1:28)?

T. F. Torrance takes the divine anger much more seriously ('the wrath of God is removed only when his righteous will has punished sin and judged it')[8] but nevertheless accepts Dodd's argument that there is a sharp distinction between the significance of *hilaskesthai* in 'profane' Greek and its significance in biblical Greek. In pagan usage the verb *hilaskesthai* is used with a god as the object (*hilaskesthai ton theon*), and means to placate or appease a deity, 'but never once is the verb used in that way of the living God – God cannot be the object of human expiation or propitiation, that is, of appeasement'.[9] The idea of conciliating or placating God was a heathen concept.

Clearly, then, Dodd's views have been widely influential, and it is important to acknowledge the truth in his position. The God of Israel *was* different from

5. Baillie, *God Was In Christ*, p. 187.

6. Kazoh Kitamori, *Theology of the Pain of God* (repr., Eugene, Oregon: Wipf & Stock, 2005 [1965]), pp. 21, 58.

7. Baillie, *God Was In Christ*, pp. 188, 189.

8. T. F. Torrance, *Atonement: The Person and Work of Christ*, ed. Robert T. Walker (Milton Keynes: Paternoster, 2009), p. 154.

9. Torrance, *Atonement*, p. 140.

pagan deities and, among other things, he was different in his anger. The deities of mythology were irascible and capricious and, when provoked, implacable. No ideas of eternal, self-giving love were ever attributed to them, far less the idea that they would take the first step towards atonement and meet its cost. Fury was their default mood, and appeasing them a costly and intimidating daily burden. The living God was completely different. He was slow to anger, reluctant to condemn and delighting in forgiveness. From the very beginning he had shown himself placable and even taken the initiative in establishing the means of atonement.

All this was already clear in the Old Testament. In the New Testament it is dramatized in the figure of the waiting father (Luke 15:11–31) and in the picture of the God who reconciled the world to himself (2 Cor. 5:19). Yet the anger of God is a reality in both the Old and the New Testament. Few would deny it with regard to the Old. Sometimes it is only implied, as in the story of the flood or the story of the destruction of the cities of the plain. But there are also numerous explicit references, many of them pointing to God's anger with his covenant people. In Exodus 32:12, for example, following the incident of the golden calf, Moses has to plead with Yahweh to turn from his fierce anger; in Psalm 90:7, the psalmist declares, 'we are consumed by your anger, and terrified by your indignation'; and in Nahum 1:6, the prophet asks, 'Who can withstand his indignation? Who can endure his fierce anger?'

There is no abatement of this emphasis when we pass from the Old Testament to the New. On the contrary, the divine anger and the need to be delivered from it provide the backdrop to the message of all the great New Testament preachers. John the Baptist, for example, challenges the Pharisees and the Saducees, 'Who warned you to flee from the coming wrath?' (Matt. 3:7), and in his letter to the Romans Paul similarly presents his message against the backdrop of the divine wrath that is being revealed 'against all the godlessness and wickedness of people' (Rom. 1:18). This is entirely consistent with the preaching of Jesus himself, who spoke vividly of apocalyptic anger: 'How dreadful it will be in those days for pregnant women and nursing mothers! There will be great distress in the land and wrath against this people' (Luke 21:23). The reality of this anger was also the background to Jesus' references to hell (e.g., Matt. 5:22; 10:28; 23:33) and to the solemn sentence he personally pronounces at the conclusion of the great judgment scene in Matthew 25: 'Depart from me, you who are cursed, into the eternal fire prepared for the devil and his angels' (25:41). Even in the Sermon on the Mount, this same note is heard: the broad road leads to destruction (Matt. 7:13).

Dodd recognized that this is an authentic strain of biblical teaching and he quite rightly sought to clear it of popular misconceptions: Paul did not

think of God as 'a vengeful despot'.[10] But Dodd also argued that the very idea
of personal divine anger was archaic and belonged to an earlier anthropic
era of religion, when people expressed their sense of the holy by attributing
to God the irrational passion of anger: 'The idea of an angry God is a first
attempt to rationalise the shuddering awe which men feel before the incalcul-
able possibilities of appalling disaster inherent in life, but it is an attempt
which breaks down as the rational element in religion advances.'[11] Indeed, so
far did Dodd carry this idea that he suggested we should always keep the
translation 'wrath', 'because such an archaic phrase suits a thoroughly archaic
idea'.[12]

To accommodate our advanced and rational stage of religion Dodd proposes,
in effect, to demythologize the idea of divine wrath. We should see it, he argues,
not as a personal attitude or emotion on God's part, but as an impersonal process
within history. In support of this he draws attention to the fact that Paul seldom
uses the phrase, 'the wrath of God', but constantly refers to 'the wrath'. He
concludes: '"the Wrath" meant not a certain feeling or attitude of God towards
us, but some process or effect in the realm of objective facts.'[13] As such it
belongs to the sphere of cause and effect: sin is the cause, disaster the effect.
He puts it even more scarily in *The Meaning of Paul for Today*: the wrath of God
'as seen in actual operation, consists in leaving sinful human nature to "stew in
its own juice"'.[14]

It is scarcely possible, however, to square this idea of an impersonal, self-
monitoring law with a providential divine order in which even the fall of a
sparrow is governed by the will of our Father (Matt. 10:29). It may indeed be
the case that such aberrations as drunkenness and promiscuity bring their own
physical and mental nemesis, but it is a nemesis which arises from the way that
God has structured his universe. Scripture certainly does not speak of a merely
impersonal wrath. Jeremiah, for example, writes, 'You have covered yourself
with anger and pursued us; you have slain without pity' (Lam. 3:43). Ezekiel
uses similar language: 'I am about to pour out my wrath on you and spend my
anger against you; I will judge you according to your conduct and repay you for
all your detestable practices' (Ezek. 7:8). The same sense of personal divine

---

10. C. H. Dodd, *The Meaning of Paul for Today* (repr., London: Collins [Fontana], 1958
    [1920]), p. 63.
11. Dodd, *Romans*, p. 50.
12. Ibid., p. 47.
13. Ibid., p. 49.
14. Dodd, *The Meaning of Paul*, p. 63.

anger is reflected in the Psalms: 'You have rejected us, O God, and burst upon us; you have been angry – now restore us!' (Ps. 60:1).

The New Testament sustains this same note. In the case of Jesus, not only does he take for granted the reality of divine anger, but on occasion he was clearly angry himself. We see this in, for example, the story of the healing of the man with the withered hand (Mark 3:1–5), when the Pharisees, completely uninterested in the sick man and concerned only to find evidence against Jesus, were waiting to see whether he would heal on the sabbath: 'He looked round at them in anger, deeply distressed at their stubborn hearts.' If anger is an irrational (or pre-rational) human passion, how can we explain its presence in the life of the incarnate Logos? And how can we explain the description of 'our God' (the God of the New Covenant) as a 'consuming fire' (Heb. 12:29), or the reference in Revelation (probably written by the same John who wrote, 'God is love') to the 'wrath of the Lamb' (Rev. 6:16)?

Even within Romans 1:18–32 the argument that 'the wrath' is an impersonal process is unsustainable. Paul's language makes plain that the anger he is speaking of was no mere reflection of a law of cause and effect, but a revelation of God's attitude towards human wickedness (Rom. 1:18). He was angry, and he showed it by actively *giving them over* to sexual impurity, shameful lusts and a depraved mind (Rom. 1:24, 26, 28). Paul clearly had in mind a judicial infliction, reflecting God's righteous decree (Rom. 1:32).

But it is precisely this that gives us hope. Were 'the wrath' an impersonal force or mechanical law it could no more be averted or placated than the law of gravity. It would operate blindly and inexorably, its whirring wheel tearing in pieces all who deviated from the moral imperatives. But because it is *God's* anger, and because his is a compassionate, personal and interactive relationship with the human race, *he* can be propitiated and *his* anger turned away. He can be pleaded with and reconciled to us.

It is this divine anger that constitutes the New Testament background to the concept of propitiation, and it is no argument against it that it was also familiar to 'the pagans'. They were absolutely right to believe that God was angry with sin and had to be propitiated. Indeed, Paul himself endorses this pagan perception. They knew 'God's righteous decree that those who do such things deserve death' (Rom. 1:32). This sense of accountability (and vulnerability) is engraved indelibly on the human conscience. This is what lay behind Hamlet's cry, 'Conscience doth make cowards of us all'.[15] For the most part, moderns are able to keep conscience at bay by minimizing the gravity of sin, dismissing the thought

---

15. William Shakespeare, *Hamlet*, Act III.1.

of life after death or re-imaging God as an all-indulgent deity. Yet, as Calvin reminds us, 'willy-nilly [people] from time to time feel an inkling of what they desire not to believe'. No one, he continues, ever burst forth into more unbridled contempt of deity than the Roman emperor Gaius Caligula, 'yet no one trembled more miserably when any sign of God's wrath manifested itself'. In this respect nothing has changed: 'he who is the boldest despiser of God is of all men the most startled at the rustle of a falling leaf. Whence does this arise but from the vengeance of divine majesty, which strikes their consciences all the more violently the more they try to flee from it?'[16]

This wrath of God, wrote Kazoh Kitamori, 'is absolute and firm. We may say that the recognition of God's wrath is the beginning of wisdom'.[17] This is the great cloud that hangs over the human race; it has to be dealt with; the process by which it is dealt with is propitiation; and the one who has to be propitiated is none other than God himself. Granted, people are also angry with God; sometimes, indeed, even the believer is angry. But it is not our anger that is the main thing. God is angry with our defiances, blasphemies and idolatries; angry with the way we treat our neighbours; angry with the way we treat the poor, the alien and the marginalized; angry with the way we treat our enemies. Far from ignoring or indulging such lovelessness God deplores it, and this is no irrational, evanescent or intemperate fury. It is the deliberate, measured, judicious response of God to our collective revolt against his rule, and to the systemic injustice which marks human society. We may pretend that our denials of the rights of our fellow human beings, our abuse of the other creatures with whom we share the planet, and our spoliation of our common habitat, are but peccadillos: only small, trivial sins. But in God's eyes, the earth is filled with violence (Gen. 6:11), and it appals him.

It would be our wisdom to propitiate God, but we have nothing to offer. This is why God the Son had to became man: to atone for our sin. Yet, as we have repeatedly seen, the incarnation, for all its wonder, could not by itself be an atonement. If it could have been, Jesus need not have proceeded beyond Bethlehem. Gethsemane and Golgotha would have been superfluous. In reality, the incarnation was but the prelude to the atonement, an absolutely indispensable prelude because only *this* man, in our place, could expiate sin and propitiate God. But his enfleshment was not itself a propitiation. He became flesh only in order to give his life as a ransom, and there could be no '*Tetelestai!*' till that life was given. He could make peace only by the blood of his cross. The union

---

16. *Institutes*, I:III, 2
17. Kazoh Kitamori, *Theology of the Pain of God*, p. 21.

of the two natures, divine and human, in the person of Christ was indeed intimate beyond our imagining, but though it was a personal (*hypostatic*) union it was not a reconciling union. The critical relationship, so far as the atonement is concerned, is not that between the two natures in the person of Christ, but the personal relationship between the Father and the Son, incarnate as the last Adam and bearing the world's sin. It is by his obedience, not by the constitution of his person, that the many are put right with God (Rom. 5:19); and that obedience must reach its climax in the cross.

In a very real sense, then, the proof of the doctrine of propitiation stands or falls with the doctrine of the anger of God. Any biblical view of salvation must take this anger seriously; and propitiation must be a central moment in the work of the Redeemer.

But how does Christ save us from the anger? It is true that Scripture never directly speaks of Christ as the object of the Father's anger, but the characteristic language of the New Testament points us unmistakeably in that direction. In Romans 8:3 Paul declares that the flesh of his own Son became the locus where God condemned sin. In Galatians 3:13 he proclaims that the way Christ redeemed us from the curse of the law was by being made a curse for us. This can mean only that he suffered the curse pronounced by God against our sin. God's Son became an accursed thing, cursed by God's own law. In 2 Corinthians 5:21 Paul is, if anything, even bolder: Christ was made 'sin', exposed to the divine displeasure which sin deserved. He died, suffering in himself as the Last Adam the curse with which God had threatened the first: 'when you eat from it you will surely die' (Gen. 2:17). Besides, the death which he died was death unmitigated. No-one, and nothing, stood between him and the wrath. He had no advocate with the Father; no great rock in whose shelter he might stand (Isa. 32:2). There was no 'sparing' (Rom. 8:32). He died the very death deserved: the condign anger of God against the sin of the race with which he had freely and lovingly identified.

No preoccupation with God's love for the human race should blind us to the dreadful paradox of God's treatment of his Son. It was no abstract law, acting as an impersonal process of cause and effect, which nailed Christ to the cross. It was God the Father not sparing his own Son. Biblically (and we have no other source) deliverance from the wrath was secured only through the grief (Isa. 53:10, ESV) of his Servant. He suffered all that our sin deserved.

The linguistic arguments

What, then, of the learned, linguistic arguments over the meaning of *hilaskesthai* and related words?

First of all, the linguistic arguments are secondary. This is not a debate about words. It is a debate about something absolutely fundamental: the Christian doctrine of God. Is he so holy that sin angers him? Dodd's primary contention is that the idea of an angry God is a pagan concept, and his subsequent arguments are an attempt to rationalize and justify that prejudgment. Clearly, if there is no such thing as divine anger there is no place for propitiation. In reality, however, the apostolic preaching clearly presupposes such anger; and, simply because it exists, it must be dealt with. The gospel, the good news, is precisely that Christ *has* dealt with it. He has saved us from the wrath as Paul makes clear in, for example, 1 Thessalonians 1:10, where he speaks of Jesus as the one 'who rescues us from the coming wrath'. The effect (the achievement, if you like) of his life, death and obedience was to avert the anger that threatened the whole human race, and this was neither more nor less than propitiation. He made peace by the blood of his cross.

Secondly, expiation and propitiation are not mutually exclusive. Evangelicals seem to have fallen, almost naïvely, into Dodd's assumption that if he can prove that *hilaskesthai* points to expiation then this rules out propitiation; hence the systemic avoidance of 'expiation' in the NIV and ESV. The older Protestant orthodoxy had no such hang-ups. In his classic work *The Atonement*, A. A. Hodge, for example, notes that the terms 'expiation' and 'propitiation' represent the same Greek word, takes for granted that in Hebrews 2:17 it is 'properly translated *expiate*', and makes plain that as far as he is concerned each of the two words has its own legitimacy:

> Propitiation removes the judicial displeasure of God. Expiation respects the bearing or effect which Satisfaction has upon sin or upon the sinner. Propitiation has respect to the bearing or effect which Satisfaction has upon God. . . . Propitiation proceeds by means of expiation, or the vicarious suffering of the penalty by the substituted victim.[18]

It is plain from this that Hodge regarded expiation and propitiation not as antitheses but as complementary. God is propitiated when sin is expiated. This is still reflected in modern non-theological usage. The very point of a political

---

18. Archibald Alexander Hodge, *The Atonement* (repr., Grand Rapids: Baker Book House, 1974 [1867]), pp. 39–40. Learned discussions of the meaning of *hilaskesthai* did not begin with C. H. Dodd. Hodge is already able to write (p. 139), 'all admit that the Greek word *hilaskesthai*, and its cognates *hilasmos* and *hilasterion*, have universally and from time immemorial, the sense, when construed with God, of *propitiation*, and when construed with sin of *expiation* in the strict sense'.

'cover-up' (expiation), for example, is to prevent or forestall public anger. This usually involves no sacrifice, but occasionally, nonetheless, a scapegoat is found, as when a junior minister or special adviser is 'sacrificed' to save a minister or even a government.

Even, then, if Dodd had succeeded in his argument that *hilaskesthai* and associated words must always be translated in terms of expiation this would not have ruled out the idea of propitiation. An expiation was offered to God, and it was offered precisely to avert his anger, or to assuage it if already aroused. Expiation was never an end in itself. It was offered only to propitiate.

But did Dodd's arguments succeed? This is where the researches of Leon Morris and Roger Nicole have been invaluable.[19] Here, the barest outline must suffice.

First, *hilaskesthai* and cognate words are never used in the Greek Bible (Septuagint or New Testament) with God as object.[20] The construction *hilaskesthai ton theon* is nowhere to be found; or, in plain English, there is no explicit biblical reference to a human subject propitiating God.

Secondly, the verb *hilaskesthai* is never used in the canonical Old Testament with 'sin' or 'sins' (*hamartias*) as its object.[21] Neither priest nor high priest is ever expressly said to expiate sin. As we have seen, however, we do find *hilaskesthai* used with 'sins' as its object in the New Testament (Heb. 2:17, where the natural translation is, 'to expiate the sins of the people').

Thirdly, in all the relevant literatures (classical Greek, the Septuagint and Hellenistic Judaism) *hilaskesthai* and cognate words are invariably associated with anger and its removal. Liddell and Scott, the standard Greek-English lexicon,

---

19. Morris, *Apostolic Preaching of the Cross*, pp. 125–185; Roger Nicole, 'C. H. Dodd and the Doctrine of Propitiation', in *Standing Forth: Collected Writings of Roger Nicole* (Fearn: Christian Focus Publications, 2002), pp. 343–385. Cf. C. E. B. Cranfield's endorsement of Morris: 'Morris has shown that in many, if not all, of the passages in which *hilaskesthai* or related words occur in the LXX the idea of God's wrath is present. Dodd failed to pay adequate attention to the contexts of these words' occurrences' (Cranfield, *Romans*, p. 215).

20. Though *hilaskesthai* does occur in Zechariah 7:2 (LXX) with 'the LORD' as object. Here, however, it carries the meaning 'to plead' or 'to entreat favour'. Cf. ESV, 'the people of Bethel had sent Sharezer and Regem-melech and their men to entreat the favour of the LORD'.

21. The form (*sy*)*hilasē* does occur, however, in Psalm 62:5, with 'our transgressions' (*tas asebeias hēmōn*) as object. But in this instance God is the subject, and the NIV renders the clause, 'you forgave our transgressions'.

point out that in Homer *hilaskesthai* is used only in relation to the gods, with the regular meaning, 'to appease', and with god (*theon*) as object. Other poets commonly use it of men, again with the sense, 'to appease' or 'to conciliate', and often with the construction 'to appease the anger of someone' (*hilaskesthai tēn orgēn tinos*).

It is, of course, precisely Dodd's point that the biblical usage is different from the classical or pagan. But the world the apostles were evangelizing was predominantly a pagan one. Why then would they use a word which would immediately suggest to their hearers a distinctively sub-Christian notion, the need to appease an angry deity, and do so without any traceable attempt to distance themselves from its pagan associations by, for example, making plain what they did *not* mean? This is certainly what Dodd would have done had he ever used the word 'appease'. He would have made clear that he was not using it in its everyday sense. May we not even say that on Dodd's assumption the gospel would have been precisely that God did not need to be propitiated and that there was no need to fear his anger? Had this been the gospel, Paul and John would have placed it in the very forefront of their message and preached it with unmistakeable clarity. Instead, they spoke of a *hilasmos*, and in their time and place there was no need to translate it. It was the everyday language of the people they were preaching to, and it meant 'to propitiate by means of an expiatory sacrifice'. Their gospel was not that God did not need to be placated, but that he had already been placated by the sacrifice of Christ.

But the use of *hilaskesthai* and related words in the sense of 'propitiate' is not confined to pagan literature. It also occurs in the Septuagint. In Genesis 32:20, for example, it is used of Jacob as he prepares to meet Esau. In view of past wrongs, the patriarch is understandably apprehensive, but he resolves, 'I will pacify (*exhilasomai*) him with these gifts I am sending on ahead; later, when I see him, perhaps he will receive me.' This is a clear instance of the classical usage, but occurring in Jewish literature. There is a similar example in Proverbs 16:14, reflecting the 'pagan' usage of appeasing the anger of someone: 'A king's wrath is a messenger of death, but a wise man will appease it.' The word continued to be used in the same way in Palestinian Judaism. In Ecclesiasticus 3:30, for example, *exhilasetai* is used with 'sins' as object, and the natural translation would be the same as in Hebrews 2:17: 'almsgiving expiates sins'. In Ecclesiasticus 5:6, the link between *hilaskesthai* and divine anger is again clear: 'And say not, His compassion is great; he will be pacified (*exhilasetai*) for the multitude of my sins. For mercy and wrath are with him, and his indignation will rest upon sinners' (RV, slightly adapted).

Later Judaism continued to use the *hilaskesthai* word-group with its classical meaning, and Arndt and Gingrich cite instances of the Homeric construction, 'to propitiate God' (*hilaskesthai ton theon*) from both Philo and Josephus.[22] The same pattern appears in early post-apostolic Christianity. The *First Epistle of Clement*, for example, uses *exhilaskesthai* with God as direct object: 'Jonah preached destruction to the people of Nineveh; but they, repenting of their sins, propitiated God (*exhilasanto ton theon*) by their supplications and received salvation.'[23] The *Shepherd of Hermas* speaks to the same effect: 'Then I said within myself, "If this sin is recorded against me, how can I be saved? Or how shall I propitiate God for my sins which are full-blown?"'[24]

If the apostles had warned of the danger of suggesting that God had to be propitiated, their successors clearly knew nothing of it. Either that, or the pagan notion had quickly reasserted itself.

This brief survey may suffice to show that in classical Greek, in the Greek Old Testament, in the Greek of Hellenistic Judaism and in the Greek of the Apostolic Fathers, the *hilaskesthai* word-group was regularly used in connection with removing the anger of God (or the gods) and ensuring his favour and goodwill. If this is so, then Dodd's argument means that the usage of the apostles is completely isolated from the language around them. They use the same words, but with a different, specialized meaning, forming, as Roger Nicole remarks, 'a sort of linguistic island with little precedent in former times, little confirmation from the contemporaries, and no following in after years!'[25]

Against such an absurdity Morris rightly protests that there is 'a definite continuity' and that 'the averting of anger seems to represent a stubborn substratum of meaning from which all the usages can be naturally explained'. He concludes: 'in view of the otherwise invariable Greek use it would seem impossible for anyone in the first century to have used one of the *hilaskomai* group without conveying to his readers some idea of propitiation.'[26]

The key New Testament passages

When we come to consider the *hilaskesthai* passages of the New Testament we must bear this last remark of Morris' in mind. Even when the correct

22. *BAGD*.
23. *The Epistle of S. Clement*, VII. See J. B. Lightfoot, *The Apostolic Fathers, Part I: S. Clement of Rome* (repr. Grand Rapids: Baker, 1978 [1890]), vol. II, p. 38.
24. Vision I.2. Lightfoot, *Apostolic Fathers*, p. 166.
25. Nicole, *Standing Forth*, p. 357.
26. Morris, *Apostolic Preaching of the Cross*, pp. 154–155.

translation is 'expiate', the idea of propitiation is never far away. There are two reasons for this.

One is that even though the reference is to 'covering' an impersonal object, sin, expiation remains an interpersonal transaction. The sin is being covered *from* someone, and the expiatory offering is being offered *to* someone. In the last analysis, the aim is not to influence sin, but to influence the God who is offended by it and to restore good relations between the sinner and God. The expiation has meaning and value only as a means of propitiation. In saying this, however, we have always to keep in mind that, in Christian terms, the expiation is offered to the God who is love, who already, indeed, loves sinners and is altogether predisposed to welcome the expiation offered to him. But grace reigns through righteousness, not in violation of it (Rom. 5:21).

The second reason why the idea of propitiation is always present whenever the New Testament uses the *hilaskesthai* word-group is that the whole idea of atonement rests on the presupposition that the human race is in serious difficulty with God. This is especially clear in Romans 3:25, which represents Christ as the *hilastērion*. The whole paragraph is dominated by the fact stated in verse 23, 'all have sinned and fall short of the glory of God'. This is the conclusion of an argument that began in Romans 1:18, where Paul set out to prove that the human race, Jew and Gentile, was universally 'under the power of sin' (Rom. 3:9), and because it was under sin it was also under the wrath of God. This, for Paul's purpose, is the most fundamental and most solemn problem facing the human race. Against our ungodliness and unrighteousness God's anger is being revealed (Rom. 1:18). This is the plight of mankind; the great shadow that hangs over all human existence. God has suspended the sentence, but he has pronounced it clearly. There will be 'wrath and anger' for all who follow evil (Rom. 2:8).

It is in this context, and as the remedy for this plight, that Christ is put forward as the *hilastērion*. Unless our sins are remitted, God's anger is inevitable, but before they can be remitted they must be expiated. Christ, by his blood, is that expiation, the place where sin is atoned for, and where God meets with us and speaks to us, justifying those who put their faith in Jesus Christ (Rom. 3:26). This is how the divine anger is averted, and this is why the *hilastērion* was provided. To speak here of an expiation which does not propitiate would be meaningless.

The same background appears in Hebrews 2:17: Christ has come 'to make atonement for the sins of the people'. Here the direct object of *hilaskesthai* is 'sins', and, as we have seen, the natural translation is, 'to expiate the sins of the people'. But these sins are not merely a problem in and of themselves. They are a problem in relation to God. This is why we need a high priest; and this is why the service of the high priest is specifically defined as a service 'towards God' (*pros ton theon*), exactly the same phrase as is used in 1 John 2:1 to describe Christ's advocacy as directed towards the Father. It is precisely because of its Godward implications that sin has to be expiated. In itself, it lies uncovered, exposed before the gaze of the Holy, whose judgment penetrates even to the thoughts and motives of the heart (Heb. 4:12). This God, warns the writer, avenges sin and judges his people. He is a 'consuming fire' (Heb. 12:29), and it is a dreadful thing to fall into his hands (Heb. 10:30).

The high priest stood between this God and the sins of his people. This is why Jesus' Levitical predecessor had to enter the Holy of Holies and present the blood before the Lord; and this is why Jesus had to pass through the heavens (Heb. 4:14) into the real, eternal presence carrying his own blood as an expiation for the sins of his people. Covering them was not an end in itself. It was a means to an end, and that end was to stay the divine anger and protect his people from the consuming fire. He expiates sin 'towards God'. Again, then, expiation is in order to propitiate, and in this case it is final and conclusive. If we despise or neglect it, there is no other: 'How shall we escape if we ignore such a great salvation?' (Heb. 2:3).

1 John 2:1–2

In 1 John 2:1–2 it is the word *hilasmos* we meet, closely associated with the work of Christ as advocate. The very fact that they need an advocate is itself a sharp reminder that those for whom Christ is acting are in serious trouble. It also makes plain that our condition is not first and foremost medical, as if our need were only for healing. The whole scene is forensic. Our problem is that we stand accused, and the fact that Christ's advocacy is directed specifically to the Father makes plain that he is the accuser. We are in trouble with God. He hates sin, and he alone can forgive it, but why should he? Sin has brought anarchy into a world which was originally 'very good' (Gen. 1:31), a world which gave God immense satisfaction and which he greatly loved. Now sin has ruined his master-piece, men and women, filled the earth with hatred and violence, and turned the world into an idolatrous, blasphemous conspiracy against himself and against all good order. How could he forgive it?

But we have an advocate. In human justice systems, defence counsels like to know the character of the judge. Has he a reputation for harshness and irrit-ability, or a special prejudice against certain groups or crimes? In our case, the advocate is fortunate. He is appearing before the Father, one who by eternal generation is his own Father, and one who from free eternal love chose to be *our* Father (1 John 3:1). The judge is well disposed, yet the advocate cannot relax. The Father is well known, even by his children, to take sin with dreadful seriousness: 'Since you call on a Father who judges each person's work impartially, live out your time as foreigners here in reverent fear' (1 Pet. 1:17). With unfailing consistency he does what is right (Gen. 18:25); and in accordance with this he has categorically endorsed the principle that to acquit the wicked is detestable (Prov. 17:15). Besides, the primal impulse in the heart of the very advocate himself is, 'hallowed be your name'. He cannot deploy any form of advocacy which might compromise that name.

What then? He has a *hilasmos*: an expiation for sin. But again, the expiation points beyond itself and beyond sin. It has no significance except as part of the advocacy. It is the key element in the case for the defence which Jesus is putting to God the Father. God already loves his clients before he hears the arguments, but their sin has grieved and angered him. Now, however, there is a new factor, and their sin is no longer the decisive factor in his bearing towards his children. What he now hears is not sin crying out to be avenged, but the persuasive advocacy of his Son, the pre-eminent one among his children (Rom. 8:29); and he now sees, not the guilt of humanity, but the *hilasmos* offered in our name by the man Christ Jesus.

The advocacy is compelling, the expiation perfect, and priceless. Sin must be forgiven. Anger, now, would be a breach of the divine faithfulness. Wrath against the expiated sin would bring dishonour to the Name.

The practical outworking of this fact, the very foundation of the gospel, is seen in Jesus' parable of the Pharisee and the tax collector (Luke 18:9–14). The pivotal moment is the prayer of the tax collector, 'God have mercy on me, a sinner'. He stands before God without pretence, excuse or boast. He is simply a sinner. Indeed, he is *the* sinner, the word 'sinner' in the original being preceded by the definite article. As he prays, this is the only relevant consideration. He has no other identity, and it is as if he thinks that when he says, 'The Sinner', God will know at once who is calling. And as he has but one identity, so he has but one possible prayer, 'God, have mercy on me'. The Greek word here is *hilasthēti*, related to *hilaskesthai*, and as Marshall suggests (quoting Hill), 'a trace of the idea of propitiation lies in the background'.[27] The Latin Vulgate reflects this with its rendering, 'be propitious' (*propitius esto*), and since the original verb is in the passive the prayer could be rendered, 'Be propitiated towards me'. However, the act of propitiation is not in the foreground here. The tax collector's hope is

---

27. I. Howard Marshall, *The Gospel of Luke: A Commentary on the Greek Text* (Exeter: Paternoster Press, 1978), p. 680.

in divine mercy, *simpliciter*, and this, no doubt, is how many of us make our first approach to God, clinging to the hope of mercy, but with no clear idea how it could ever reach us.

'Have mercy on me,' cried David, 'according to your great compassion' (Ps. 51:1). It is the plea of one who has no defence, who has exhausted all legal arguments and whose only hope is sovereign clemency. But behind the clemency lies, for the Christian, not only the eternal love of God but the advocacy of Jesus and the blood of the Lamb.

7. RECONCILIATION: GOD'S WAY OF PEACE

Paul is the only New Testament writer who uses the language of reconciliation (the verb *katallassō* and its derivatives, *apokatallassō* and *diallassomai*, and the noun form, *katallagē*). It is a familiar enough concept, however, in daily life. Estranged husbands and wives, members of quarrelling families, and erstwhile friends are said to be reconciled when good relations are restored. The concept is also familiar in industrial relations, where parties in dispute may be reconciled through arbitration; and in the political arena, where warring nations, divided by ancient hatreds, may be reconciled through peace-talks and diplomacy.

The same basic presupposition underlies the Christian doctrine of reconciliation. There has been a breakdown in relations between God and the human race. A state of enmity now exists between us, and this is true both of the race collectively and of each individual human being.

On whose side is the enmity?

The question is, on whose side does the enmity lie? Are the barriers only on our human side, or are there also barriers on God's side? It is often noted that the New Testament never speaks of man reconciling God; indeed, it never speaks of God being reconciled at all. He is always the reconciler, never the reconciled. For example, in 2 Corinthians 5:20 the apostolic appeal is, 'be reconciled to

God'; an appeal directed to us and requiring action on our part. There is no corresponding appeal to God.

This has led many scholars to take it as axiomatic that all the enmity and all the misunderstanding are on the side of the human race. The nineteenth-century commentator, J. B. Lightfoot, set the tone: 'It is the mind of man, not the mind of God, which must undergo a change, that a re-union may be effected.'[1]

It is, of course, true that there is enmity on the human side: 'the mind governed by the flesh is hostile to God' (Rom. 8:7). More broadly, we are by nature followers of God's arch-enemy, 'the ruler of the kingdom of the air' (Eph. 2:2). Resentment of divine rule, disobedience of his law, mistrust of his ways, rejection of his gospel and hatred of his followers are all fundamental aspects of the human condition. Mankind lives in a state of chronic revolt against their Maker. Any meaningful concept of reconciliation must, therefore, include the removal of this enmity, replacing hatred with love and blasphemy with doxology.

Yet the New Testament makes plain that there are barriers on God's side, too. He cannot condone sin. He hates it, condemns it and opposes it. It is so abhorrent, indeed, that he cannot look at it (Hab. 1:13), much less can he be expected to walk in concord with the children of darkness. He deems them aliens and foreigners (Eph. 2:12), impenitent rebels against his kingdom.

All this is highlighted in the Genesis account of the fall of mankind. Sin immediately brought resentment and fear. When Adam and Eve 'heard the sound of the Lord God as he was walking in the garden' they immediately hid among the trees; and when they were challenged Adam answered, 'I heard you in the garden, and I was afraid' (Gen. 3:8–10). The relationship is in tatters, and from this moment onwards mankind's attitude to God is a mixture of guilt, fear, hatred and paranoia. But the Genesis account does not end there. It ends with the words, 'God drove the man out' (Gen. 3:24). John Milton paints a charming picture of the fallen couple's departure from Paradise:

> They hand in hand, with wandering steps and slow,
> Through Eden took their solitary way.[2]

But they were not voluntary exiles. They were 'banished' (Gen. 3:23); and not only were they banished, but the road back was closed: 'After he drove the man

---

1. J. B. Lightfoot, *St Paul's Epistles to the Colossians and Philemon: A Revised Text with Introductions, Notes, and Dissertations* (8th ed., London: Macmillan, 1886), p. 159.

2. *Paradise Lost*, Bk. XII, 64–69.

out, he placed on the east side of the Garden of Eden cherubim and a flaming sword flashing back and forth to guard the way to the tree of life' (Gen. 3.24). It is a defining moment. The human race can never go back to the womb. Innocence, once lost, is lost for ever. And there can be no cheap grace, though at that point Adam and Eve could scarcely have imagined what the cost of their sin would be. Yet even in the moment of expulsion, there is grace. The human pair are not banished from the earth, only from the garden; and they are not left without provision. No longer will they enjoy the lush provision of paradise, but the ground will still support them, though by the sweat of their brow.

Yet the divine anger towards the disobedient pair is plain enough. God does not simply order them to leave, he forcibly expels them, and bars their return. Eden was the place where God walked, where humans lived in harmony with their Maker, with each other and with their environment, and where eternal life was within their grasp. Now, their situation is changed irrevocably. Eden is behind them, and at the gate stands a flaming sword. The divine holiness, the flaming anger of God, now stands between mankind and paradise. Humanly speaking, the way back to eternal life is closed; and closed, not by mankind's 'No!' to God, but by God's 'No!' to mankind. Anyone who dares to go back must reckon with the flaming holiness of offended deity.

That would be the mission of Christ. He would approach the Holy in the name of mankind, the sword would flash, the curse would be endured, and a new way would be opened back to paradise. But it would not be a way opened through a change of heart on mankind's part. It would be opened through the blood of Jesus (Heb. 10:19).[3]

But if it is the holiness of God that guards the way to the tree of life, why does Paul plead with *us* to be reconciled to God (2 Cor. 5:20)? Is this not a clear plea that *we* should lay aside *our* enmity against God?

There is a close parallel to Paul's form of words in Matthew 5:24, where Jesus lays down the principle, 'first go and be reconciled to your brother'. The key point here is that the person who is being urged to 'be reconciled' is not the one who harbours the resentment. Quite the contrary: 'If you are offering your gift at the altar and there remember that *your brother or sister has something against*

---

3. There is no reason to think the cherubim and the flaming sword anything but historical. True, they are not to be seen today, but Eden, too, was part of the ground that was cursed, and as the thorns and thistles took over it became a place that no one would want to go back to. The curse spread only gradually, but in the meantime Eden was securely guarded. While the symbols of man's banishment were temporary, the theological reality they point to was permanent.

you, leave your gift there in front of the altar. First go and be reconciled to them; then come and offer your gift' (italics mine). In this context, reconciliation clearly does not mean changing your own personal attitude to someone: it means changing their attitude towards you. 'Be reconciled', here at least, is equivalent to, 'deal with what your brother or sister has against you'. In view of the overall teaching of Scripture, Paul's appeal, 'be reconciled to God', must be seen in this light. God has banished man; now we must deal with what he has against us. We must make peace with the one we have provoked by our sin.

2 Corinthians 5:18–21

The seminal New Testament text on reconciliation is 2 Corinthians 5:18–21. The first thing that stands out here is the emphasis on the divine initiative. It pervades the whole context: 'all this is from God' (v. 18). He it is who makes us new creatures (v. 17); he it is who reconciled us to himself; he it is who gave us the ministry of reconciliation; he it is who does not count our sins against us; he it is who makes his appeal through the apostles; and he it is who made Christ 'sin' for us. All this brings out with overwhelming force that it is the offended, not the offender, who not only takes the first step, but carries the whole process through to its conclusion. But, then, this simply underlines what we have already noted so often: the love of God is the source of the atonement, not its intended outcome. He does not wait for the offender to take the first, apologetic step. Instead, he is the one determined to do all that has to be done to heal the broken relationship. And not only does he take the initiative, delegating the work to Christ and then standing back, but he was actively involved throughout (as, indeed, was the Holy Spirit): *God* was reconciling *in Christ* (v. 19).

The passage also makes clear what exactly Paul understood by reconciliation: 'God was reconciling the world to himself in Christ, *not counting people's sins against them*' (v. 19, italics mine). This cannot be a reference to some inward, subjective change in the human heart. It is a divine act of non-imputation. The key word here, *logizomenos*, is a bookkeeping term. Paul sees sin as a debt; reconciliation consists of God cancelling the debt. It is not that he *has* nothing against us, but that he *holds* nothing against us. Reconciliation is a comprehensive act of divine forgiveness, and Paul's language here is the equivalent of his statement in Romans 8:1, 'there is now no condemnation for those who are in Christ Jesus'. Nor is there any hint that the erasure from the debit column of the ledger is God's response to a change of attitude on the debtor's part. The debt is cancelled in Christ and for the sake of Christ. This connection should not be overlooked. If reconciliation were the result of a change of heart on the part of the sinner it would be the work of the Holy Spirit, whom Scripture consistently portrays as the agent of renewal. This, the transformation of the sinner, is an essential element in the plan of salvation, but it is not the reconciliation spoken of in 2 Corinthians 5. There it is the work of Christ that is prominent; the reconciliation consists not in a change of hearts on our parts but in a cancellation of debt on God's part, and the reason the debt is cancelled is not that we have laid aside our enmity but that Christ has paid our debt in full.

But the most remarkable feature of the passage is Paul's account of the procedure by which God reconciled the world to himself. He did indeed take the initiative, but he did not proceed directly from love to forgiveness. Instead, he took this extraordinarily costly route; he reconciled us through Christ and in Christ.

What exactly this means becomes clear in verse 21: 'God made him who had no sin to be sin for us, so that in him we might become the righteousness of God.' The structure of the verse is chiasmic, contrasting 'him who knew no sin' with 'us' who knew it only too well; and his being made 'sin' with our being made 'righteousness'. At the heart of the verse lies the boldest statement to be found anywhere in the New Testament. Not only was Christ made 'flesh', as John declares (John 1:14); he was made 'sin'.

Any exegesis of this statement requires one instant disavowal. Christ was not made 'sinful', a point which Paul carefully safeguards when he speaks of him as the one who 'knew' no sin. He never committed sin, he never confessed it and he never inherited it. Instead, the human nature he took was perfectly holy from its very inception. He had no affinity with sin and bore not the slightest taint of corruption. But he was 'made sin'. He took responsibility for it, was identified with it, charged with it and paid for it. He endured its curse (Gal. 3:13), being banished to a place where he could not see God walk or hear God talk. What sin deserved, Christ suffered; and all he suffered was because of sin. Yet, once again, we confront the paradox: it was not for his own sin, but 'for us'. That 'for' brought a deadly entail.

But as he was made sin, so we are made 'righteousness': not simply righteous, but *righteousness*. Though it is not explicit, the idea of imputation underlies the whole passage. Reconciliation, as Paul sees it, means the non-imputation of our sins to us (v. 19); conversely, Christ's being made sin means the imputation of our sins to him. It is hard to see how it can bear any other meaning: our debts were debited to his account. Here, the prepositions are crucial. *For* us, he was made sin; *in* him, we are made the righteousness of God. This last phrase is remarkable. Righteousness is an absolute. God's righteousness means that he never deviates from his own norms or falls short of his own standards. He is absolutely true to himself as his own law. Can such righteousness possibly be ours? Can we be *that* righteous? Yes, in Christ! His righteousness is ours, not only because his obedience is that of a divine person but because the human life he lived (albeit as the Son of God) was a perfectly sinless and absolutely holy life over which God could unhesitatingly pronounce the verdict, 'very good'. In him, that righteousness is ours. We are as righteous as God himself: perfect, our sins blotted out.

But it is here, too, that the divine paradox climaxes: it was God who made Christ 'sin'. This is the most challenging of all the biblical statements portraying God the Father as not a mere spectator at Calvary, but as the key participant. Here is the ultimate expression of God not sparing his Son. God treated him as the sin of the world deserved to be treated. But here (here above all) we must also remember Christ's willingness. His love prompted him to become the representative and substitute of his people. And here, too, we must remember the twofold identity of the Messiah. He is 'the man Christ Jesus' (1 Tim. 2:5), and in him the human race offered the obedience and sacrifice it owed. It was in the nature that sinned that Christ was made sin, and it was in the nature that had disobeyed that he was obedient even to the point of dying (Phil. 2:8). Christ, dreadful though it sounds, is a human sacrifice, God's own Isaac; but this time there is no voice to stay the slayer's hand (Gen. 22:12).

Yet the Mediator is also God the Son, and, since there is but one God, in him God offers himself, becoming man so that in his own personal humanity (the humanity of God) he can offer himself: God not sparing *himself*. Christ is both 'Other than God' and 'Not Other than God'; God the Son *and* the Last Adam. However counter-intuitive such a vision, the two great, basic points are clear: our sin is covered by the sacrifice of the one who knew no sin, and God bears the whole cost.

It is not, then, to sinners as such that God is reconciled, but to sinners 'in Christ': sinners who are 'the righteousness of God' in him. Between eternal love and reconciliation there intervene these two momentous steps: Christ is made sin, and sinners are made righteous. It is to those who are thus righteous that God is reconciled. He cannot count their sins against them because these sins are theirs no more. The debts have been paid in full, or, to revert to the imagery of Genesis 3, as the risen Christ approaches Eden the flaming sword cannot touch him or the divine holiness rebuff him. There is *shalom* because there is righteousness. And when we approach, we, too, have safe conduct. The flaming sword cannot touch us because we are 'in him'. Now the sword, once so threatening, is our defence, poised to strike any accuser who dares to defy God's word: 'There is no condemnation for those who are in Christ Jesus' (Rom. 8:1).

This is the core Christian message, and Paul takes time to elaborate on the responsibility of the messenger. God, he says, has given us 'the ministry (*diakonia*) of reconciliation' (v. 18). This is our diaconate. God has accomplished it. At that level, we have nothing to do. It is not ours to reconcile God to man. But we serve this reconciliation; serve it up, almost. Like table waiters, we wait upon the world, and what we offer is peace with God. Nothing may divert us from this. It is humanity's greatest need, we have it, and apart from it we have nothing.

But how do we exercise this diaconate? Through the message (*logos*) of reconciliation! This is what God has placed 'among us' (v. 19); and it is no vague thing, as if our only 'word' were that some Christ or other has delivered us in some way or other from some sin or other. The message is specific, and it involves not only proclaiming the fact of reconciliation and holding out the offer of it, but explaining it and making plain its underlying logic. It has been secured at a price, and that price must be proclaimed: 'Be reconciled to God, because he made the one who knew no sin to be sin for us.' Sinners need to know not only that there is peace, but that that peace rests on a secure foundation: in this case, the righteousness of God.

Nor is this to be done in some detached, matter-of-fact way, as if the preacher cared not at all whether people welcomed the peace and accepted its terms. The language of verse 20 is the language of passion. It is not merely a matter of delivering the message faithfully, important though that is. The outcome matters, too, and matters urgently. Preachers are not only servants but ambassadors, authorized to speak for Christ and charged with protecting and advancing his interests; as ambassadors they must respect their Master's instructions not only as regards the content of their message, but as regards its tone. That tone is the tone of exhortation, as if 'God were making his appeal through us' (v. 20), exhorting and urging men and women to accept his peace. The preacher is 'imploring' on his master's behalf. The verb here is *deometha*, and it is the language of prayer. Jesus used it when he told Peter he had prayed for him (Luke 22:32); Paul used it (in its noun form) when he told the Philippians not to be anxious, but instead to make their requests known to God with prayer and 'entreaty' (*deēsis*) (Phil. 4:6). Here is the paradigm for evangelism: earnest, imploring entreaty, addressed this time not to God, but to the sinner in the far country. It is as if Christ, through his ambassadors, were on bended knee, pleading with men and women to accept God's peace. No preoccupation with our own dignity, or even with the dignity of the gospel, should tempt us to drop this tone. Preachers in the apostolic mode preach with tears (Acts 20:31).

But is the appeal not limited to the Corinthians and as such aimed at the saints ('holy people'), not at the world (2 Cor. 1:1)? There can be no denying that the saints often need to be reconciled (or re-reconciled) to God, but we should note the precise language Paul uses. When the KJV adopted the rendering, 'we pray you in Christ's stead, be ye reconciled to God', it quite rightly put the word 'you' in italics, because there is no 'you' in the original. Instead, we have the impressive programmatic statement: 'We plead on behalf of Christ, be reconciled to God.' It is a plea without restriction, addressed to the whole human race.

Romans 5:10–11

Paul's other main reference to reconciliation between God and man is in Romans 5:10–11:

> For if, while we were God's enemies, we were reconciled to him through the death of his Son, how much more, having been reconciled, shall we be saved through his life! Not only is this so, but we also boast in God through our Lord Jesus Christ, through whom we have now received the reconciliation.

Once again, the key question is, on whose side is the enmity? In the previous chapters, Paul has already spoken of our human antagonism to God. We neither glorified him nor gave him thanks (Rom. 1:21), and instead of worshipping him we turned to idols of our own making (Rom. 1:25). We suppressed the truth he revealed to us (Rom. 1:18) and dismissed him from our minds (Rom. 1:26). We are God-haters (Rom. 1:30) and persist in patterns of behaviour we know to be abhorrent to him (Rom. 1:32). We show contempt for his kindness, tolerance and patience (Rom. 2:4). None of us seeks him (Rom. 3:11) or shows him the reverence he deserves (Rom. 3:18).

This is a damning indictment of man's hostility to God, and Protestant theology has accepted it unreservedly. Indeed, many would argue that by adopting the doctrine of 'total depravity' Protestant theology has burdened itself with an altogether too gloomy view of human nature. Yet that doctrine accords fully with Paul's perspective. Our depravity is a reality, it is universal and it crystallizes in hostility to God. It follows, then, that reconciliation must include an end to this hostility on man's part.

But the fact that there is hostility on our part against God does not rule out the possibility that there is opposition on his part toward us. On the contrary, our enmity against him (which is never merely against him, but also against our neighbour) inevitably wounds his love and provokes his holiness. Paul has already made this clear. It is precisely against our *asebeia*, our contempt for the majesty of God, that his anger has been revealed from heaven (Rom. 1:18). God is not at peace with us, and will not be until there is reconciliation.

All that Paul says of reconciliation in this passage points away from its being a pacification of human beings and towards its being a once-for-all peace-making with God. Apart from this moment, 'the death of his Son', God would have kept us at a distance and demanded that we reap what we sow. Now he is at peace with us, and invites us to draw near.

The key points are as follows.

First, it is clear, once again, that it was not the function of the atonement to make God love us. The cross is a 'demonstration' of his love (Rom. 5:8), not its cause. The love was utterly unconditional, focusing on us not as capable, righteous or good people (vv. 6–8), but as helpless and ungodly sinners. Yet though God loved us when we were still powerless and ungodly, he was not at peace with us. Peace came only through justification (Rom. 5:1), and justification came only through the blood of Christ (v. 9).

Secondly, Paul identifies both the time when we were reconciled and the means by which we were reconciled. It took place when Christ died. This was the great reconciling moment: not our change of heart and attitude, but Calvary. Christ made peace by the blood of his cross (Col. 1:20). The alternative view that reconciliation is a spiritual change in believers would require a massive shift in theological focus away from, 'we were reconciled to God by the death of his Son' to, 'we were reconciled to God by the work of the Holy Spirit in our hearts'. This is exactly what Paul does not say. What he says is that peace came through the sacrifice of Christ, offered not to us, but to God; and offered once for all on Good Friday. There, and then, Christ reconciled the world and God. God always loved it (John 3:16). Now he is at peace with it.

Thirdly, Paul speaks of reconciliation as something we are to 'receive' (v. 11). He uses a similar expression when he speaks of 'receiving' the apostolic tradition. In 1 Corinthians 15:3, for example, he reminds the believers that he had passed on what he had received, and they in turn had received what he had passed on. This clearly refers to the fixed and well-defined message that Christ died for our sins and rose again on the third day, a message which is true irrespective of whether or not people receive it. He speaks to similar effect of 'receiving' Christ: 'just as you received Christ Jesus as Lord, continue to live your lives in him' (Col. 2:6). In this case again the receiver contributes nothing. Like his death and resurrection, the lordship of Christ is an objective, unalterable fact. But so, too, is the reconciliation referred to in Romans 5:10. It has already been achieved in Christ (2 Cor. 5:19). God has made peace, it comes to us from his side, and what is asked of us is only that we receive it.

It would be impossible to speak of reconciliation in this way if it consisted only of a change of attitude on the part of the sinner. We can 'receive' another person's offer to lay down his enmity and be at peace. We could not 'receive' our own laying down our enmity against him or her. Nor can we 'receive' our own cessation of hostilities against God. In terms of the Christian doctrine, we accept a peace which God has placed on an eternally secure foundation in the sacrifice and service of his Son.

Fourthly, Paul's *a fortiori* argument in verse 10 (arguing from the greater to the lesser) would make no sense if reconciliation meant only a change in our attitude to God. It would then need to read as follows: 'For if, when we were God's enemies, we laid aside, through the death of his Son, our enmity against God, how much more, having laid aside our enmity against him, shall we be saved by the life of his Son?' This throws everything into confusion because it puts the emphasis on what *we* have done. The greater then becomes the fact that we have laid aside our enmity against God; the lesser, that we shall be saved through his life. The former is a human action, the latter a divine. We laid aside our enmity; he will save us. We did the greater; he did the lesser. This is utterly incoherent. Paul's argument has to be that since God has already done the greater we can be confident that he will do the lesser. The greater is that he has reconciled us, and there are two things that make it greater: first, that he did it when we were still 'enemies'; secondly, that he did it even though it cost the death of his Son. The lesser is that God will complete his salvation, and this is lesser, first, because we are no longer enemies and, secondly, because the completion of our salvation requires only that his Son shall live (to continue his ministry), not that he shall die. It cost God the death of his Son to make peace with the world. Now that there is peace, and now that no further sacrifice is required, God's blessing will flow freely. It is precisely the same argument as is stated succinctly in Romans 8:32: 'He who did not spare his own Son, but gave him up for us all – how will he not also, along with him, graciously give us all things?' If he gave us his Son, he will hold back nothing.

The final point to note in this passage is that Paul clearly equates reconciliation with justification. Indeed, the two are virtually synonymous throughout Paul's letters, as Calvin noted: 'The righteousness of faith is reconciliation with God, which consists solely in the forgiveness of sins.'[4] This appears clearly in 2 Corinthians 5:19, where Paul defines reconciliation in terms of forgiveness, the key element in justification: 'God was reconciling the world to himself . . . not counting people's sins against them'. It is equally clear here in Romans 5, where the statement, 'we have now been justified by his blood' (v. 9) is synonymous with the declaration, 'we were reconciled to [God] through the death

4. *Institutes,* III:XI, 21. Cf. Calvin's comment on Paul's language in 2 Corinthians 5:19–21: 'Here he mentions righteousness and reconciliation indiscriminately, to have us understand that each one is reciprocally contained in the other . . . he reconciles us to himself by not counting our sins against us.'

of his Son' (v. 10). The two concepts do, of course, have different starting points. Justification implies guilt; reconciliation implies alienation and enmity. But the one implies the other. It is precisely the enmity that causes the guilt, and the (divine) enmity will persist so long as the guilt remains. Once the guilt is removed, the (divine) enmity ceases. The whole point of being justified by faith, as Calvin points out, is that, being reconciled to God through Christ's blamelessness, 'we may have in heaven instead of a Judge a gracious Father'.[5]

But justification is no inward, spiritual transformation. It is a change in status, not a change of nature; not a change in our attitude to God but a change in our relationship with him. Instead of condemning, he now acquits and vindicates us, declaring us to be in the right and by that declaration putting us in the right. To the extent that justification is synonymous with reconciliation it, too, marks not a change of heart on our part but a change of relationship on God's part. He becomes our friend. He welcomes and embraces us. Indeed, to the two great moments, justification and reconciliation, there must be added a third: adoption. The three are inseparable. The Judge is now our vindicator, our friend and our Father. Love has made peace.

Yet this reconciliation is accomplished only when God is reconciled to his Son. There was, of course, no enmity in Christ's heart towards God, nor was the Son ever anything but the object of his Father's love. Yet when the Son became the sin-bearer, and even 'sin' itself, the Father is alienated; and he cannot hide that alienation. Even when it is his Son who bears it, God cannot condone sin. He condemns it; and even though in this case it is pre-eminently true that while he hates the sin he loves the sin-bearer, yet it is the sin-bearer who is forsaken and put to grief. God turns away his face and invokes against him the curse of his law (Gal. 3:13). Here at Calvary, it is impossible to argue that all the enmity is on man's side. Here, there is no enmity on the human side; not in the man, Christ Jesus. But here there is rejection and banishment on God's side. Here, and here alone, in the flesh of his own Son, does God treat sin as it deserved. Here it is made unmistakeably plain that God's attitude to sin is one of uncompromising hostility. He loves the sin-bearer, but he is not at peace with him; and he will not be at peace with him (he will not be *reconciled*) to him till the sacrifice is consummated and Christ pours out his soul unto death (Isa. 53:12).

But from that moment, the sin-bearer is secure under the full protection of the law. He died to sin once for all, and he cannot die again (Rom. 6:9–10). Here there can be no double jeopardy. Sin and death no longer have any claim on

5. *Institutes*, III.XI, 1.

him. He is protected by his own blood and by the absolute rectitude of God. God is at peace with him. God is reconciled. And all who are in him enjoy the same protection. There is *now* no condemnation for Christ Jesus, though once there was; and there is *now* no condemnation for those who are *in* Christ Jesus, though once there was. Not only does God love us. He is now at peace with us.

Ephesians 2:11–22

The reconciliation effected by the cross embraces more, however, than our relations with God. It also transforms our human relationships with each other, as Paul makes clear in Ephesians 2:11–22. The basic principle is unmistakeable: all those who have been reconciled to God are also reconciled to each other, or, not only have the barriers between God and the human race been broken down, but the barriers between human and human have also been demolished.

The background to this statement is the great divide between Jew and Gentile, which spread tensions throughout the ancient world and posed a serious threat to the peace and unity of the church in the early days of Christianity. To the Jew, a Gentile was an inferior creature, ritually unclean, socially beyond the pale and spiritually beyond hope, and these ancient hatreds were institutionalized in what Paul calls the 'dividing wall': the complex of boundary-markers by which Jews distanced themselves from the Gentiles and jealously preserved their own identity. These included circumcision, temple rituals, the holy days and the food laws. To a Jew it was unimaginable that one could fraternize with anyone who refused to observe these laws. The problem for the church was that within her own bounds a party had emerged which argued that these barriers were still in place and that Gentiles could not be admitted into fellowship unless they agreed to be circumcised and keep the law of Moses (Acts 15:5). This was the problem which was addressed by the Council of Jerusalem (Acts 15:6–29), and which was resolved by the clear decision that salvation was by grace for both Jew and Gentile, and that disciples (all disciples) were now free from the yoke of Moses (Acts 15:10).

By the time Paul wrote Ephesians, priorities had changed and instead of trying to convince Judaisers of their errors he was trying to convince the Gentile believers of their privileges. The boundary markers have been revoked, there is no longer a dividing wall and the Ephesians must see themselves not as aliens or as second-class Christians, but as those who have been brought near and fully adopted into the family of God.

And all this, says Paul, came about through the blood of Christ (Eph. 2:13). God's love embraced both Jew and Gentile; Christ's blood was shed for both

Jew and Gentile; both Jew and Gentile can draw near to God; and both Jew and Gentile draw near on the same terms. Under the cross the church is a barrier-free household (Eph. 2:19). This is not a demand that God makes; it is a statement of fact, part of the gospel itself. Indeed, it is the very 'mystery' made known to God's holy apostles and prophets (Eph. 3:4–5). In God's commonwealth all citizens have equal rights, so that as in the Trinity itself, 'none is greater and none is lesser'.[6]

This has clear ethical implications. Christ himself set the pattern of non-exclusion and non-discrimination by so often doing the unthinkable: for example, by discussing the Torah with a Samaritan women (John 4:4–26), and arranging for Matthew the collaborator and Simon the freedom-fighter to sit together at the Last Supper. Each had to recognize that whatever wrongs they had committed against each other had been atoned for by the blood of Christ, and whatever debts they owed each other, he had paid. They had no right to hold against each other sins that Christ had paid for and God had forgiven. This is, surely, a thrillingly liberating vision. I may be, I am, I must be, at peace with every member of the church universal because even their unconfessed violations of my rights have been expiated at the cross of Calvary. In God's eyes, their sins are covered. My eyes, like his, must see not the offence, but the blood.

It may not be wise to attach too much symbolic value to the outspread arms of Christ on the cross, but it is true that his love embraces the whole world, and just as that embrace reconciles sinners to himself, so it reconciles them to each other. The embrace breaks down all barriers. The problem is that while totally captivated by the beauty of such a vision we seem to have no difficulty finding a thousand different reasons for not implementing it at a daily level. In the abstract, Jew and Palestinian, Afrikaaner and Xhosa, Serb and Croat, Loyalist and Republican, *should* set aside their ancient hatreds and sit together to give thanks for the body and blood of Christ. But what of the myriad instances where Christians have found 'good cause' not to worship as one, and not to recognize each other's 'orders' and 'ministry'? What petty differences in doctrine and liturgy, what trivial clashes of personality, what absurd hubris, have been used as pretexts for schism and separation! And how often have we, to whom so much has been forgiven, found it so difficult to forgive private wrongs!

Where are we to begin the road to recovery? By realizing that whatever the wrong committed against us by fellow believers, all has been dealt with at the cross. Forgiveness and reconciliation are not then matters of mere indulgent forbearance. They are matters of theological rigour. God is at peace with 'them'

---

6. Athanasian Creed, 25.

through the blood of the cross. They are my Father's friends. They must be my friends.

Colossians 1:19–20: cosmic reconciliation

In Colossians 1:19–20 Paul introduces yet another dimension of reconciliation, the cosmic: 'God was pleased ... through [Christ] to reconcile to himself all things ... by making peace through the blood of his cross'. The phrase, 'all things' (*ta panta*), refers to the whole created order, the definite article indicating that what is in mind is not the unconnected aggregate of individual things, but the ordered universe: what Genesis 1:1 calls 'the heavens and the earth'. In the beginning, that universe was perfect, and gave God total satisfaction. It was 'very good' (Gen. 1:31). But as Genesis 3 makes plain, the revolt of mankind had calamitous consequences for the earth as well as for themselves. The ground is cursed because of the man and his whole relationship with it thrown out of joint: 'through painful toil you will eat food from it all the days of your life' (Gen. 3:17). A world which formerly produced abundance now produces thorns and thistles, and only by the sweat of their brow will humans eat their bread (Gen. 3:19). By the time the human story reached Genesis 4:10, blood was crying out to God from the ground. By the time of Noah, the earth was filled with violence, and mankind had dragged even the sub-human creation down to ruin: 'I will wipe from the face of the earth the human race I have created – and with them the animals, the birds and the creatures that move along the ground – for I regret that I have made them' (Gen. 6:7).

Paul takes up this theme in Romans 8:18–21. His starting-point is 'our present sufferings'. But just as believers ('the children of God', v. 19) are suffering, so is the creation, which, no less than man, is in bondage to sin. Instead of giving satisfaction and pleasure to God, and benefiting from the care and stewardship of man, it is frustrated, out of harmony with man and consequently out of harmony with God's original purpose for the world. Its beauty is being spoiled, its resources recklessly squandered, its fertility and wealth prostituted to sin, greed and cruelty. Evil stalks where once God walked (Gen. 3:8), and the creation stands by helpless while idolatry, blasphemy and oppression proliferate. The creation, against its will (Rom. 8:20), has been enlisted in the service of sin and shares in the curse with which God threatened human disobedience.

But just as the children of God are supported in their sufferings by hope of the glory of God (Rom. 8:18) so the creation suffers in hope, straining forward eagerly to the day when it will be liberated and brought to share in the glorious freedom of the children of God (Rom. 8:21).

It is the basis of this hope that Paul exposes in Colossians 1:19–20. In Christ, God has reconciled everything to himself: not only humanity, but also the sub-human creation and the entire material universe. As the disobedience of the first Adam had significance for the whole cosmos, so did the obedience of the Last. The only thing excluded from the reconciliation is hinted at rather than expressed. When, in Philippians 2:10, Paul speaks of every knee bowing at the name of Jesus, he expands that to indicate that he means every knee 'in heaven and on earth and under the earth'. In the corresponding list in Colossians 1:20, there is no reference to 'under the earth'. The reconciliation is limited to all things 'whether things on earth or things in heaven'. Things 'under the earth' (the demonic and satanic) are subjugated, but not reconciled. There will never be peace between heaven and hell.

However, what Paul wants to emphasize with all the force at his command is that this reconciliation took place 'through him': Christ.

There are two key points here. First, as a matter of God's good pleasure, all the fullness of the godhead was in Christ: 'for God was pleased to have all his fullness dwell in him' (Col. 1:19). This cannot mean that Christ owed his deity to the good pleasure of God; he was 'God' in the beginning (John 1:1). Paul's meaning is clarified in Colossians 2:9, where he declares that 'in Christ all the fullness of the Deity lives in bodily form (*sōmatikōs*)'. It was the dwelling of deity 'in the body' that was God's good pleasure, and Paul's language probably takes its colour from the false teaching that was beginning to infiltrate the church at Colossae. Our knowledge of this false teaching is very limited, but it is likely that it bought into the widespread idea that matter is evil, and thus recoiled from the message that the fullness of godhead could dwell in the physical body of Christ. It is equally likely that it recoiled from the idea that there could be only one mediator. Instead, the gap between the infinite and the finite was so immense that it could be bridged only through countless intermediaries, of whom Christ could be but one. Alternatively, the divine had to be manifested in innumerable forms, of which, again, Christ could be only one (the others being the various 'thrones or powers or rulers or authorities', Col. 1:16).

Over against such speculations Paul insists that the fullness of deity *was* present, incarnate, in the body of Christ; not confined to that body, but present in it. But he is also insisting on the completeness, finality and exclusiveness of this presence. God is fully present in Christ, and God is present only in Christ. In the Old Testament, the polytheistic idea that the divine is so manifold that it must be distributed among 'gods many' is countered by the use of the plural *'ĕlōhîm* to describe the living God, the God of Israel. The whole of 'god-ness' is concentrated in him; he completely exhausts and fulfils the idea of 'god', so that there can be no other. Paul is thinking within this paradigm. Over against the idea that the 'fullness' is distributed through poly-intermediaries, he insists that all the 'fullness' is present here: not distributed vaguely through time and space, but in the body of Christ. Here the one God is revealed; here alone is he revealed; and here he is fully revealed.

Secondly, it was not merely for the purposes of revelation that all the fullness dwelt in Christ. There was another purpose beyond that: through Christ God would reconcile all things to himself. In the divine good pleasure, the incarnation is in order to reconcile. All things go back to the divine pleasure (*eudokēsen*), and all things are through Christ. He is the one reconciler. All syncretism is ruled out. There is no room for the notion that Christ is but one of many reconciling agents. Syncretism (or pluralism) implies that behind all the world's religions there lies an ultimate, never-fully-disclosed deity, who works in a fragmented way through all faiths, but never gives himself fully in any. Paul will have none of this. In Christ, there is fullness: fullness of revelation and fullness of reconciliation. That reconciliation is complete and world-embracing. The creation became accursed through disobedience, but that disobedience was expiated by the blood of Christ: not without blood, and not with many bloods, but by the blood which flowed in the veins of this one man in whom the fullness of the godhead dwelt bodily.

If we ask, in what capacity did he shed his blood, the answer may lie in Colossians 1:17. It was as the one 'in whom all things hold together'; as the one who bears a special relation to the material universe as well as to the human race. This is emphasized from a different point of view, but equally strikingly, in Hebrews 1:2, which refers to Christ as the 'appointed heir of all things'. It was his own inheritance which had acted in defiance of God; and it was on behalf of that inheritance, therefore, that Christ had to make peace.

The reconciliation of the cosmos is closely linked to the reconciliation of the human race. The ground was 'cursed' because of mankind's sin, but now that God no longer counts our sins against us the ground may be freed from its curse. It may seem unfair that the ground was cursed in the first place. The earth, after all, is innocent. But we must remember the bond between the human race and the material universe. Human beings were fashioned from the dust of the ground (Gen. 2:7), and are biochemically linked to every plant and to every star. They live off it, drawing their sustenance from the soil. Its productivity, beauty and good order provided them, un-fallen, with a magnificent habitat. Now, defiant, they have forfeited all right to it. But the environment in turn depended on mankind. Humanity was not only its appointed head, but its servant and guardian (Gen. 2:15), charged with conserving and developing it. After the fall, however, they quickly became dysfunctional, grasping and irresponsible; their whole habitat suffered, and in that suffering every other species shared. All became disorder. The environment no longer cared for humanity, and humanity no longer cared for it.

The effects of this curse are still with us, just as suffering and death are still the lot of the reconciled sinner. But in the case of the universe, as in the case of mankind, the curse itself has been lifted. The reconciled sinner no longer fears eternal death, and the reconciled universe no longer fears destruction. Instead, there will be what Peter in Acts 3:21 described as an *apokatastasis*: a restitution or restoration. The universe will be returned to its original condition, 'very good'. In Matthew 19:28, Jesus speaks of it as a *palingenesia*, or regeneration. The only other instance of this word is in Titus 3:5, where it refers to the regeneration of the sinner by the Holy Spirit. Just as the sinner experiences new birth, so the universe, too, will be born again; and we can be sure that in the one case, as in the other, the Holy Spirit will be the agent, as he was in the original creation, when he hovered over the waters (Gen. 1:2). But just as in the case of the human soul the work of the Spirit is based on the removal of the curse by the blood of Christ (Gal. 3:13–14), so in the case of the universe the regeneration rests on the fact that God has made peace through the cross.

The parallel between the Spirit's work in renewing the soul and his work in renewing the universe is fascinating. The regeneration of the universe and its restoration to its splendour is an integral part of God's plan of salvation. The meek are to inherit the earth, but it will be a transformed earth; transformed, not by a process of historical evolution, but by the intrusion of divine power. The New Jerusalem comes 'down out of heaven from God' (Rev. 21:2) and the result will be the restoration of perfect harmony between humanity and its environment. What God has in mind, and what the cross secured, is total salvation: a new soul in a new body in a new universe. This is our 'hope of glory'. We look for a new heaven and a new earth, where the God who once banished us will condescend to walk again among us, where the ground that once defied us will gladly yield its harvest (Rev. 22:2), and where we who once were drudges will reign for ever and ever.

What Peter describes as a 'restoration' and Jesus spoke of as a 'regeneration', Paul speaks of in Romans 8:19–21 as a 'liberation', and here again the link between the redemption of humanity and the redemption of the universe is maintained. In Galatians 5:1 Paul describes the saving work of Christ as a liberation: 'It is for freedom Christ has set us free.' That freedom is already a reality, but for the present it is a veiled freedom, yet to be fully revealed. The world does not recognize the children of God (1 John 3:1). One day, however, their glory will be disclosed; and that hope sustains believers as they struggle to cope with their present sufferings (Rom. 8:18).

But it is not only believers who long for that day, says Paul. The whole creation longs for it, hoping to catch a glimpse of the freedom which glory will bring to the children of God. Nor is creation's longing born of mere curiosity. It has a vested interest in the final liberation of the children of God because their liberation will also be the liberation of creation itself. At the moment, while the children of God suffer, creation groans, frustrated and enslaved, condemned to bear thorns and thistles, labouring and yet getting nowhere, and no longer able to give satisfaction to its Maker. So long as the human race, the rational agent in creation, is dysfunctional, the world will continue on its absurd, discordant way. But when humanity is finally delivered from its enslavement to sin and futility, creation, too, will be free under new leadership: the leadership of the Last Adam, the Son of God.

This is the vision we see in Hebrews 2:5–9. Jesus, having tasted death, is now crowned with glory and honour, and all things have been put under him. These words are a clear allusion to Psalm 8:6: 'You made [mankind] ruler over the works of your hands; you put everything under their feet.' For the time being, pending the parousia, this is but a promise, governed by a 'not yet'; 'at present we do not see everything subject to him' (Heb. 2:8). Satan, though bound, still prowls, the world is still ravaged by war and plagued by pestilence, and the earth (and beyond) is plundered by human greed. But on the day of liberation, Satan, and all his works, will be destroyed, and the Last Adam will resume the great mandates given to the First. Then the universe will once again be free, and fit for purpose.

It may seem an anticlimax when, having spoken of the reconciliation of all things, Paul continues the reconciliation theme in Colossians 1:21–23, but refers it this time to the reconciliation between themselves and God: 'now he has reconciled you by Christ's physical body through death' (v. 22). But there is a clear connection. Just like the Ephesians, the Colossians need to be reminded of their new relationship with God. The NIV, unfortunately, misses the stress on the words 'you also' with which the Greek sentence begins: 'You also he reconciled'. He is saying, in effect, 'Not only has God reconciled the cosmos. He has also reconciled *you*.' The Colossians might have found this hard to believe, partly because as Gentiles they had been alienated from God, and partly because they didn't qualify under the terms laid down by the false teachers (for example, the asceticism prescribed in Col. 2:20–23).

Here again we encounter J. B. Lightfoot's rubric that when it comes to reconciliation: 'It is the mind of man, not the mind of God, which must undergo a change.'[7] This is now the received orthodoxy, and there is indeed no denying

---

7. Lightfoot, *Epistles to the Colossians and to Philemon*, p. 159.

that the mind of man must be changed. But there is a *prima facie* absurdity in the idea that God would be indifferent to hostility on the part of his creatures, and an even greater absurdity in the notion that the Judge of all the earth would be acting out of character if outraged by the 'evil behaviour' Paul refers to in Colossians 1:21. Hostility against God is not some trivial matter, easily forgiven. It is a clear breach of the greatest of all commandments, the commandment to love God: the sum, indeed, of all breaches, and the root cause of the futility and enslavement of which Paul spoke in Romans 8, and of the violence depicted so graphically in Genesis 4 and 6. The very thorns and thistles are eloquent testimony to God's displeasure with sinful humanity.

But Paul assures the Colossians that despite their hostility God is now reconciled to them. The 'now' is important: '*Once* you were alienated . . . But *now* he has reconciled you by Christ's physical body through death' (vv. 21–22). It was ordained and planned from eternity, but it was accomplished (and, as far as the Colossians were concerned, only a few years previously) through the physical death of Christ at Calvary. In the case of the Colossians, as in the case of 'all things', peace was made only through the sacrificial blood of the cross.

Conclusion

Two final points should be noted.

First, God's ultimate purpose in reconciliation is to present us 'holy in his sight' (Col. 1:22). It is not on the basis of our holiness that peace prevails, but the peace is in order to holiness. This brings out once again the link between the two great aspects of salvation, the forensic and the transformational. Reconciliation and justification belong to the forensic, whereby we are brought into a right relationship with God: no longer condemned, but acquitted; no longer enemies, but friends; no longer aliens, but children. But this forensic change is always accompanied by inward transformation. Indeed, according to Romans 8:29, this was the whole point of God's eternal plan of salvation: 'Those God foreknew he also predestined to be conformed to the image of his Son.' The cross is clearly set within this purpose, which means not only that *remission* and *renewal* are organically linked, but that remission itself is an intermediate step towards the greater goal of restoring us to the divine likeness we lost in the fall. In the last analysis it is this renewal (including the resurrection of the body) that constitutes salvation. This is why Paul in Romans 5:10 distinguishes between reconciliation and salvation. We *were reconciled* to God by the death of his Son; we *shall be saved* through his life.

The forensic and the transformational are interdependent. Reconciliation is in order to transformation: everyone who is 'brought near' will ultimately bear God's image. But, equally, the transformation is secured by the great act of atonement. In other words, the ministry of the Spirit rests upon the sacrifice of Christ. Only when the blood has made peace can the ministry of the Spirit begin, and the transformation he brings about will be commensurate with the price that Christ paid at Calvary. We shall be as glorious as the blood of Christ deserves, and once again God will smile and say, 'Very good!'

The second and final point to note is Paul's stress on perseverance. God will present us holy in his sight only if we continue in our faith, not constantly shifting, but firm and stable. The activity of the false teachers, and the risks they pose, are clearly on the apostle's mind. There are, of course, other emphases in the New Testament, particularly the promise that God will keep us. But we should leave this warning in Colossians 1:23 as Paul left it, and let it speak its own word to us. If we abandon the gospel we shall never know that final salvation which God promises. As Calvin reminds us, 'we are still only *en route* and have not yet reached the goal'.[8]

But the warning applies not only to those who give up on the gospel but also to those, like the false teachers at Colossae, who believe that there are multiple mediators between God and humanity. For Paul, the only one in whom we can find peace and reconciliation is Christ. To abandon him is to abandon all hope. But conversely, in the moment of union with him there is what the older theologians called *duplex gratia*: the double grace of remission and renewal, both secured by the blood of the cross and together constituting one seamless salvation.

---

8. John Calvin, *The Epistles of Paul the Apostle to the Galatians, Ephesians, Philippians and Colossians*, tr. T. H. L. Parker (Grand Rapids: Eerdmans, 1996), p. 315.

8. SATISFACTION: ENOUGH TO JUSTIFY FORGIVENESS

Unlike propitiation and reconciliation the word 'satisfaction' is never used in Scripture in connection with the atonement, though it does occur twice in the KJV in a passage (Num. 35:31–32) which warns against commuting the capital sentence which was then mandatory for murder: 'ye shall take no satisfaction for the life of a murderer, which is guilty of death: but he shall surely be put to death'. The underlying Hebrew word, however, is *kopher*, which the NIV and ESV correctly translate as 'ransom': 'Do not accept a ransom for the life of a murderer'. Neither the Levitical sacrifices nor the sacrifice of Christ are referred to anywhere in Scripture as satisfactions to the deity.

Yet though the word is absent the idea is not altogether alien to the Old Testament. It is implied in the description of the Levitical sacrifices as 'an aroma pleasing to the LORD' (Lev. 1:13, language which is also applied to Christ in Eph. 5:2, which speaks of him as a 'fragrant offering and sacrifice to God'). It is also implied in Psalm 51:17: 'My sacrifice, O God, is a broken spirit; a broken and contrite heart, you, God, will not despise.' A similar reference to the kind of sacrifice which pleases God is found in Micah 6:6–8, where the prophet asks,

> With what shall I come before the Lord
>   and bow down before the exalted God?

and replies,

He has showed you, O mortal, what is good.
   And what does the Lord require of you?
To act justly and to love mercy
   and to walk humbly with your God.

The converse, making pain what does *not* please the Lord, is found in Isaiah 1:11,

'The multitude of your sacrifices –
   what are they to me?' says the Lord.
'I have more than enough of burnt offerings,
   of rams and the fat of fattened animals;
I have no pleasure
   in the blood of bulls and lambs and goats.'

Such passages make plain that God is satisfied with some sacrifices and not with others, but even more interesting is the use of the word 'satisfied' in Isaiah 53:11, a passage which has posed a problem for translators. The KJV reads, 'he shall see of the travail of his soul and shall be satisfied'; the NIV, 'after he has suffered, he will see the light of life and be satisfied'. Both these renderings suggest that the sacrifice of the Servant gave satisfaction to himself, but it could have done so only if he was confident first of all that it gave satisfaction to his heavenly Father, and was acceptable to him as, indeed, a fragrant offering. This again fits in with Genesis 1:31: the sacrifice of Christ, like the original work of creation, was 'very good'. It was everything that God could have desired.

But theology is not limited to specifically biblical terminology or forbidden to introduce new words into the discussion of the truth. Sometimes there is no single biblical word which can sum up what we understand the Bible to be saying: hence the need to coin a new vocabulary. The word 'atonement' itself is one example of such new coinage, the word 'sacrament' is another, and the word 'Trinity' is yet another. We must always bear in mind, of course, that no human words (not even those of Scripture) can 'contain' the truth. To paraphrase the language of Solomon at the dedication of the temple, 'the heavens, even the highest heavens, cannot contain you. How much less this *terminology* that I have chosen' (see 2 Chr. 6:18). But the glory of the Lord can fill our manmade language as it filled the manmade temple. The criterion is whether, and for how long, our non-biblical words can help to conserve and deliver the biblical message.

Anselm

The concept of satisfaction was first introduced to the formal theology of the atonement by Anselm, an Italian monk who served as Archbishop of Canterbury from 1093 to 1109 and whose seminal work, *Cur Deus Homo?*, was completed around 1100. Prior to Anselm, there had been virtually no rigorous or systematic treatment of the atonement. The one exception was Athanasius' *On the Incarnation* (published around 318), which had clearly understood the cross in sacrificial terms and portrayed Christ as our substitute. But no-one had built on this. Christian thinkers had simply accepted that the cross redeemed from sin, death and Satan, but there had been little reflection on what precisely the cross had achieved, or how, or why.

It is fair to say that when Anselm addressed these questions he was more concerned with the metaphysical than with the exegetical foundations of Christian doctrine. His aim was to show, with 'great logicality', that the incarnation and death of Christ flowed by necessity from the very nature of God: God being what he was, his Son had to become man and die. At the same time, Anselm was anxious to reject the idea, common among the early Fathers, that the atonement consisted of a ransom paid by Christ to the devil. This was absurd, he argued. The devil had no rights, his government was entirely illegitimate, and neither God nor man owed him anything. On the contrary, it was God, not the devil, who had claims that had had to be satisfied: 'whatever was demanded of man, his debt was to God, not to the devil'.[1]

There has been much discussion of the source of Anselm's theory of satisfaction, but whether it was Roman law, Germanic jurisprudence or the medieval sacrament of penance (with its three components of confession, contrition and satisfaction) the basic idea is clear: Christ did enough (Lat. *satis fecit*) to justify God in cancelling the debt that man owed him and in conferring on him the blessing of eternal life. The debt, as Anselm portrayed it, was a debt of honour. The human race owed God the debt of obedience. Instead, we had dishonoured him by disobeying him, and now we had no way of repaying that debt. Neither, however, could God simply cancel it. To allow the human race to sin with

---

1. *Cur Deus Homo?*, II:19. The most accessible edition of *Cur Deus Homo?* is in *Anselm of Canterbury: The Major Works*, ed. Brian Davies and G. R. Evans (Oxford: Oxford University Press, 1998). This volume uses a variety of translators. The translation of *Cur Deus Homo?* was by Janet Fairweather. The passage quoted is on p. 354 of this edition, but in view of the many extant translations future references will be to book and chapter. The translation will be that of Fairweather.

impunity would be to put sin above and beyond the law. The debt had to be paid, and it could be paid only by a sacrifice of even greater value than the original debt itself: 'It is not sufficient merely to repay what has been taken away: rather, he ought to pay back more than he took, in proportion to the insult which he has inflicted.'[2] This meant that only a sacrifice of 'infinite value' would suffice, and the only one able to offer such a sacrifice was God himself. This is precisely why God became man. No one *can* make satisfaction or pay the recompense except God, and no one *ought* to offer satisfaction except man; 'it is necessary that a God-Man should pay it'.[3] Anselm continues: 'In order, therefore, that a God-Man should bring about what is necessary, it is essential that the same one person who will make the recompense [Lat. *satisfactionem*] should be perfect God and perfect man. For he cannot do this if he is not true God, and he has no obligation to do so if he is not a true man.'[4]

The great strength of Anselm's doctrine lies in that it takes sin seriously, a point which is underlined by his famous remark to Boso, his dialogue partner. When Boso suggests that a single sin might be cancelled by a single moment of repentance, or that sin in general might be atoned for by penitence, fasting, a contrite heart and many bodily labours, Anselm replies, 'You have not yet considered how heavy the weight of sin is.'[5] This is why it is 'an absolute certainty that God cannot remit a sin unpunished, without satisfaction'.[6] This satisfaction, in Anselm's view, was made by Christ, the God-man, who by sacrificing himself 'did enough' to reconcile the world with God.[7] This 'enough' included satisfying the justice and holiness of God, but it also gave supreme expression to the divine mercy. For God to have forgiven sin without satisfaction would have undermined the moral universe, leaving sin (and therefore the universe itself) unregulated: 'if sin is neither paid for nor punished, it is subject to no law'.[8] On the other hand, for God to have demanded satisfaction from sinners personally and individually would have been to make salvation impossible. For God himself, however, to provide the satisfaction and bear its cost, was both holy and merciful. The mercy of God, writes Anselm,

---

2. *Cur Deus Homo?*, I:11.

3. Ibid., II:6.

4. Ibid., II:7.

5. Ibid., I:21.

6. Ibid., I:19. The idea of satisfaction is frequently obscured in Fairweather, who tends to render *satisfactio* by 'recompense' (as she does in this passage).

7. I have drawn here on the language of Barth, *Church Dogmatics*, IV:1, p. 276.

8. *Cur Deus Homo?*, I:12.

we have found to be so great, and so consonant with justice, that a greater and juster mercy cannot be imagined. What, indeed, can be conceived of more merciful than that God the Father should say to a sinner condemned to eternal torments and lacking any means of redeeming himself, 'Take my only-begotten Son and give him on your behalf', and that the Son himself should say, 'Take me and redeem yourself.'[9]

But Anselm's doctrine is not without its problems. Underlying it is the (to us) bizarre idea that what moved God to redemption was that in order to fully repopulate heaven he had to make up with humans the number of angels who had fallen. More prosaically, the language of 'infinite value', which would persist among Anselm's successors, is uncomfortably commercial, and jars in the context of such an interpersonal transaction as the atonement. In addition, it is not clear in what sense Christ's death was vicarious. Anselm appears to have no clear doctrine of union with Christ. He is clear that human nature suffered in Christ, but how does that suffering connect to us as individual human beings? Lacking the idea of a covenant connection between Christ and his people, Anselm can propose only that the sacrifice of Christ creates a superfluity of merit which God has to reward; and since the Son himself lacks nothing, logic demands that the reward be given to those whose nature he took. Logical it may be, but it is a far cry from Paul's, 'I have been crucified with Christ' (Gal. 2:20).

There also appears to be a serious inconsistency in Anselm's doctrine. Despite his argument that Jesus satisfies the holiness of God, it sometimes looks as if, instead of cancelling our debt, the satisfaction offered by the God-man merely put us in a position where we can imitate him; and by imitating him we satisfy God for ourselves. On whom, he asks, is it more appropriate for him to bestow the reward for his death than on those for whose salvation he made himself a man and for whom 'he set an example, by his death, of dying for the sake of righteousness'? He adds, 'for they will be imitators of him in vain, if they are not to be sharers in his reward'.[10] We are still a long way from the point where the vicarious obedience of Christ is seen as laying a perfect and secure foundation for justification by faith alone.

Yet these are but the sorts of blemishes that accompany all ground-breaking and pioneering work, such as Anselm's undoubtedly was. His doctrine would require appraisal and adjustment at the hands of his successors, but its core idea quickly became the orthodoxy of Western Christianity, both Protestant and

---

9. Ibid., II:20.
10. Ibid., II:19.

Catholic. A century and a half after Anselm it was taken for granted by Thomas Aquinas (1224–74), who wrote, 'Christ's Passion was sufficient and super-abundant satisfaction for the sins of the whole human race; but when sufficient satisfaction has been paid, then the debt of punishment is abolished.'[11] We find it repeatedly in Luther. For example, in his *Lectures on Romans* (1515–16) he comments (on Rom. 4:25), 'The death of Christ is the death of sin, and His resurrection is the life of righteousness, because through his death He has made satisfaction for sin, and through his resurrection He has brought us righteousness.'[12] In Calvin, the idea of satisfaction is closely linked to the ideas of propitiation (appeasement), expiation and redemption. 'Christ's grace,' he writes, 'is too much weakened unless we grant to his sacrifice the power of expiating, appeasing, and making satisfaction.'[13]

At the time of the Reformation the doctrine that Christ by his death satisfied the justice and holiness of God was formally adopted not only in the confessions of the Reformed churches (including the Anglican *Articles of Religion*, Art. XXXI), but also in the creeds and confessions of Roman Catholicism and Lutheranism. The Council of Trent, for example, declares that the meritorious cause of justification is 'our Lord Jesus Christ . . . who merited Justification for us by his most holy Passion on the wood of the cross, *and made satisfaction for us unto God the Father*'.[14] This is similar to the language of the Augsburg Confession (Lutheran), which lays down that people are justified through faith when they believe that 'their sins are forgiven on account of Christ, *who by his death made satisfaction for our sins*'.[15]

Clearly, then, the doctrine of vicarious satisfaction was not, as it is often seen today, the shibboleth of a marginal fundamentalist stream within the Christian church. It was the doctrine of Anglican priests as well as revivalist preachers, and underlay the Lutheran Communion Service and the Roman Mass as surely as it did the Presbyterian Lord's Supper. On this doctrine, everyone was an evangelical. Only when theology began to seek its sources and its norms outside Scripture was the doctrine of vicarious satisfaction abandoned.

---

11. Thomas Aquinas, *Summa Theologica*, Pt. III Q. 49, Art. 3.

12. *Luther's Works, Vol. 25: Lectures on Romans*, p. 284.

13. *Institutes*, II:XVII, 4.

14. Italics mine. *The Canons and Decrees of the Council of Trent*, Sixth Session, Chapter VII (see Philip Schaff, *The Creeds of the Greek and Latin Churches*, vol. 2 of *The Creeds of Christendom* (London: Hodder and Stoughton, 1877), p. 95.

15. Article IV, italics mine. See Leif Grane, *The Augsburg Confession: A Commentary*, tr. John H. Rasmussen (Minneapolis: Augsburg Publishing House, 1987), p. 58.

Presupposes divine goodwill

But what were its leading features as developed by Anselm's successors?

First, it clearly presupposed goodwill on God's part towards the human race. Had there been no such goodwill, God would have punished sin instantly. Instead, as we saw from Romans 3:25, he was already forgiving sin even before any atonement had been offered: a remarkable tribute to his forbearance. But, as Romans 3:25 also makes clear, this forbearance rested on the fact that God had himself made provision for atonement, appointing Christ as a *hilastērion* through his blood, in order to justify his 'leniency' towards sin. That atonement would, in Anselmian terms, make full satisfaction to God.

But it also had at its heart a further adjustment which, once again, bespoke God's goodwill. In strict justice, every human being should have suffered for their own sin. This, after all, was what the letter of the law stipulated: 'the soul that sins shall die'. Instead, God arranged for a vicarious bearing of the penalty. He would accept a substitute; and he did so, not in response to desperate pleas from the human side, but entirely on his own initiative. What Gabriel said to the virgin Mary applied to the whole human race: 'You have found favour with God' (Luke 1:30). Mankind, spiritually bankrupt, has nothing to offer, but God, prompted by pure grace, and drawing on his eternal wisdom, prepares a counsel of salvation in which the Father, the Son and the Holy Spirit are united in redeeming love and pity for the human race. The triune God resolves to save the world, and to accept the good offices of a Mediator who shall act for mankind as their representative and suffer for them as their substitute: so accommodating is the divine will, and so predisposed to forgive our transgressions.

But the Three-in-One, acting to save the world, go further: they resolve that the salvation shall be free to the human race. It will cost them nothing. For them, it will be an act of pure love and mercy. From sinners as such no satisfaction will be required. Instead, everything will flow from the loving-kindness of God. He will bear the whole cost. He will provide the one who will take the sinner's place. But he will go even further: he will *become* the one who takes the sinner's place. God the Son will suffer for the world's sin. God the Father will suffer in the Son's pain. God the Holy Spirit will share in the pain of both. At Gethsemane and Golgotha the Three will be One, as God, not sparing himself, takes blood, his own blood, and sheds it to redeem the world.

But did God's goodwill go further, and prompt him to accept as satisfaction something less than what sin deserved? This was one of the questions which occupied the minds of European theologians in the sixteenth and seventeenth centuries, and though their interest in the precise status of Christ's sufferings may seem to us like arid speculation, it was driven by a reverent desire to appreciate more fully the cost of salvation.

Four answers were offered to the question of the value of Christ's sacrifice. Some argued that Christ suffered the exact penalty with which God had threatened to punish sin; others that Christ suffered an equivalent penalty; yet others that he offered a partial satisfaction which God graciously accepted; and, finally, Socinians (the rationalists of the day) argued that God required no satisfaction, but simply considered the debt paid.

The core question is whether Christ suffered exactly what the finally impenitent will suffer eternally; and the moment it is put in these terms we have to answer, 'No!'. Christ's sufferings were temporary, confined to the thirty or so years of his earthly life; he never had to endure the pangs of an accusing conscience; he was never physically in hell. Instead, he went from the cross to the tomb (and even while his body lay there, his soul was in paradise), and from the tomb to the right hand of God. He never, like the rich man in the parable, opened his eyes in hell (Luke 16:23).

But none of this detracts from the fact that Christ experienced in all its awfulness the curse that our sin deserved, as Paul makes clear in Galatians 3:13. Christ redeemed us only by enduring the curse we deserved. He suffered from the curse pronounced on the ground and on human labour (Gen. 3:17). He suffered from the enmity between the seed of the woman and the seed of the serpent (Gen. 3:15). Above all, he suffered death (which was itself, precisely, the curse); suffered the taste of it and the fear of it and the weakness of it and the dishonour of it. And then he allowed death to bind him and to 'hold' him for three days (Acts 2:24).

But only for three days! No more! Death had to let him go. There were three reasons for this.

First, he was the Prince of Life. This goes back to his divine identity. He was not only the source of life. He was life itself and all other life lived in him (John 1:4). As such, he had authority to pour out his life in death, but death could never hold him as it might hold a conquered foe. He chose the circumstances of his dying, and he chose its moment; and in the same way he would choose the moment when he would take his life back again, and in what circumstances (including the post-resurrection appearances). The eternal Logos could taste death. But it was inconceivable that he could be held by it, or even detained a moment longer than he wished.

Secondly, by dying Christ expiated sin. So long as he bore it and answered for it, death could hold him, but by dying he atoned for it, and by atoning for it he broke its power. Sin no longer had dominion over him, and neither did death. Granted, he continued under its power (in the state of death, and among the dead) for a time. But over against this we must set the supreme dignity of the sacrifice he offered. Had it been but the blood of bulls and goats, it would have had to be offered repeatedly; had it been but the sinner bearing what was due to his own sin, it would have had to be borne eternally. But Christ gave himself: not anything external to himself, such as his suffering or his human nature, but his self. His blood is the blood of the Son of God, indeed, the very blood of God, and as such it has a unique 'preciousness' (1 Pet. 1:19). Granted, there is something not quite right about speaking of the 'infinite value' of his sufferings cancelling out the 'infinite guilt' of our sin. It is hard to attach any clear meaning to 'infinite' sufferings, especially when they were of finite duration. In any case God doesn't use such scales; he is hardly a grocer. But that the self-sacrifice of his Son was uniquely precious in the sight of God is beyond dispute. His was not an offering to which God arbitrarily attributed a high value. It was intrinsically 'enough'. It was the obedience the law required, and the curse the law denounced. It was, perhaps, even more than the law could have asked, because here the law finds God's own Son submitting to it (Gal. 4:4). Here, one who was in the form of God was obedient even to the point of death (Phil. 2:8). Here was something so remarkable that even the angels peered down to look; so remarkable, indeed, that we can even picture God the Father and God the Spirit gazing in wonder at the glory of the Son's obedience.

Thirdly, Christ could not be held by death because his work as redeemer had to continue long beyond Calvary. From this point of view, God's 'deliberate plan and foreknowledge' (Acts 2:23) involved not only that he be crucified and slain but also that he should rise again. This, too, was part of his obedience: he must lay down his life, but he must also take it again (John 10:17). Similarly, the Father must vindicate and affirm the Son, declaring him 'Son of God in power' (Rom. 1:4). There must be an enthronement of the Messiah; and there must be a resumption of his redeeming work. Only if he holds the reins of power can his church evangelize the world (Matt. 28:18); only from a position of glory can he give eternal life to those the Father has given him (John 17:2); only from the centre of the throne can he open the scroll and control the march of history (Rev. 5:6); only as the risen one can he live in the hearts of his people (Gal. 2:20); and only as the conqueror of death can he lead his people in triumph (2 Cor. 2:14). No wonder Paul declares, 'If Christ has not been raised, your faith is futile; you are still in your sins' (1 Cor. 15:17).

Satisfied the justice of his Father

The second leading feature of Anselm's doctrine as developed by his successors was the insistence that by his 'obedience and sacrifice' Christ fully satisfied the justice of his Father.[16] The phrase, 'obedience and sacrifice', reflects a distinction between *active* and *passive* obedience which used to be familiar to hearers of Christian preaching and which still serves to remind us that the obedience of Christ involved both doing and suffering. However, the distinction needs to be handled with care. Such a phrase, for example, as 'the obedience of his life and the suffering of his death', can be misleading, suggesting that his life was devoid of suffering and his dying devoid of obedience. On the contrary, as we have already seen, his whole life from the cradle to the cross was lived in the shadow of the fall and under the conditions into which it had plunged the human race. He was liable to all the ills that flesh is heir to, and this certainly did not begin at Calvary. But neither, on the other hand, did his obedience end there. Instead, his dying was the climax of his obedience (Phil. 2:8); his very greatest *doing*. His ministry must be seen as a seamless whole, in which the active and the passive were inextricably woven together.

'Obedience', as we have seen, is clearly a major category when it comes to describing Christ's work of atonement. His obedience expiates our collective sin (Rom. 5:19). He came as the Servant, and he redeemed us by his service (Mark 10:45). But this raises a question which, yet again, was much discussed in the heyday of Protestant theology. Is the active, as well as the passive, obedience of Christ imputed to justified sinners? The followers of Jacob Arminius (1560–1609) argued that only the righteousness of Christ's sacrificial death was imputed to believers; his active righteousness (his life-long compliance with the will of God) was not. In its chapter on justification, the Westminster Confession (11:1) took the opposite position: both Christ's *obedience* and his *sacrifice* are imputed to believers.

All this may seem like the proverbial theological hair-splitting, but there is a real gospel issue at stake here. The Arminian position implied that while Christ had endured the curse of the law in our place he had not positively obeyed the law in our place. It followed, therefore, that God still required some sort of obedience as a condition of justification. But what sort? The answer proposed by those sympathetic to Arminius was that Christ by his death had secured a concession: God had relaxed his law and introduced new and easier terms of salvation for the whole human race. He no longer required 'legal obedience', that is, compliance with the whole moral law. Instead he now required only 'evangelical obedience'; in other words, faith and repentance. This was in effect a new legalism (our seventeenth-century forebears dubbed it 'Neonomianism'), and it meant that the righteousness of Christ had to be supplemented by

---

16. Westminster Confession, 8:5.

something of our own. Justification was no longer *through* faith (*per fidem*); it was *on account of* faith (*propter fidem*).

This may look like a subtle shift involving no spiritual risks, but it quickly came to mean that faith was no longer faith in Christ alone, but faith in our own faith. Faith, or, more broadly, our own conversion experience (dramatized in personal 'testimonies') became the rock on which we stood, and this had far-reaching consequences. It fatally shifted the focus from Christ to personal experience, and by doing so it bred an introspection which in too many instances proved fatal to Christian assurance. To Luther and Calvin, faith *was* assurance: assurance that God loved us and forgave our sins because of the obedience and sacrifice of Christ. But now many were troubled by a new question. Am I a true believer? Am I born again? At the same time others were only too confident. They were sure they were right with God because they had had dramatic conversions and heart-warming experiences. It became increasingly hard to resist such currents and to steer by the apostle's compass, 'God forbid that I should glory, save in the cross of our Lord Jesus Christ' (Gal. 6:14, KJV). That cross was a perfect atonement for sin, and no defect in our own faith and repentance can ever detract from it. His blood covers even the shortcomings of our faith and the worrying irregularities in our conversion experience. He did it all.

As he lay dying on a cold winter's night in a North Dakota hospital in December 1936, J. Gresham Machen wrote to his young colleague, John Murray, 'I am so thankful for the active obedience of Christ. No hope without it.'[17] The Messiah had to fulfil *all* righteousness (Matt. 3:15), and within that commission the obedience and the sacrifice, the active and the passive, the doing and the suffering, cannot be separated.

Yet this active obedience of Christ in our place can never mean that we ourselves are no longer bound to live by the divine law. On the face of things, such antinomianism would seem logical enough: if Christ's vicarious suffering relieves us from the obligation to suffer for our own sins, does his vicarious obedience not release us from the obligation to comply with the moral law? And is it not illogical to portray the believer as under grace and under law at the same time?

But there is an inherent absurdity in antinomianism. Sin is, precisely, lawlessness (*anomia*, 1 John 3:4). How then can we be redeemed from lawlessness to live a life of lawlessness? On the contrary, the very reason that God condemned sin in the flesh of his own Son was 'in order that the righteous requirement of

---

17. *Collected Writings of John Murray, Volume Three: Life of John Murray; Sermons & Reviews* (Edinburgh: Banner of Truth, 1982), p. 64.

the law might be fully met in us'. There can be no antithesis or tension between being under the law and being in the Spirit. On the contrary, it is those who live according to the Spirit who fulfil the requirements of the law (Rom. 8:3–4).

This agrees fully with the perspective of Jesus himself. When rumours were circulating that he was destroying the law and the prophets, he faced the charge head on and repudiated it utterly: 'Do not think I have come to abolish the Law or the Prophets; I have not come to abolish them, but to fulfil them' (Matt. 5:17). He then went on to say, 'unless your righteousness surpasses that of the Pharisees and the teachers of the law, you will certainly not enter the kingdom of heaven' (Matt. 5:20). Pharisaism was a system of evasion, majoring on the external and obsessed with the exceptions ('When do I *not* have to love my neighbour?'). Jesus demands sincere, inward and rigorous compliance, and he spells it out in detail in the great antitheses of the Sermon on the Mount (Matt. 5:21–48), where he makes plain that on such matters as murder, adultery, divorce, oaths and vengefulness he sets far higher standards for his followers than the Pharisees ever set for theirs. He leaves no place whatsoever for distinguishing between love and law. If we love him, we keep his commandments (John 14:15).

Yet, right beside this there lies the equally momentous truth that it is not because we have kept the law that God loves us. His love is entirely a matter of free grace. But once he adopts us into his family, we are bound by his house rules. The imperatives of the law always rest on the indicatives of redemption. Like the Israelites of old, we were not redeemed because we had kept the law, but once liberated we come under its regime, and are bound to love the Lord our God with all our hearts and our neighbours as ourselves; and for 'neighbours', says Jesus, we must also read, 'enemies'.

The necessity of satisfaction

But was the sort of satisfaction contemplated by Anselm really necessary? Surely God, all-merciful, could have forgiven sin freely and unconditionally? Is this not the picture we find in the parable of the prodigal son: a father who makes no fuss about the profligate's past life but welcomes him warmly and gladly on his return? Is this not, indeed, what God requires of ourselves: to turn the other cheek, to exact no retribution and to forgive seventy-seven times (Matt. 18:22)?

It cannot be stressed often enough that as far as we are concerned forgiveness is absolutely free. Whatever the cost, God himself has met it. For us, justification is a free gift (Rom. 3:24), as it has to be, because we have absolutely no way of earning it. Nor do we have to engage in complicated negotiations. Instead, we have the assurance, 'whoever comes to me I will never drive away' (John 6:37). It is this very fact that we have been forgiven freely that puts us under obligation to forgive freely: 'Freely you have received; freely give' (Matt. 10:8).

Alongside of this, however, we must remember why we are forbidden to repay evil with evil. It is not because retribution is inherently wrong, but because it is God's prerogative: 'Do not take revenge, my friends, but leave room for God's wrath, for it is written: "It is mine to avenge; I will repay," says the Lord' (Rom. 12:19). This is why all of us will one day appear before the judgment seat of Christ (2 Cor. 5:10); and this is why God has appointed 'governing authorities' (Rom. 13:1) for the very purpose of punishing wrongdoers (Rom. 13:4). These authorities derive their authority not from human convention, public utility, popular consent or social contract, but from divine institution; and that institution rests in turn on the very nature of God himself. He is holy and righteous in all that he does. This is why we can be confident that he will keep his every promise; and equally confident that he will never condone sin. This is not merely a matter of the divine will, as if we were to picture God pondering whether or not he should punish sin. Such hesitation is no more possible on God's part than it would be possible for us to watch someone abuse a child and calmly ponder whether or not we should be upset by it. It is our nature to be upset, and it is God's nature to be upset when he sees godlessness and violence fill the earth. His whole nature recoils from sin. It is darkness, he is light, and there can be no concord between them. Hence the banishment from Eden, and hence, at last, the dread sentence, 'depart from me, you who are cursed' (Matt. 25:41).

This means that if God forgives sin he can do so only as the holy and righteous God. He was under no obligation to save the human race: God has no duties. The undertaking was an act of sovereign clemency, entirely optional on God's part. But once he embarked on this enterprise, it would be done in accordance with his nature as the holy and righteous one. He can pardon sinners only when he is satisfied that it is right.

It was to satisfy this righteousness (Lat. *iustitia*) and thus make it right for God to be at peace with sinners, that Christ, according to Anselm, had to become man, live, suffer and die: 'Consider it, then, an absolute certainty that God cannot remit sin unpunished, without recompense [Lat. *sine satisfactione*] that is, without the voluntary paying off of a debt, and that a sinner cannot, without this, attain to a state of blessedness, not even the state which was his before he sinned.'[18]

---

18. *Cur Deus Homo?*, I:19.

Today, such language is widely deplored, but the doctrine that it was necessary for Christ to die if he were to save the human race rests on solid biblical foundations.

First, unless the death of Christ was necessary it is hard to see how it could be a demonstration of the divine love. In Galatians 2:20 Paul describes it as an expression of the love of Christ, 'who loved me and gave himself for me'; and Jesus himself spoke of it in similar terms: 'Greater love has no one than this: to lay down one's life for one's friends' (John 15:13). Such a love makes sense if the friend is in mortal peril; it makes no sense if it is merely a demonstration. It is one thing for someone to risk her life by diving into the sea to rescue a drowning child; quite another to risk it by diving from a cliff merely to express solidarity with a strong swimmer who is in no trouble at all. Paul was in mortal spiritual peril, liable to the curse of the law. He needed to be redeemed from that curse, and the Son of God showed his love by taking his place and saving him at the cost of his own life. Had his death not been necessary, absolutely necessary, it would have been meaningless.

But the deeper issue is how, if the death of his Son was not necessary, it could ever serve as a revelation of the *Father's* love for the world. Yet this is undoubtedly the love emphasized in the New Testament: not the love of the Son primarily, but the love of the Father. At the same time, however, it stresses the love of the Father for the Son. He was the 'beloved Son' (Mark 1:11), loved with a love of which Abraham's love for Isaac was but a pale shadow. Abraham sacrificed Isaac because God commanded him (Gen. 22:2). But why did God sacrifice his own Son? Our first reaction has to be pure horror.[19] There was no higher power to command it, and it is horrific to think of it as a mere demonstration. There must have been an underlying reason, a necessity; a crisis which could not have been resolved in any other way.

The nature of that crisis is laid down in John 3:16: God gave his Son to save the world from perishing. This is the ultimate *decretum horrible*, the utterly awesome, holy, divine action; the place where we tremble in the presence of the uncanny and the unbelievable; the final impenetrable mystery, where there is darkness over the whole land, God not sparing his own Son. If God resorted to such a way of salvation, it had to be because there was no other way. No

---

19. Cf. Ratzinger, *Introduction to Christianity*, p. 281: 'Many devotional texts actually force one to think that Christian faith in the Cross imagines a God whose unrelenting righteousness demanded a human sacrifice, the sacrifice of his own Son, and one turns away in horror from a righteousness whose sinister wrath makes the message of love incredible.'

father or mother ever sent their son off to such a war, and if God could have spared him, he would. But there was no alternative. The cup could not pass, for either the Father or the Son. If the law, promising salvation on the basis of personal rectitude, could have offered a solution, God would have used it. Indeed, he would have been culpable not to: 'if righteousness could be gained through the law, Christ died for nothing!' (Gal. 2:21). But 'the law was powerless' (Rom. 8:3). It could command, but it could never empower. Nor could repentance offer a viable route to eternal life: partly because we are by nature incapable of it; partly because it is forgiveness itself that breaks our hearts; but above all because repentance itself is always profoundly conscious of the need to make restitution. The Prodigal offers to work as a 'hired servant' (Luke 15:19), but neither labour nor tears can atone for sin. The powerlessness of the human race was such that we could never put ourselves in the right with God, and the holiness of God was such that he could never condone sin. There had to be a mediator who would suffer and obey.

But secondly, unless the death of Christ was the only possible remedy for the human predicament it could never serve as a revelation of the righteousness of God. It certainly was such a revelation, as Paul makes plain in Romans 3:25: the reason why God put Christ forward as an expiatory sacrifice (*hilastērion*) was to demonstrate both that he was right to remit the sins of Old Testament believers and equally right to justify those have faith in Jesus. But how could the fact of the Father sacrificing his own Son prove that God is just? On the face of things, Calvary was a travesty of justice: perjured testimony, a corrupt judge, a lynch mob, a barbaric execution. How can this demonstrate justice, especially when we know that it happened by the deliberate purpose of God (Acts 2:23), the Judge of all the earth? When truth and goodness are taken to the scaffold, how can this show the righteousness of God? Only if it serves some higher purpose: a purpose which could be served in no other way. Christ's death, despite its dark, horrific backdrop, was just, because it was the death of the voluntary, divine sin-bearer, whose sacrifice satisfied God that it was right for him to forgive the sin of the world.

Thirdly, the death of Christ was necessary because sin, inherently, deserves condemnation. This takes us back again to Anselm's word to Boso, 'you have not yet considered how heavy the weight of sin is'.[20] We see no need for atonement because we see, not sin, only peccadillos. Why should God require atonement for a few sexual indiscretions or a few white lies or a few moments of overindulgence?

---

20. *Cur Deus Homo?*, I:21.

But Christ bore the sin of the world: not only its minor indiscretions but rape, child abuse, patriarchy, murder, torture, fraud, corruption, extortion and genocide. No civilized society tolerates these. They distress us. We deplore them and find it hard to forgive them. We insist that they be punished and that the punishment fit the crime.

But what of God? Should he not mind? Should he leave it to us to exact justice, untrammelled by divine restraint and regulation? We should remember the words of David: 'Let us fall into the hands of the LORD, for his mercy is great; but do not let me fall into human hands' (2 Sam. 24:14).

And what of those sins aimed directly at God himself? The question itself is of doubtful validity. Every sin is a sin against God, as David recognized in confessing his murder and adultery. These were no victimless crimes, yet David's words are, 'Against you, you only, have I sinned and done what is evil in your sight' (Ps. 51:4). One reason for this is that the commandment to love our neighbour as ourselves is as much a divine imperative as the command to love the Lord our God with all our hearts. Another is the fact that every violation of human rights is a violation of a right conferred by God; additionally, every crime against a person is a crime against that image of God in which every creature is made. Every sin, therefore, is a defiance of God's majesty.

There is an analogy to this in British jurisprudence. Very few crimes are committed against the actual person of the sovereign. The Queen, after all, is not normally the victim in a mugging. Yet every criminal prosecution takes the form, 'the Crown against . . .' The reason for this is that the Crown is the custodian of law and order, and if crime were allowed to pass unchallenged and unpunished society would collapse in anarchy. Anselm made the same point with regard to the divine government. If God allowed sin to go unpunished this would amount to a declaration that sin is above the law, 'and the incongruity extends even further: it makes sinfulness resemble God. For, just as God is subject to no law, the same is the case with sinfulness'.[21] This rewrites the so-called Karamazov Hypothesis, 'if there is no God, anything goes', which now becomes, 'even though there is a God, anything goes'. He has no interest in restraining or punishing sin; in which case, the sinner will not reap what he sows, but the saint may find himself thrown to the infernal lions. The final twist is that the fact that there is no justice in the world then becomes itself an argument against God's existence. God is damned if he punishes sin and damned if he doesn't.

---

21. *Cur Deus Homo?*, I:12.

Yet there are sins which are, not indirectly, but directly, assaults on the majesty of God, and every one of us is guilty of them. The most obvious of these are idolatry and blasphemy. There can be no doubt as to the seriousness with which the Bible views such sins. By contrast, modern culture views them lightly. We are surrounded by temples to other deities, our media pride themselves on their bold blasphemies, and even the demurest mouth utters obscenities. It is not surprising if in such a culture we regard God's sensitivity as mere pique. But matters are not that simple. Blasphemy and idolatry are contemptuous repudiations of the governance of God: the ultimate expression, indeed, of contempt of court. Once again we encounter the paradox that while human judicatories must be accorded the highest respect, the divine judicatory may be dismissed with impunity. This is secure enough if the Most High does not exist and if the very idea of a supreme judge is a nonsense. But if there is in fact a judge of all the earth, it is at our peril that we treat him with defiance and contempt, especially when the criterion at the great assize will be whether we loved him with all our heart. Blasphemy registers as hatred of God. How can he satisfy himself that it is right to forgive it and to admit the blasphemer into the most intimate circles of his love?

Objections to the idea of penal satisfaction have invariably focused on its underlying assumptions as to the nature of justice. We are told, for example, that the satisfaction 'model' of the atonement makes no sense to a generation which has abandoned the idea of universal moral law. It is not immediately obvious, however, that what a generation has or has not abandoned is a reliable criterion of truth. It would certainly be perilous to judge the cross by the wisdom of a prevailing culture. From the standpoint of divine revelation the logic must go in the exact opposite direction, allowing the cross to be itself the judge of the culture. This is what Luther meant when he declared, *crux probat omnia* ('the cross is the test of everything');[22] and this is what Paul meant when he wrote that because he gloried in the cross, the world was crucified to him (Gal. 6:14). Its wisdom had made a fool of itself at Calvary. And, on the other hand, the cross itself was a vindication of universal moral order. It condemned sin; it vindicated righteousness.

The grain of truth in the observation that there is no universal moral order is that we, with our limited human faculties, have but a very partial grasp of

---

22. This statement occurs in Luther's comment on Psalm 5:11, part of his second series of lectures on the Psalms (1519–21). See Martin Luther, *Werke: kritische Gesammtaugabe* (Weimar: Hermann Böhlau, vol. 5, 1892), p. 179. Unfortunately this series is not included in the 55-vol. *Luther's Works*.

justice, and it would be arrogant for any of us to claim that we know what is
right always and in all circumstances. But the fact that our perception of justice
is partial does not mean that the moral order does not exist. In fact, we constantly assume that it does, just as we assume that truth exists even though our
grasp of it is extremely limited. As C. S. Lewis pointed out, 'human beings, all
over the earth, have this curious idea that they ought to behave in a certain
way'.[23] This is why we instinctively apportion praise and blame. Universal moral
law condemns Adolf Hitler and admires Mother Teresa. But in accordance with
this very same principle we also insist that when the universal moral law is
breached, justice must be satisfied. This is why we have war crimes tribunals,
and this is why every nation on earth has its penal code and its justice system.
These, sadly, are often arbitrary and even corrupt, but when we say that it was
wrong for the seventeenth century to burn witches but right for us to incarcerate
terrorists in 'supermax' prisons, we are assuming that there is a universal moral
law by which all penal systems must themselves be judged. Whether or not the
sacrifice of Christ offered an appropriate satisfaction to this law may remain an
open question. But it cannot be dismissed on the basis that there is no universal
moral law. We invariably assume that there is.

It is objected, again, that the satisfaction theory portrays God as the prisoner
of an abstract notion of justice, as if it were something external to himself
which he had to be careful not to offend. But God's righteousness is neither
abstract, nor external to himself. Nor is it a separate component of deity, far
less an independent heavenly department able (like, for example, the Treasury
in secular administrations) to dictate to other departments. 'Righteous' is what
God is. Justice means that by his very nature he consistently acts justly; righteousness means that he invariably does what is right. But justice and righteousness
are not his only attributes. He is also loving, gracious, merciful, kind and good.
There is no tension between these different qualities of the divine being. We
humans may suffer from tension between head and heart, but God knows
nothing of such tension or of any internal clamour to put justice above mercy
or mercy above justice. When he forgives sin, it is with the consent of his whole
nature. All that he is, is engaged in the act of pardon. It is loving, gracious,
merciful and wise; but it is also right. He is prisoner to no external law. He *is*
good, and he *does* right.

A third objection is that advocates of penal satisfaction operate with an
unbiblical understanding of justice. Brown and Parker, for example, apply this

---

23. C. S. Lewis, *Mere Christianity*, C. S. Lewis Signature Classics Edition (London:
HarperCollins, 2012), p. 21.

criticism to Anselm: 'his view of justice is not that wrong should be righted but that wrongs should be punished.'[24] Behind this objection lies a profound aversion to the idea of justice as retribution, and this brings us back to the idea discussed earlier[25] that there is a gulf between the biblical and the classical ideas of justice. According to the classical idea, justice means giving everyone what is due to them, in which case the criminal will get what he deserves: retribution. The biblical idea, it is said, is quite different. It means that God is always faithful to his covenant, and since his covenant is gracious, God's righteousness pledges him, not to punish people, but to stand at their side, committed to act for their protection and salvation.

We need to go back to basics here. God does indeed keep his covenant, but the correct order, surely, is not that God is righteous because he keeps his covenant, but that he keeps his covenant because he is righteous. What he *is* comes first; what he *does* follows: 'I, the LORD, do not change. So you, the descendants of Jacob, are not destroyed' (Mal. 3:6).

In accordance with this righteousness, God will fulfil every gracious promise he has ever made. This is why, particularly in the Psalms and in Isaiah, righteousness is closely linked to salvation, justifying Cremer's description of it as *iustitia salutifera* ('salvation-bearing righteousness').[26] It also fits in with the idea of God intervening to put things right or to restore things to what they should be. This sense of 'righteousness' occurs in, for example, Psalm 4:1, where the psalmist bases his appeal for relief on the divine righteousness. In Psalm 103:17–18 this righteousness is virtually equated with God's love:

> But from everlasting to everlasting
> the LORD's love is with those who fear him,
> and his righteousness with their children's children –
> with those who keep his covenant.

The same link between righteousness and salvation appears clearly in the second half of Isaiah. We see it in, for example, Isaiah 46:13, 'I am bringing my righteousness near, it is not far away; and my salvation will not be delayed' (cf. Isa. 45:8; 51:6). McGrath is justified, then, in concluding that the Old

---

24. Brown and Parker, 'For God So Loved the World?', p. 7.

25. See pp. 91–92.

26. Quoted in Alister E. McGrath, *Iustitia Dei: A History of the Christian Doctrine of Justification* (2nd ed., Cambridge: Cambridge University Press, 1998), p. 8.

Testament concept of the 'righteousness of God' has strongly soteriological overtones.[27] His faithfulness impels him to act for the protection and vindication of his people, and this goes back to the very beginnings of Israel's history, when God heard the groaning of his people in Egypt and 'remembered his covenant with Abraham, with Isaac and with Jacob' (Exod. 2:24). Later deliverances, particularly the return from the exile, were expressions of the same covenant loyalty (Heb. *ḥesed*).

But within this, there is another strand. God acts for the oppressed: 'The Lord works righteousness and justice [Heb. *mišpāṭîm*] for all the oppressed' (Ps. 103:6). The same point is made in Psalm 72:4: 'May he defend the afflicted among the people and save the children of the needy.' In the first instance, this referred to the poor within Israel: the slaves, widows, orphans and immigrants whose needs are highlighted in the Book of the Covenant (Exod. 21:1 – 23:33). However straitened in circumstances, and however marginalized in society, they bear the image of God, and as such they have certain inalienable rights which constitute a claim on every human being.[28] This is not so far removed from the Ciceronian principle, 'to each his own'. Justice to the poor means giving them what is due to them.

Yet God's defence and vindication of the oppressed almost invariably means retribution for their oppressors. This stands out clearly in the picture of the righteous king in Psalm 72: in defending the needy he will crush the oppressor (v. 4). Jeremiah can even portray God as vowing to punish the nation precisely because it has not defended the rights of the poor (Jer. 5:28–29). Here the righting of wrongs clearly implies the punishing of wrongs, and in practice this is recognized even by groups which are among the most vocal in objecting to the Anselmian doctrine of the atonement. Feminists, for example, insist that the wrongs committed against women can be righted only by criminalizing gender discrimination: any breach of equality legislation is punishable by the full force of the law. Divine justice operates in the same way. The Lord who loves justice inevitably hates injustice (Isa. 61:8). This is why he is utterly true to himself when he maintains the cause of the needy precisely by executing judgment (*mišpāṭ*) on their oppressors (Ps. 140:12).

At first glance, this has little bearing on the doctrine of the atonement. Let us remember once again, however, that Christ bore the sin of the world, and let us remember, further, that in the whole range of sin there is nothing more

---

27. McGrath, *Iustitia Dei*, p. 8.

28. 'A human right is a right such that the only status one needs to possess the right is that of being a human being' (Wolterstorff, *Hearing the Call*, p. 291).

abhorrent to God than the oppression of the poor, the widow and the immigrant. How can the guilt of such sin be remitted? Only if God is satisfied that it is right to forgive it; and it can be right only if it is expiated. This is why Christ bore it, including the guilt of patriarchy, racism and every other form of discrimination. And this is why such a passage as Romans 8:3 has to be interpreted in the light of *mišpāṭ*: when God condemned sin in the flesh of his own Son he was executing judgment on the oppressors whose crimes have blighted human history, as well as on the myriad blasphemies and idolatries which have made man's religions his greatest crimes.

The mere fact of a link between righteousness and covenant should not, then, betray us into the fallacy that God's righteousness is never retributive but always protective. The divine covenant implies curses as well as blessings, threats as well as promises. In Exodus 34:28, the Decalogue is defined as 'the covenant', and nothing could be clearer than that violation of this covenant brings condign punishment: 'Cursed is everyone who does not continue to do everything written in the Book of the Law' (Gal. 3:10; cf. Deut. 27:26). It would be hazardous, in view of this, to dismiss the idea of divine retribution on the basis of some specialized Old Testament concept of justice. That specialized concept is certainly there, as we have seen. When God says that he loves justice (Isa. 61:8) he certainly does not mean that he loves punishing. He means that he will keep his pledge to save his people. But while this is a distinctive Old Testament meaning, it is not the only one, or indeed the predominant one, being largely confined to Isaiah and the Psalms. Human language existed before the Torah, and God did not bypass that language when he spoke to his people. Had he done so, his revelation would have been unintelligible. Instead, he availed himself of the language which was already there, and in that language justice clearly included retribution for those who violate law and break their covenants.

Scripture never abandons this principle. 'Do you think,' Paul asks those who so readily pass judgment on their fellow human beings, 'that you will escape God's judgment?' (Rom. 2:3). How can God simultaneously right the world's wrongs and condone the wrongs that have been perpetrated? How can he forgive the sin of a race corporately guilty of blasphemy, idolatry, vanity, selfishness, violence, rape and child abuse? Only in response to the mediation of his Son, who has pleaded the cause of those that hated both God and their neighbours, and who has backed up his pleading by taking personal responsibility for our violation of other people's rights. God's rectitude can be salvation-bearing only because Christ has atoned for our breaches of the covenant.

Does the cross glorify suffering?

But does the satisfaction theory of the atonement not glorify suffering, even to the extent that the Christian doctrine of redemption itself needs redemption? This is certainly the view of such Christian feminists as Joanne Carlson Brown and Rebecca Parker: 'Christianity is an abusive theology that glorifies suffering.'[29]

Far from glorifying violence, however, the gospel narrative of the passion makes no concession to the macabre human fascination with gruesome detail. The fact of the crucifixion is recorded, but virtually nothing of the procedure. What is emphasized, instead, is the sheer evil of the event, implicating every level of society: the common people, baying for blood; the religious leaders, mocking; the military, sheltering behind orders; and, above all, a corrupt judicial system, sacrificing innocent blood for political expediency.

But the point must be made once again that when we speak of Christ bearing the sin of the world, a large part of what this means is that Christ bore the guilt of the violence that humans perpetrate against each other, and this is by no means confined to the brutal oppression practised by tyrannical regimes. It applies equally to domestic violence and to the bullying which is endemic to so many workplaces. It is precisely in these contexts that we must remember Anselm's *nondum considerasti*. The very reason that God's judgment fell on the world of Noah's day was that the earth was filled with violence (Gen. 6:11), and things have improved little in the meantime. It is well for us that Christ bore the guilt of the abuses that, individually and collectively, we daily heap upon each other.

But if the cross does not quite glorify violence, does it not glorify passive acquiescence in violence? This is a serious issue, particularly if it can be shown that part of the message of Calvary is that victims of abuse should endure it silently, soak up the pain, offer no resistance and demand no justice. The charge gains plausibility from the fact that too many Christian men have seen meekness as a distinctive feminine virtue and quiet submission as the crowning glory of womanhood, and too many Christian women have accepted this role definition. Even where they have not been abused and violated, they have taken it for granted that they exist to serve their husbands and children, and should sacrifice their own personal fulfilment to those objects.

---

29. Brown and Parker , 'For God So Loved the World', p. 26. They add, 'Is it any wonder that there is so much abuse in modern society when the predominant image or theology of the culture is of "divine child abuse"'?

The cross certainly commends non-violence and non-resistance to the extent that it portrays Christ as one who went like a lamb to the slaughter and who suffered without any threat of retaliation (Isa. 53:7; 1 Pet. 2:23). This fits in with the great *kenotic* perspective which Paul describes in Philippians 2:6–11. Far from insisting on his own divine rights, Christ made himself a no-person, devoid of rights, and there can be no doubt that the apostle lays this down as the paradigm for all believers. But that is precisely the point. It is the paradigm for *all* believers, above all for the powerful, who must renounce their own rights and strive for the rights of others. No man who takes the cross as his paradigm can make it an excuse for demanding that women acquiesce under his authority and submit to servility and abuse. Christ has exactly the same destiny in mind for the woman as for the man, and in the meantime, each of us, male and female, is called to do everything in our power to encourage the other in his or her journey towards that destiny. At the foot of the cross, the husband is bound to subordinate his own interests to those of his wife no less than she is bound to subordinate hers to those of her husband. It is patriarchy, not the doctrine of the atonement, that needs to be redeemed.

Yet here, too, there is a paradox. Many of those who deplore the cross as a paradigm for non-resistance also applaud the programmes of non-violent resistance advocated by Mahatma Gandhi and Martin Luther King, and there can be no doubt that these tactics proved effective against a certain type of oppression. Meekness delivered what armed resistance could not. But if we applaud such tactics, is the cross not the archetypal instance of power through weakness? Paul certainly understood it in these terms: 'The foolishness of God is wiser than human wisdom, and the weakness of God is stronger than human strength' (1 Cor. 1:25).

What underlies such a statement is that the cross was not the last word. It looked like the last word, and the bewildered disciples certainly thought that it was. In reality it was but the penultimate word, the word before the last, because God spoke another word, the resurrection. This was the vindication of the innocent, and if at first glance it looks like a glorification of suffering ('if we suffer we shall also reign', 2 Tim. 2:12, KJV) what it is in reality is the very ultimate in righting wrongs. The sufferer is vindicated; the oppressor humiliated. The Lamb is no longer on the cross, but on the throne (Rev. 5:6), and when he pronounces his final judgment, patriarchy, racism and discrimination will be put to an open shame.

9. NO OTHER WAY?

The doctrine that sin could not be remitted unless God's justice was satisfied by the sacrifice of his Son has never been without its critics. As we have already seen,[1] Anselm's younger contemporary Abelard (1079–1142) deplored the idea of penal substitution and thought it abhorrent that God should consider the death of his Son 'so agreeable that by it he should be reconciled to the whole world!'[2] The barrier, he argued, was not in God, but in human beings, and what was needed, therefore, was not that God be propitiated but that our whole attitude be changed. This is exactly what the blood of Christ achieved. By taking our human nature to himself and suffering in that nature, Christ has demonstrated to us the perfection of love, and as a result we are joined to him by an 'indissoluble bond of affection'. This love (*amor*) becomes our righteousness, and through this righteousness ('which is love') we gain remission of sins. The effect of the cross is thus entirely subjective: 'He has more fully bound himself to us by love; with the result that our hearts should be enkindled by such a gift of divine grace, and true charity [Lat. *caritas*, love] should not now shrink from enduring anything for

---

1. Ch. 3, p. 61.
2. From Eugene R. Fairweather (ed.), *A Scholastic Miscellany; Anselm to Ockham*, Library of Christian Classics (London: SCM Press, 1956), p. 283.

him.'[3] Freed from slavery to sin, we now do all things out of love rather than fear, since Christ has shown us such grace that no greater can be found. Everyone who honestly and purely loves the Lord is predestined to life.

Abelard's approach appears to give relief from the more demanding aspects of Anselm's doctrine, particularly its penal element, and it has had, and continues to have, a wide appeal. Among its most influential modern exponents have been the American Congregational preacher, Horace Bushnell,[4] and the Anglican moral philosopher, Hastings Rashdall.[5] Rashdall warmly endorsed the formulation of Peter the Lombard (one of Abelard's students): 'So great a pledge of love having been given us, we are both moved and kindled to love God who did such great things for us; and by this we are justified, that is, being loosed from our sins we are made just. The death of Christ therefore justifies us, inasmuch as through it charity is stirred up in our hearts.'[6] The Abelardian doctrine was also set forth at a more popular level by William Barclay in *The Plain Man Looks at the Apostles'Creed*.[7] Because Jesus has showed us God as he is, fear has turned to trust.

This understanding of the atonement is appropriately referred to as the moral influence theory, since it bases the atonement on the change for the better which the cross brings about in ourselves. This avoids the idea of sacrificial blood, which our human sensibilities find repugnant, and it also appeals to our predilection for a doctrine which links the idea of forgiveness to self-improvement. But despite these apparent advantages, it is beset with serious difficulties.

We should note, first of all, that as compared with Anselm's doctrine Abelard's theory does not abate one whit the actual suffering of Christ. It is easy to become confused on this, as if by describing Christ's sufferings as 'penal' we actually make them worse. In reality, no theory affects the facts. The sufferings of Jesus

---

3. *A Scholastic Miscellany*, p. 283.

4. Horace Bushnell, *The Vicarious Sacrifice* (London: Strahan and Co., 1871). Bushnell argued (p. 109) that the one, comprehensive aim of Christ, 'in the industry of His life and the pangs of His cross', was 'the change He will operate in the spiritual habit and well-being of souls'. The way this change is effected is indicated in the words, 'we look on him whom we have pierced, and are pierced ourselves' (p. 113).

5. Hastings Rashdall, *The Idea of Atonement in Christian Theology* (London: Macmillan, 1919).

6. Ibid., p. 438. The 'charity' referred to is the Latin *caritas*, love.

7. William Barclay, *The Plain Man Looks at the Apostles' Creed* (London: Collins, 1967), pp. 95–114.

remain the same whatever the theory. Doctrines of the atonement merely attempt to explain the facts, and no theory can make them more, or less, horrific. Christ was as surely crucified under Pontius Pilate on the Abelardian view as on the Anselmian.

We also need to note that the death of Christ was as necessary on the one theory as on the other. All the classical theories of the atonement presuppose the necessity of the cross. Abelard did not believe that this link was necessary in order to satisfy divine justice, but he did think it necessary as a demonstration of the love and mercy of God. In no other way could God have made his sympathy with sinners so plain.

The difference is that on the moral influence theory the cross is a *mere* demonstration. God does not demonstrate his love by saving us; he saves us by demonstrating his love. But can the cross ever be a demonstration of redeeming love unless, first of all, it is a redeeming act? This is certainly how the New Testament portrays it. It bears clear witness to the fact that the cross was indeed a demonstration (indeed, *the* demonstration) of God's love. We have already seen this in 1 John 4:10, but this passage is not content to say 'this is love: not that we loved God, but that he loved us'. It says, 'this is love: not that we loved God, but that he loved us *and sent his Son as an atoning sacrifice for our sins*' (italics mine). If we take away the reason for his dying (to expiate sin) the love becomes an empty gesture. The cross must be a saving act before it can be a saving word.

Other difficulties cluster around this core difficulty. For example, while it is relatively easy from Abelard's point of view to see how the cross can demonstrate the love of Jesus, it is extremely difficult to see how it can demonstrate the love of the Father. Yet this, as we have seen repeatedly, is what the New Testament emphasizes. It throws the Father's love into the foreground. Yet it was not the Father who came into the world and shared its woes. It was the Son. The Father 'merely' delivered him up. How does this comport with his love for his Son? In reality, the Father's love for the Son is the base point. This is the register of his love for the world, the fact that he gave his Son and what he gave him to. He gave him to die. But why? Was this merely God saying to the world, 'I love you'? How could the cross say any such thing if the sacrifice was unnecessary in the first place? Calvary speaks of the love of God only because it portrays him as not shrinking from that great costly act by which alone the world could be redeemed. Would he have delivered up his Son to abuse and crucifixion – would he have forsaken him – merely to show solidarity or to provide humans with a role model?

We are back with the fundamental protest: what right did God have to sacrifice his own Son? Only the most desperate crisis, only the structures of the moral universe, could justify what God sanctioned at Calvary.

Linked to this is the fact that Abelard's approach requires us to revise all that the New Testament says about the reasons for Christ's coming into the world. Both Bushnell and Rashdall argue that Christ's suffering and death, far from being the primary object of his mission (as Anselm had insisted) were in fact entirely incidental. According to Rashdall,

> the death came to Him as the direct and necessary consequence of His faithfulness to His Messianic calling, of a life devoted to the doing of God's will and the service of His fellow-men. To the very last, according to the Synoptists, our Lord conceived it as possible that he might accomplish that task without the necessity of dying a violent death.[8]

Bushnell is even bolder: 'The sacrifice, taken as an act in time, was not set before Him as the end or object of His ministry – that would make it a mere pageant of suffering, without rational dignity or character – but, when it came, it was simply the bad fortune such a work, prosecuted with such devotion, must encounter on its way.'[9] As if this were not enough he then goes on to compare the 'sacrifice' of Christ with that of a missionary going off to spend his days among a heathen people. He does not go for the express purpose of laying down his life, but he is willing to do so, should the work require it.

That may be so. But how many missionaries ever sailed believing that their sacrifice was of the same order as that of Christ at Calvary? 'There is a Gethsemane hid in all love,' wrote Bushnell, and therefore, 'what we call the vicarious sacrifice of Christ is nothing strange as regards the principle of it, no superlative, unexampled, and therefore unintelligible grace. It only does and suffers, and comes into substitution for, just what any and all love will, according to its degree.'[10]

Extraordinary though this sounds, it follows naturally from Abelard's understanding of the atonement. If Christ looses people from their sins by the moral force of his personality and the power of his love, then it is his life and example that matter, not his death, which in itself achieved nothing. It is impossible, however, to square this with the New Testament. The recorded utterances of Jesus make plain that he himself was utterly convinced that his death was the express purpose of his mission. He had come to give his life as a ransom for many (Mark 10:45). In accordance with this, the certainty of a violent death was

---

8. Rashdall, *Idea of Atonement*, p. 441.

9. Bushnell, *Vicarious Sacrifice*, pp. 90–91.

10. Ibid., pp. 12–13.

not something that dawned on him only gradually. It was present to his mind from the very beginning of his ministry, as we have already seen in Matthew 9:15, where, even before the beheading of the Baptist, Jesus refers to a time when he will be 'taken away' from his disciples. This shows, as Leon Morris points out, that 'from quite early in his ministry Jesus faced the fact that it would end in rejection and death'.[11]

On the other hand, even at a late hour there was no mere historical inevitability about his death. When he entered Jerusalem after the long trek from Caesarea Philippi, he made a triumphal entry, and had he chosen to capitalize on his popularity, the visit could, humanly speaking, have had a very different outcome. He chose, instead, to lay down his life; and over and above this human decision stood divine foreordination itself. The lamb 'was slain from the creation of the world' (Rev. 13:8); or, as Peter put it in his Pentecostal sermon, he was handed over 'by God's deliberate plan and foreknowledge' (Acts 2:23). Jesus did not die as a missionary martyr, overwhelmed by circumstances beyond his control. Instead, his death had been, from the beginning, the foundation of God's plan for the world. Whatever the parts played by Judas, the Jews and Pontius Pilate, Calvary is above all the locus of a divine action: a place where God the Father presented his Son as a *hilastērion*; and he was a *hilastērion*, not by the force of his character and the pathos of his death, but by his blood (Rom. 3:25).

Four further points deserve a brief mention.

First, Abelard's theory cannot explain how the cross conquered the powers of darkness (Col. 2:15). Did he do this by his example? Or is Satan conquered by the transformed lives of those who follow Jesus? Not according to the New Testament, which categorically declares that it was Christ's death that destroyed the devil (Heb. 2:14).

Secondly, far from being morally and spiritually transformed by witnessing the life and death of Jesus Christ, the vast majority of his contemporaries (who, after all, saw him most closely) were scandalized by him. He brought out not the best, but the worst, in human nature, and to the appalling catalogue of human crimes they now added deicide. They crucified the Lord of glory (1 Cor. 2:8). Far from being mollified and won over by the life of Christ, people mocked, hated and rejected him; and from this point of view the majesty and fragrance of his life bred judgment, not blessing. This is why he pronounced such solemn woes over such cities as Chorazin and Bethsaida. They had witnessed his

11. Leon Morris, *The GospelAaccording to Matthew*, Pillar NT Commentary (Grand Rapids: Eerdmans and Leicester: Apollos, 1992), p. 225.

miracles, but not repented. Now it would be worse for them than for Tyre and Sidon (Matt. 11:20–24).

Thirdly, there is the objection that may be raised against all exemplarism: it means that God used a human being as a means to an end. Christ was crucified to teach a lesson. Even if this had been effective (which it was not) it would have been profoundly immoral, implying that Jesus was exploited and victimized in the fragile hope of thereby rendering others more righteous.

Fourthly, the moral influence theory quickly dissolves into the old theory of salvation by works. The basis of our acceptance with God becomes not what Christ did for us, but what we do ourselves under the inspiration of his example. We are justified because we are more loving. This is pure legalism. Love, after all, is the fulfilling of the law, and precisely because it is legalism it can lead only to despair. How can we ever match the example of Christ? Fortunately, we do not have to. There is a new and living way into the Holiest: not via our own transformed lives, but via the blood of Jesus (Heb. 10:19–20), and it is uniquely suited to those who are profoundly conscious that they have been but miserable imitators of God (Eph. 5:1).

Abelard's theory sets out to moralize the doctrine of the atonement. It dissociates itself from the notion of penal justice; it eliminates the priesthood of the Father; it joins the chorus of derision against the concept of redemption by blood. This may secure it some credit among the wise and the righteous, but it instantly ceases to be a word of the cross. Calvary no longer saves; it merely educates and influences, and its last word is no longer the triumphant, '*Tetelestai!*' ('It is finished!'), but the overwhelming challenge, 'Go and do likewise!'

The rectoral theory: vindicating divine justice

While Abelard portrayed the cross as primarily a demonstration of divine love and mercy, others portrayed it as first and foremost a demonstration of God's justice. The underlying premise, however, remains the same: the cross is effective because it changes human beings. By showing God's abhorrence of sin it leads us to repentance, and thus creates the conditions in which God can be satisfied that it is right for him to forgive the sinner.

The most notable exponent of this theory (known as the rectoral or governmental theory) was the Dutch jurist, Hugo Grotius (1583–1645), whose *Defence of the Catholic Doctrine of the Satisfaction of Christ* was published in 1617.[12] As the

---

12. See R. S. Franks, *The Work of Christ* (London: Thomas Nelson, 1962), pp. 389–409.

title suggests, this was intended as a vindication of the received doctrine, but in attempting to vindicate it Grotius also modified it. The necessity to punish sin arose, he argued, not from the divine nature as such, but from God's position as Rector, or Moral Governor, of the universe. As such, his overriding concern is the public good, and particularly the maintenance of public order. The cross is to be set within this framework. Gratuitous forgiveness would have undermined the authority of the law, but the vicarious death of Christ upheld it by declaring God's abhorrence of sin. Even though Christ's sufferings were not (in Grotius's view) either identical with the curse originally pronounced against sin or even an exact equivalent, they were sufficient (because God deemed them so) to constitute a 'conspicuous example'[13] and as such a deterrence to sin. From this point of view the cross clearly served the interests of public order.

The best known English-speaking advocate of the rectoral theory was the Congregational preacher R. W. Dale (1829–95), whose work *The Atonement* was first published in 1875. Dale's language sometimes echoes that of the older Protestant doctrine, and his exposition is further complicated by the prominence he gives to the idea that besides declaring God's abhorrence of sin the cross also secures the death of sin in the believer. Yet, like Grotius, he argues that the ground for divine forgiveness is that the crucifixion provided a revelation of the righteousness of God and at the same time a revelation of the ill-desert of sin. The great register of this ill-desert is death, the penalty denounced from of old against sin, and it is by submitting to this penalty on behalf of humanity that Christ vindicates the honour of the law and thus makes it right for God, as Moral Governor of the universe, to forgive iniquity.

As the example of Dale indicates, this view of the atonement, precisely because it takes sin seriously, has a strong appeal to evangelicals.[14] Yet, no less than the moral influence theory, it is beset with serious difficulties.

First, God already makes plain his abhorrence of sin quite independently of the cross. In fact, he made it plain in the very beginning, when he warned Adam, 'in the day you eat from it you will certainly die' (Gen. 2:17); a warning repeated times without number throughout Scripture. But he also makes it plain through his ordinary providence. His 'wrath', as Paul reminds us in Romans 1:18, is

---

13. Franks, *The Work of Christ*, p. 398.

14. B. B. Warfield was of the view that James Denney's work, *The Atonement and the Modern Mind* (as distinct from his earlier volume, *The Death of Christ*) also reflects the Grotian or rectoral theory. See B. B. Warfield, *Critical Reviews* (London and New York: Oxford University Press, 1932), pp. 102–105.

already revealed against all human ungodliness and unrighteousness. His judicial abandonment of the Roman Empire to unbridled promiscuity was one clear instance of such anger. It is also revealed in the way he disciplines his people. This was a large part of the message of the Old Testament. The sins of Israel led to rejection, and those of Judah to exile, precisely to make plain that the seed of Abraham could not sin with impunity. This remains a rule as much under the New Testament as the Old: 'Those whom I love I rebuke and discipline' (Rev. 3:19).

Clearly, then, while the cross was the supreme revelation of God's abhorrence of sin it was not the only one. Nor was it necessarily any more effective than the deterrents implicit in God's word and providence. The Roman soldiers who crucified Jesus were in no way solemnized by the event, nor were the spectators who bayed for his blood. The cross upholds the majesty of law only if it is understood, and those involved in the crucifixion had no such understanding, as Jesus himself makes clear: 'Father, forgive them, for they do not know what they are doing' (Luke 23:34). The bare event of the cross does not convince people either of the majesty of the law or of the guilt of sin. Only the 'word' (*logos*) of the cross can convey this message. Apart from it we are merely among the passersby, totally unaffected by the solemnity of Calvary.

But no word could give the cross its power as a vindication of the law unless the penalty was right in the first place; and it could be right only if it was deserved. Dale is aware of this, which is why he refuses to endorse the idea that the purpose of punishment is to deter others from doing wrong. He makes his point in an unattributed quotation: '"The suffering of a criminal," it has been said, "benefits the public because it is deserved; it is not deserved because it benefits the public."'[15] Exemplary punishments are, unfortunately, no uncommon thing even in modern judicial systems, but they are immoral to their core. No authority has the right to use a human being as an instrument of social policy; or, to put it crudely, to impose deterrent sentences *pour encourager les autres*. Such a policy smacks of the worst atrocities of Nazism and is a world away from the word of the cross. God did not enact Calvary to make an example of his Son, nor was Christ's death merely a warning about what happens to sinners. It was a suffering of what sin deserved, and the primary purpose of that suffering was not revelation, but redemption. What the cross *does* comes before what it *says*. Only by redeeming (at such a price) does it show the seriousness with which God takes sin. Were it not that it redeems, it would be dumb.

---

15. R. W. Dale, *The Atonement* (21st ed., London: Congregational Union of England and Wales, 1900), p. 377.

Further difficulties remain. First, the rectoral theory portrays God as constrained by the moral universe. Were it not for the pressures of the common good he might have ignored sin, or forgiven it gratuitously. Instead, Christ has to be sacrificed: not, however, to satisfy *God* that it was right to forgive sin, but to satisfy *us*, his subjects, as if what really mattered was that our sense of justice should not be offended by the wonder of free grace. This is not far from the thought-process that says, 'I would like to, but what would people think?' This completely inverts the biblical order; God does not demand satisfaction, the public do.

Secondly, the rectoral theory, like the moral influence theory, collapses into pure subjectivism: our reconciliation with God depends not on what Jesus did towards God, but on the effect he has on us by revealing the uncompromising divine rectitude. But on these terms the cross was scarcely necessary. Christ's whole life was an homage to the law and a testimony to the holiness of God. No one has expressed this better than Dale himself:

> The whole of His ministry is a revelation of the righteousness and of the love of God, an authoritative appeal to the heart and conscience of the human race, a mighty force constraining men to repent of sin and to trust in the infinite love of the Father. And if his death contributed to our eternal redemption only by producing in us those dispositions which render it right and possible for God to forgive us, it would be no more intimately related to the remission of sins than every part of his public ministry.[16]

Yet Jesus himself makes plain (and Dale is fully aware of this) that his death bore on the remission of sins in a way that, for example, the parable of the rich man and Lazarus did not (Luke 16:19–31).

Thirdly, in making our repentance the decisive thing, the rectoral theory is merely a sophisticated variant on the doctrine of salvation by works. Legalism takes many forms, but at its heart lies the belief that our relationship with God depends on something commendable in ourselves, something that allows us to say, 'I am not like other people' (Luke 18:11). It may be the pure moralism that thinks it has kept all the commandments or the easier moralism that is prepared to stake everything on having done our best. It may be ethnic identity, as in the case of those who boasted that they were children of Abraham. Or it may, more subtly, be some spiritual change we have undergone ourselves: something we have felt or experienced, or some supposed revolution in our attitudes. The rectoral theory belongs within this last variety of legalism, assuming that what matters in the last analysis is our repentance, our abhorrence of sin, our

16. Dale, *The Atonement*, pp. 69–70.

acknowledgement of all that sin means to God, and thus our meeting all the psychological conditions in which it is right for God to forgive us.

There are two problems with this. One is that repentance (even if perfect) can be no adequate atonement, and no-one knows this better than the penitent himself, who would love to offer satisfaction to God for his sin, but would never dream that his repentance itself could qualify as such a satisfaction:

> Not the labours of my hands
> Can fulfil thy law's demands;
> Could my zeal no respite know,
> Could my tears for ever flow,
> All for sin could not atone:
> Thou must save, and thou alone.[17]

But it is not a question merely of inadequacy; it is a matter of impossibility. The penitent can never produce within herself a repentance deep enough even to satisfy her own conscience. The heart can never be broken enough. This is why the rectoral theory, like the moral influence theory, is ultimately a counsel of despair. We can never glory in our own repentance, nor would we dare present it before the Eternal Light as the reason why God should give us the crown of righteousness (2 Tim. 4:8). 'Nothing in my hand I bring' includes our repentance. We can glory only in the cross (Gal. 6:14).

Yet it is never the cross, in and of itself, which evokes repentance, and this highlights another weakness of the rectoral theory. It bypasses the ministry of the Holy Spirit. He alone can produce repentance, and the repentance he produces is not the cause of the atonement, but its consequence. The cross, resurrection and ascension of Jesus secure the ministry of the Spirit, with all the gifts and blessings which that brings with it. Foremost among these is the gift of repentance; never a human achievement, but a divine *given* (Acts 5:31), produced not by a mere demonstration, but by the intimate touch of grace in the depths of the human heart. This touch, of course, produces its own psychological narrative as the sinner faces the truth about himself, accepts that his life is indefensible and acquiesces unquestioningly in the judgment of God (Ps. 51:1–4). The cross may be one of the cognitive elements in this journey. It may highlight the ugliness of sin. It may bespeak God's abhorrence of it. It may make us ashamed of our past attitudes to Christ. It may fill us with wondering appreciation of the love of God. But none of these is what constitutes

---

17. 'Rock of Ages, cleft for me', Augustus Toplady, 1740–78.

atonement or purchases redemption. Instead, in the language of the older evangelical piety, repentance is itself a 'blood-bought' grace, created in our hearts by the mysterious agency of the Holy Spirit. The psychological journey which marks the sinner's recovery is but the outward expression of the inner touch of the supernatural. Yet the real foundation of assurance and joy is the knowledge that whatever the shortcomings of our repentance (or of our conversion-narrative) God accepts us for Jesus' sake.

Vicarious repentance?

Suppose, however, that there could be a perfect repentance, and suppose that someone offered it to God in our place: would this not be an adequate atonement? This was the doctrine proposed by the Scottish theologian, John McLeod Campbell, in his work *The Nature of the Atonement*, first published in 1855. Campbell, ordained to the ministry of the Church of Scotland in 1825, was deposed for heresy in 1831, the key charge against him being that he taught universal pardon and redemption. Throughout his trial Campbell insisted that his views were entirely consistent with the Westminster Confession of Faith, including its doctrine on the extent of the atonement. By the time he wrote *The Nature of the Atonement*, however, he had clearly moved to a position where he rejected not only the doctrine of definite atonement, but the very presuppositions of the evangelical understanding of the cross (associated in his mind with John Owen and Jonathan Edwards). This doctrine rested, in Campbell's view, on a false doctrine of God: he punished sin by necessity of his nature, but showed mercy only at his own discretion. On the contrary, Campbell argued, not only was God's love universal, but his forgiveness, too, was universal. Everyone was born in a state of pardon, and the atonement, far from being the ground of this pardon, was but its expression: the revelation of the loving, fatherly heart of God, and the declaration of his forgiveness. Campbell stopped short, however, of preaching universal salvation. We can reject God's pardon, and this is the ultimate and irremediable condemnation.

From this, other denials followed: the denial of substitution, the denial of imputation and, above all, the denial that Christ's sufferings were in any sense penal. Campbell viewed with abhorrence the idea (which he attributed to 'the older Calvinism') that the atoning element in the sufferings of Christ was, '*sufferings as sufferings*, the pain and agony as *pain and agony*'.[18] He continued:

---

18. John McLeod Campbell, *The Nature of the Atonement* (repr. 2nd ed., Edinburgh: Handsel Press, 1996 [1867]), p. 106. The italics are Campbell's.

While Christ suffered for our sins as an atoning sacrifice, what he suffered was not –
because from its nature it could not be – a punishment. [Instead,] it was the spiritual
essence and nature of the sufferings of Christ, and not that these sufferings were
penal, which constituted their value as entering into the atonement made by the Son
of God.[19]

It was in this context, as a moral and spiritual alternative to the doctrine of
vicarious punishment, that Campbell introduced the idea of vicarious repentance (though he himself never used this phrase). The idea had been suggested
to him by a passage in Jonathan Edwards's discussion of 'The Christian Doctrine
of Satisfaction for Sin' in his *Remarks on Important Theological Controversies*. There,
Edwards had written that sin is so heinous that God must punish it 'unless
there be something in some measure to balance this desert; *either some answerable
repentance and sorrow for it,* or other compensation'.[20] Edwards himself instantly
dismissed this alternative as out of the question, 'for all the repentance men are
capable of is no repentance at all, or is as little as none, in comparison with the
greatness of the injury'. Campbell, however, seized on it and developed it as
the key element in Christ's 'dealing with God on behalf of men'. Christ's oneness
of mind with the Father would, he argued, take the form of a perfect confession of our sins. He then added the famous sentence: 'This confession, as
to its own nature, must have been *a perfect Amen in humanity to the judgement of
God on the sin of man*.'[21] This 'amen', Campbell continued, is the perfect response
of his 'divine' humanity to the wrath of God,

> *and in that perfect response he absorbs it.* For that response has all the elements of a perfect
> response in humanity for all the sin of man – a perfect sorrow – a perfect contrition
> – all the elements of such a repentance, and that in absolute perfection, all – excepting
> the personal consciousness of sin; and by that perfect response in Amen to the mind
> of God in relation to sin is the wrath of God rightly met, and that is accorded to
> divine justice which is its due, and could alone satisfy it.[22]

Campbell's views commanded little assent at the time. Later, however, they
were received sympathetically by the liberal Anglo-Catholic, R. C. Moberly, who

---

19. Ibid., pp. 107–108.
20. *The Works of Jonathan Edwards,* rev. Edward Hickman, 2 vols. (repr. Edinburgh:
    Banner of Truth, 1974 [1834]), vol. 2, p. 565 (italics mine).
21. Campbell, *The Nature of the Atonement,* p. 118 (italics his).
22. Ibid. (italics Campbell's).

wrote, 'to me it seems difficult to estimate too highly the debt which Christian thought owes to that reverent spirit'.[23] Among twentieth-century Scottish theologians, Campbell became a cult figure, the late James B. Torrance even going so far as to compare *The Nature of the Atonement* with Athanasius's *De Incarnatione* and Anselm's *Cur Deus Homo?* as 'one of the classics of all time on this doctrine'.[24] The idea of vicarious repentance also appealed to C. S. Lewis, who, although reluctant to endorse any particular theory of the atonement, devoted a whole chapter of *Mere Christianity* to the 'The Perfect Penitent': 'Only a bad person,' he wrote, 'needs to repent: only a good person can repent perfectly.'[25] This, he suggests, is what Christ did for us. He took our nature so that he could identify with us rebels, willingly surrender himself to God, say, 'sorry!', and give himself to humiliation and death; and because he was God, he could do all this perfectly.

Campbell's idea was driven by a concern to find a more 'moral and spiritual' understanding of the atonement, but for all its apparent reverence his presentation is distinctly polemical, reflecting all the prejudice the world feels against the idea of divine retribution and its even deeper prejudice against the idea of redemption by blood. But we have already seen how improbable it is that repentance could constitute an adequate atonement. Certainly no human court would recognize it. An individual charged with causing death by dangerous driving might well be deeply penitent, but such penitence would never be accepted as an alternative to a custodial sentence. The idea of vicarious repentance is even more improbable. As Campbell himself acknowledged, the one element lacking in Christ's repentance was 'the personal consciousness of sin'.[26] The concession is, surely, fatal? Repentance is in its very nature an intensely personal thing, as appears clearly in Psalm 51. Here, David is certainly saying 'amen!' to God's condemnation of his sin: 'You are right in your verdict and justified when you judge' (v. 4). But the sin confessed is *my* transgression, *my* iniquity, *my* sin (vv. 1–2). It is easy to see why such a sense of personal guilt should make him feel 'crushed' (v. 8) and create a broken spirit and a contrite heart. But it is extremely difficult to understand how there could be such feelings, such contrition, where the sin is not one's own. Indeed, far from confessing sin, Christ protests his innocence: 'Can any one of you prove me guilty of sin?' (John 8:46); and St Paul speaks of him as one 'who had no sin' (2 Cor. 5:21). Nor is there any hint of a word of confession or repentance uttered by Christ on the cross.

---

23. Moberly, *Atonement and Personality*, p. 402.

24. See Campbell, *The Nature of the Atonement*, p. 2.

25. Lewis, *Mere Christianity*, p. 57.

26. Campbell, *The Nature of the Atonement*, p. 118.

Indeed, at the climax of his suffering what we hear is not 'amen!', but 'why?'. On the other hand when, as in the prayer of Daniel (Dan. 9:4–19), we hear an expression of collective (vicarious?) repentance, the penitent is himself a sinner who cannot distance himself from the iniquity of his people. When Daniel says, 'we have sinned and done wrong. We have been wicked and have rebelled' (v. 5), the *we* must be taken as meant sincerely. On the other hand, there is no suggestion that Daniel's confession, no matter how sincere, and no matter how contrite, could serve as an atonement for the sins of his people, any more than David's repentance could be seen as an atonement for his own.

To add to the difficulty, repentance is not merely a matter of feeling. It does, indeed, involve grief and sorrow for sin, but it also involves a turning away from sin: not only *metallomai*, a feeling sorry, but *metanoia*, a radical change of mind and attitude, leading to a complete change of direction. This is why one of the key Hebrew words for repenting is *šûb*, to turn or to return; and the New Testament reflects the same usage. Repentance is a conversion, as appears in the words of Jesus to Peter, 'when you have turned back, strengthen your brothers' (Luke 22:32). It is impossible to attribute this kind of repentance (the only biblical kind) to Jesus: he had no sin or idol to turn from (1 Thess. 1:9), and no previous sinful lifestyle to abandon. Yet the only repentance which could remotely serve as an atonement would have to be one which included such a turning.

Even supposing Jesus to have been capable of such a repentance, however, in what sense could it have been vicarious? How could the repentance of one man two thousand years ago avail for me? Though Campbell regarded Christ's repentance as vicarious he did not regard it as substitutionary. We ourselves are still bound to repent, each one for him or herself, and as Campbell develops his doctrine the impression grows that the key element in the atonement is, in fact, our own repentance, and the key element in the work of Christ is that, by bearing witness to the Father, he elicits this repentance. We are enabled to accept, 'as a most welcome part of the gift of God in Christ, the power to confess our sins *with an Amen to Christ's confession of them*'.[27] But this is not all. Moved by Christ's declaring of the Father's name, we also say 'amen!' to Christ's filial spirit. Campbell contrasts this filial spirit with what he regards as the merely 'legal relationship' implied in the concept of adoption. Instead, we are reconciled children, trusting not in a legal status but in the Father's heart. Christ's own confession of sin, and Christ's righteous trust in the Father are reproduced in us, and this becomes, not the *basis* of our communion with God, but the very communion itself.

---

27. Ibid., p. 143 (italics mine).

It is hard to avoid the conclusion that this takes us back to the moral influence view of the atonement: the core of Christ's work is prophetic, he reveals the heart of the Father, and he moves us to repentance and trust. Thus, our sense of peace with God has nothing to do with vicarious sacrifice or obedience on Christ's part. Instead, God's *name* gives us peace.

How does this square with the New Testament emphasis on the centrality of the cross? In the theory of vicarious repentance the cross becomes incidental to Christ's revealing of the Father's name: collateral damage, virtually, as a result of his bearing witness to his Father's name. The apostles, by contrast, place the cross in the very forefront of their message as the purpose of his mission and the key moment in his work. Time and again it is to his blood and to his death that they attribute our salvation. They say little, or nothing, of Jesus repenting, but much of his dying. It is hard to imagine St Paul writing to the Corinthians and declaring, 'I delivered to you first of all that Christ said amen to God's condemnation'.

But the centrality of the cross is not the only problem here. We face, once again, the question of the Father's role in the death of Jesus. That role is clear. The Father was in effect the officiating priest at Calvary. It was he who delivered up his Son; and he delivered him up not only to the bitterness of repentance but to the bitterness of the curse (Gal. 3:13). Why, if repentance was all that is necessary, did Christ have to die?

Let us go back to the story of Abraham offering up Isaac. Just as the patriarch took the knife to kill his son, a voice comes from heaven, 'Do not lay a hand on the boy. Do not do anything to him. *Now I know that you fear God, because you have not withheld from me your son, your only son*' (Gen. 22:12, italics mine). Should the same not have applied at Calvary? If repentance was all that was necessary, ought not God to have halted the ritual and cried, 'Now I know that you say amen to my condemnation because you have not withheld yourself from me'?

Instead, God abandons his Son. Campbell plays down the forsakenness of Jesus. Even Moberly goes so far as to say that according to Campbell, 'the suffering Christ never felt himself forsaken at all'.[28] Instead, he speaks of Christ enjoying 'the unbroken sense of the Father's favour' and seems to regard the cry of dereliction as signifying only that 'God leaves him in the hands of the wicked, and interposes not on his behalf'.[29] He dismisses any idea that there was a hiding of the Father's face, or God looking upon him in anger or treating him as a sinner.

---

28. Moberly, *Atonement and Personality*, p. 407.

29. Campbell, *The Nature of the Atonement*, p. 201.

Instead, he argues, the key phrase is 'my God', and the whole point of the moment is merely that the Son's trust in the Father was being put to the test.[30]

But why should the Father put him to such a test? Why should God choose to show his love not only by *giving* his Son, but by giving him as a *hilasmos*, an expiatory sacrifice (1 John 4:10)? Why, if the forsakenness of the Son was such a non-event did Paul describe him as being made a 'curse' for us (Gal. 3:13)? Above all, why did God have to condemn sin not only in the *mind*, but 'in the *flesh*' of his own Son (Rom. 8:3, ESV)?

This last passage exposes a contradiction at the heart of the idea of vicarious repentance. If Christ was saying 'amen!' to God's condemnation, he was not merely saying 'amen' to God's fatherly heart towards the human race. He was saying 'amen' to his condemnation, acknowledging that God was right to condemn sin; and right to condemn it precisely here, on the cross, in the flesh of his own Son, who carried our sins in his own 'body' on the cross (1 Pet. 2:24). At that moment God was treating him not primarily as his Son, but as 'sin' (2 Cor. 5:21). It is to the very retributive justice which Campbell says is no necessary part of God's nature that Christ was saying 'amen!' on the cross of Calvary.

Nor is this all. While Campbell rejects outright the idea of the imputation of sin, Christ's 'repentance' implies that he is imputing the world's sin to himself. It also implies his acknowledgment that God is right to impute it to him. He can say 'amen' only because in the eyes of both himself and his Father that sin is his own. He is acknowledging the rightness of what the Father is doing in 'crushing' him (Isa. 53:10), and this acknowledgement is an essential element in the atonement. The Lamb of God, brought to the slaughter, does not open his mouth (Isa. 53:7). But in the last analysis, the power of the cross lies, according to the New Testament, not in the mind with which it was accepted, but in the sentence it executed: 'in him we have redemption through his blood, the forgiveness of sins' (Eph. 1:7). We cannot reduce, 'Christ died for the ungodly' (Rom. 5:6) to, 'Christ repented for the ungodly'.

Campbell's treatment does, however, raise an issue which is serious for both personal religion and evangelism: what is the relation between repentance and forgiveness? We have already seen that repentance itself cannot constitute an atonement, but neither does the atonement dispense with the need for repentance. This is already made plain in the ritual prescribed in Leviticus 16 for the Day of Atonement (*yôm kippur*). While it was the sacrificing of the sin offering and the sin-bearing of the scapegoat that atoned for the sins of Israel, the people

---

30. Ibid., p. 203.

were also required to afflict themselves (KJV, 'ye shall afflict your souls', Lev.
16:29). The full extent of this affliction is not spelt out, but it clearly involved
the observance of a solemn Sabbath, and in later Jewish tradition (transmitted
orally via the Mishna) it meant that eating, drinking, anointing, putting on sandals
and marital intercourse were forbidden.[31] Yet the signs are that this self-
humbling before God was not part of the atonement, but a response to it. The
people were solemnized by the ritual itself.

Nor did the firmest grasp of the divine love and mercy preclude such
self-abasement. In Psalm 51 David speaks unambiguously of a broken and
contrite heart as more acceptable to God than any ritualized offerings (Ps.
51:16–17), yet the opening verses make plain that he placed his confidence not
in his broken and contrite heart, but in God's mercy and unfailing love. It is in
the presence of this mercy (and in response to it, indeed) that David is heart-
broken over his own sin. He already knows that he is forgiven, because the
prophet, Nathan, had brought the message, 'the LORD has taken away your sin'
(2 Sam. 12:13). It was this announcement of forgiveness that had, in David's
own words, crushed his bones (Ps. 51:8). It was against this God, this faithful,
loving, forgiving God that he had sinned; and this is what broke his heart.

We need to be clear, of course, what is involved in repentance. It is not mere
guilt-feelings, or a change in outward lifestyle, or a fear of retribution, human
or divine. Nor, again, is it simply regret over the pain we may have caused to
others and the shame and embarrassment we have brought upon ourselves. It
does indeed mean facing the truth about ourselves, but the paramount truth we
have to face is the pain we have caused to a loving God; grief and anger against
the sin that hurt *him*. By the same token, the action we have to take is not merely
to turn from the sin, but to turn to him, confident that he will forgive us.

This means that repentance is rooted in faith: faith in God's willingness to
accept and forgive us. The prodigal son not only came to himself. He recalled
the nature of his father's house and he returned home because, knowing his
father, he entertained the hope that he might be welcome, if not as a son, then
as a hired hand. Biblical repentance is always rooted in such hope, and the hope
itself arises from faith in the promises of God. 'Let the wicked forsake their
ways,' cried the prophet, 'and the unrighteous their thoughts. Let them turn to
the LORD, *and he will have mercy on them, and to our God, for he will freely pardon*' (Isa.
55:7, italics mine). The same note continues in the New Testament, as we see in,
for example, 1 John 1:9: 'If we confess our sins, he is faithful and just and will

---

31. See John E. Hartley, *Leviticus*, Word Bible Commentary, vol. 4 (Dallas: Word Books,
1992), p. 242.

forgive our sins.' Puritan theology grasped this truth equally clearly: repentance is rooted not only in a true sense of sin but in an 'apprehension of the mercy of God in Christ'.[32] In all these examples, repentance is evoked by the gospel, not by the law; prompted, not by fear, but by faith in God's mercy and love.

This faith has, however, a specific focus: Christ himself. Only through him can we turn to the Father; and we will come through him only when we believe that he is indeed the way, the truth and the life: the great High Priest through whom we may come with boldness to the throne of grace (Heb. 4:14–16). But this faith also knows that Christ lays down no conditions before undertaking to act for us before God. He takes us on, just as we are, 'poor, wretched, blind'. He does not ask that we first be penitent, or broken, or hungry, or seeking, or 'prepared'. His clients are all sinners: sinners, and nothing else. When they come, they bring nothing, because they have nothing to bring. Only by coming, and only in him, can they find all they need; and that includes even penitence itself. He gives repentance as well as forgiveness (Acts 5:31).

But repentance is rooted in love, no less than in faith. The greatest example of this is the story of the anointing of Jesus by 'a woman who had lived a sinful life' (Luke 7:36–50). The incident occurred in the house of a Pharisee who had invited Jesus to dinner. The woman stood behind him, weeping, and began to wet his feet with her tears. The she wiped them with her hair, kissed them and poured perfume on them. The Pharisee was horrified, but Jesus defended her stoutly. Her tears flowed from her love, and she loved much because she had been forgiven much. He might equally have said that she loved much because she was loved much: the very point made in 1 John 4:19, 'we love because he first loved us'. Equally, however, it is from this love that penitential sorrow flows. The penitent laments, not the injury sin has inflicted on him or herself, but the pain it has caused to the Love that loves us; and in the end we grieve for our sin because it created a situation which God could resolve only by sacrificing his own Son. It is our sense of this love, in all its extravagance, that drives the Christian life: 'I live by faith in the Son of God, who loved me and gave himself for me' (Gal. 2:20).

Vicarious humanity

Some Christian thinkers, however, have not been content to speak only of the vicarious repentance of Christ, but have gone on to speak of his 'vicarious

---

32. Shorter Catechism, Answer 87.

humanity' and even of his 'inclusive humanity'. The most distinguished exponent of this development has been the Scottish theologian, T. F. Torrance, aided and abetted by his brother, J. B. Torrance. Both were ardent admirers of Campbell, and both were driven by an animus against not only federal theology and 'Westminster Calvinism', but against what they saw as the legalist tendency endemic in Western theology since Tertullian and Augustine.[33]

T. F. Torrance used the ancient Christological concept of the 'impersonal' (*anhypostatic*) humanity of Jesus to convey the idea that he was not only *a man* but *man*. Not only did Christ possess a true and complete humanity (a human mind as well as a human body), and not only was he the federal head of humanity, representing other human beings in some external sense, he *was* humanity, onto-logically one with us. He included the whole race in himself, so that in him it was not a man, but Mankind, who obeyed and suffered. This is what J. B. Torrance appears to mean by the 'inclusive humanity of Christ': Jesus was 'not only a man but *the Man* in whom God has given *himself* to the world and for the world'.[34] Human nature as such, humanity in its entirety, humanity in its essence, acted and atoned in him, the God-man.

One immediate problem with this is that it leads, logically, to universalism, but we are not allowed to draw this conclusion (and Torrance himself does not draw it) because it savours of what he deplores as 'the logic of causal relations' which has bedevilled Western theology. The Apostle Paul, however, had no such aversion to logical inference: witness his wholesale use of the word 'therefore'. It would seem fair to infer that if humanity inclusively fully redeemed itself in the inclusive humanity of Christ, then humanity inclusively is fully redeemed. If the conclusion is unacceptable, the premise that leads to it should be abandoned.

There are, however, deeper problems. Humanity is an abstraction, the essence of human beings, but the essence as such does not *exist*, any more than the 'form' (Gk *morphē*) of something exists. Christ took the form of a servant (Phil. 2:7), but it was not that form that became 'obedient to death' (Phil. 2:8), but the man Jesus, the Servant of the Lord. By the same token, it was not the essence of humanity, or humanity inclusively, that said 'amen!' to God's condemnation on the cross of Calvary, but Jesus, 'Mary's boy', the fruit of her womb: united

---

33. See especially T. F. Torrance, 'Karl Barth and the Latin Heresy', *Scottish Journal of Theology* 39, no 4 (1986), pp. 461–482.

34. James B. Torrance, 'The Vicarious Humanity of Christ', in Thomas F. Torrance (ed.), *The Incarnation: Ecumenical Studies in the Nicene-Constantinopolitan Creed* (Edinburgh: Handsel Press, 1981), p. 140.

to her by the umbilical cord, but not including even her in his own humanity. His work will avail for her only if she believes in it.

Human nature as such cannot think, feel, will, decide or act. It can do so only in individual human beings. Jesus did not give humanity for us: he gave *himself* (Gal. 2:20). To universalize his humanity, portraying him not as a man, but as Everyman, is to destroy his humanity. There is indeed community of nature between Christ's humanity and ours, and this is clearly reflected in the language of the Formula of Chalcedon, which declared him 'consubstantial [*homoousios*] with the Father according to the Godhead, and consubstantial with us according to the Manhood'. But there is a vital difference between the sense in which the Son is *homoousios* with the Father and the sense in which he is *homoousios* with us. The unity between the Son and the Father is numerical: they are one being. The unity between Jesus and us is merely generic: the same in kind. The Father and the Son are not two gods, but Jesus and I are distinct beings. It is impossible, by any sleight of language, to collapse this distinction to the point where my being is included in his. He is my representative, and his righteousness is imputed to me, but it is imputed to me as the righteousness of another (*iustitia aliena*). His obedience was no more my personal obedience than the sin of Adam was my personal sin.

Alongside the idea of 'inclusive humanity' lies the idea of 'incarnational and atoning union'.[35] In traditional Christian thinking, the incarnation was in order to make atonement: the Son of God became man in order to give his life a ransom for many. In this new thinking, however, the incarnation is a key part of the atonement, leading to the idea of 'incarnational redemption': 'we are sanctified in the purity of his Incarnation through union with him in his humanity' and 'this perfect purity of our nature in his Person covers our impurity'.[36] But, again, the meaning is far from clear. It may mean that God's act of uniting himself to human nature was an affirmation of his nature as a loving and merciful Father who has already forgiven us and is already at peace with us. Alternatively, it may mean that the union of the divine and the human in Christ was itself the reconciling act, the two natures coexisting and concurring in the one being. What is clear, however, is that according to the idea of incarnational redemption, God, in the very moment of the incarnation, acts on the human nature he takes, and transforms it. He sanctifies and heals it.

---

35. Thomas F. Torrance, *The Mediation of Christ* (Grand Rapids: Eerdmans, 1983), p. 98.
36. Thomas F. Torrance, *Scottish Theology: From John Knox to John McLeod Campbell* (Edinburgh: T&T Clark, 1996), pp. 57, 56.

This is put at its most dramatic by James Torrance:

> Christ does not heal us by standing over against us, diagnosing our sickness,
> prescribing medicine for us to take, and then going away, to leave us to get better by
> obeying his instructions – as an ordinary doctor might. No, He becomes the patient!
> He assumes that very humanity which is in need of redemption, and by being
> anointed by the Spirit in our humanity, by a life of perfect obedience, by dying and
> rising again, for us, our humanity is healed *in him*.[37]

At the heart of this construction lies the highly problematical idea that Christ took not merely a true and complete human nature, but *fallen* human nature. The word 'fallen' has a well-established use in Christian theology. Applied to the first Adam, it means that he 'fell' from his original state of righteousness; applied to us, it means that we are born in a state of original sin, morally and spiritually corrupt. Torrance makes plain that this is not the sense in which he applies the term 'fallen' to Christ, the Last Adam. He never fell, and he knew no sin. But if that is the case, then human nature as individualized in him was not fallen. He did not suffer from the disease. In what sense, then, did he heal the nature by taking the disease? As Christ faced temptation and suffering, he did so with a mind unclouded by sin, undistracted by lust, and totally at one with the mind of God. He was whole, and though he took the guilt of sin and shared in the misery it brought upon his brothers and sisters (Heb. 2:17), he never contracted the contagion, disease or corruption of sin. He heals sinners, and that is his glory, but he does not do it by descending into the 'ontological depths of humanity' and making sin part of his own being. He does it by his atoning sacrifice which restores our communion with God and secures for us the ministry of the Holy Spirit; and he, in turn, leads us in our campaign to mortify sin, till at last we are as pure as God himself is pure (1 John 3:3).

There remains the problem that there is absolutely no empirical evidence that the incarnational union healed and sanctified humanity. Human nature after Bethlehem, and even after Calvary, remains the same as it was before. Indeed, if Christ healed our humanity by taking it, we end up with the fascinating paradox that he was crucified by the very nature he had healed. The reality is that the sanctifying has simply not taken place. Humanity is still dead in transgressions and sins (Eph. 2:1), which means that, despite all that may be said of Christ's 'inclusive humanity', human beings are still gratifying the cravings

---

37. J. B. Torrance, 'The Vicarious Humanity of Christ', p. 141. Cf. T. F. Torrance, *The Mediation of Christ*, p. 94.

of their sinful nature, still separated from Christ, still without God and still without hope (Eph. 2:3–12).

Oddly enough, what is offered to us in this idea of the vicarious, inclusive humanity of Christ is a mirror-image of what was set forth historically in the orthodox doctrine of the union between the first Adam and his descendants. According to that doctrine, Adam was the representative of all mankind, and the whole human race therefore sinned in him and fell with him. But he was also the *root* of all mankind,[38] and through natural procreation he transmitted to all his descendants a sinful and sickly nature. Now, it is suggested, the work of Christ offers a close parallel. He is ontologically united to humanity and imparts to them the holiness and purity of his own human nature. The problem is that while the depravity we inherit from Adam stares us in the face, the holiness flowing from Christ does not. Human existence is still marred by endemic, universal and structural sin.

The idea of Christ as the physician becoming the patient has also fostered a whole new interpretation of Paul's statement in Romans 8:3, where he refers to sin being condemned in the flesh. According to T. F. Torrance, this means, first, that the sin referred to is the sickness that Christ took; secondly, that it was Christ himself who condemned it; and, thirdly, that he condemned it by saying 'no' to the flesh and living, instead, a life of perfect faith, worship and obedience.

This takes Paul's idea completely out of the sphere of Calvary. The condemnation of sin did not take place on the cross, but in the daily life of Jesus. Yet in the apostle's original statement it is not Jesus, but God the Father, who condemns sin in the flesh; and while it was indeed in the flesh of his Son that God condemned sin, it was not merely in his Son as incarnate, but in his Son as a sin offering. It was precisely in this capacity that God sent him: *peri hamartias*, a sin offering. God condemned sin not merely by excluding it from his own incarnate life, but by passing judgment on his Son, who bore our sin to the cross. Because he bore it, he became an accursed thing (Gal. 3:13); and because he became an accursed thing, we are free.

Yet salvation in the full sense does include the total transformation and healing of human nature: a point made with remarkable lack of qualification in 2 Peter 1:4, which speaks of our participating in the divine nature. This is what the Greek Fathers spoke of as *theōsis* (lit., God-making),[39] but it is not

---

38. Westminster Confession, 6:3.

39. See, for example, Athanasius, *The Incarnation of the Word of God*, 54 (p. 93): 'He, indeed, assumed humanity that we might become God.' Cf. his *First Discourse against*

fundamentally different from what St Paul meant by our being conformed
to the image of his Son (Rom. 8:29), or Jesus' promise to give us the very glory
the Father has given him (John 17:22).

But three things must be borne in mind.

First, this *theōsis* is not some direct result of the incarnational union of divinity
and humanity in the person of Christ. It is the result, according to Peter, of the
fact that his divine power has given us all we need for the life of godliness (2 Pet.
1:3); and far from being a transformation of human nature as such, it is limited
to those who share the apostle's faith (2 Pet. 1:1) and who strive to make their
calling and election sure (2 Pet. 1:10).

Secondly, this *theōsis* is not the reason for God being reconciled to us. We are
justified as 'ungodly' (Rom. 4:5), not as partakers of a 'nature' which has already
been ennobled by union with the divine.

Thirdly, *theōsis* is not immediate and instantaneous, as if it took place the very
moment the Son of God united himself to our nature. On the contrary it is the
outcome of a life-long war between the Spirit and the flesh (Gal. 5:17). Only as
God builds us up do we attain 'the whole measure of the fullness of Christ'
(Eph. 4:13).

The most complicated part of Torrance's construction still remains, however:
the role played by the vicarious, inclusive humanity of Christ in our human
response to the grace of God. Torrance insisted, quite rightly, that both the
active and passive obedience of Christ were essential to the work of atonement;
and this active obedience included the whole of his human history from the
moment he assumed our nature (at his conception) to the moment he reassumed
his body (at the resurrection). During his earthly life Jesus was, clearly, a believer,
trusting implicitly in his Father, and, equally clearly, he was a worshipper,
thanking his Father for his every mercy, including his mercy towards the
messianic community he represented. But Torrance goes beyond this and argues
that not only did Christ save us: he also offered in our place a total response
to that salvation. He repented for us, believed for us, was born again for us, was
converted for us and worships for us.

---

the Arians, 39 (NPNF, Second Series, vol. IV): 'Therefore He was not man, and then
became God, but He was God, and then became man, and that to deify us.' Calvin's
comment on the passage is striking, bordering on the incredulous: 'indeed, it is, so
to speak, a kind of deification.' (*The Epistle of Paul The Apostle to the Hebrews and the
First and Second Epistles of St Peter*, tr. William B. Johnston, ed. David W. Torrance and
Thomas F. Torrance, Calvin's New Testament Commentaries [Grand Rapids:
Eerdmans, 1994], p. 331).

Even allowing for Torrance's penchant for paradox this is a challenging innovation. He himself loved to tell the following story:

> During my first week of office as Moderator of the General Assembly of the Church
> of Scotland when I presided at the Assembly's Gaelic Service, a highlander asked me
> whether I was born again, and when I replied in the affirmative he asked when I had been
> born again. I still recall his face when I told him that I had been born again when Jesus
> Christ was born of the Virgin Mary and rose again from the virgin tomb, the first-born
> from the dead. When he asked me to explain I said: 'This Tom Torrance you see is full of
> corruption, but the real Tom Torrance is hid with Christ in God and will be revealed only
> when Jesus Christ comes again. He took my corrupt humanity in his Incarnation,
> sanctified, cleansed and redeemed it, giving it new birth, in his death and resurrection.'[40]

In other words, as Torrance himself went on to explain further, our new birth, our regeneration, our conversion, has taken place in Jesus Christ himself, and when we speak of our own conversion we are really referring to our sharing in the conversion which he brought about in humanity: 'we must think of him as taking our place even in our acts of repentance and personal decision'.[41]

It is easy to understand the Highlander's jaw dropping. Even allowing that Christ stood as our representative before a gracious and forgiving God, there were things he could not do with them or for them because there was one great discontinuity between him and them: they were sinners and he was not. He could not personally trust in God's forgiveness because he had no need of it; could not be born again because he required no change of heart; and could not be converted because his life demanded no change of direction. For all his identification with humanity, at the heart of his every communication with his Father there lay the fundamental distinction between '*my* Father and *your* Father, *my* God and *your* God' (John 20:17). There was a unique ontological unity between Jesus and his Father (and the Holy Spirit) and that unity made it impossible (and undesirable) to replicate in *his* life every aspect of ours.

The question of the vicarious humanity of Christ becomes even more complicated when we move from the idea of Jesus as a believer to the idea of Jesus as the one who is believed *in* (the object of faith). Does he believe, vicariously, in himself? Here Torrance offers a peculiar interpretation of Galatians 2:20, 'I live by faith in the Son of God'. In the original, the phrase, 'the Son of God', is in the genitive case, and the grammatically literal translation would be, 'by

---

40. Torrance, *The Mediation of Christ*, pp. 95–96.
41. Ibid., p. 96.

faith *of* the Son of God'. The question, as in many similar cases, is whether the genitive is subjective or objective. Does it refer to the faith Jesus had, or the faith of which he is the object? Torrance takes it as a subjective genitive: we live by the faith which Jesus had (and has).[42] The consensus among commentators, however, is that this is an objective genitive 'expressing the object of the faith',[43] and this certainly seems to be what the context requires. The whole tenor of the passage points to the moral and spiritual change which has taken place in the believer, and this is emphasized by Paul's use of the preposition 'in'. Faith in Christ, not faith in the law, is the atmosphere in which the believer lives: the orientation of her whole existence.

When we move away from Galatians 2:20, it becomes unmistakeably clear that Christ is the object of faith. Indeed, it is clear in verse 16 of this very chapter itself, where, once again, Paul uses the phrase, '[the] faith of Christ Jesus', and immediately clarifies his meaning: 'we, too, have put our faith in Christ Jesus'. Clearly, it is the believer's own action that is in view ('we believed'), and the word for 'in' is *eis*, which could be translated 'into': 'we believed into Christ'. Other key New Testament passages likewise portray Christ not as a vicarious believer, but as the one believed *in*. In Acts 16:31, for example, Paul and Silas respond to the jailer's anguished question, 'Sirs, what must I do to be saved?' with the emphatic message, 'Believe in [*epi,* upon] the Lord Jesus, and you will be saved'. The Apostle John is equally unambiguous: 'This is his command: to believe in the name of his Son, Jesus Christ' (1 John 3:23).

It is possible, and even likely, that Christ had faith in himself, even though he had no personal need of the work which he performed for sinners. But the faith emphasized in the New Testament is *our* faith: faith in him, faith into him, faith upon him. It is also faith in the whole Christ: God and man; prophet, priest and king; active and passive obedience. But above all, it is faith in the core message of the apostolic tradition, 'Christ died for our sins' (1 Cor. 15:3). It is

---

42. Even if the phrase be taken as an objective genitive the most likely interpretation would not be that we are saved by the *faith* of Christ, but that we are saved by his *faithfulness.*

43. Ernest De Witt Burton, *A Critical and Exegetical Commentary on the Epistle to the Galatians* (Edinburgh: T&T Clark, 1921), p. 139. Cf. Hans Dieter Betz, *Galatians* (Philadelphia: Fortress Press, 1979), p. 125; James D. G. Dunn, *A Commentary on the Epistle to the Galatians* (London: A & C Black, 1993), p. 146; Ronald Y. K. Fung, *The Epistle to the Galatians* (Grand Rapids: Eerdmans, 1988), p. 124. C. E. B. Cranfield, in his comment on the same phrase in Romans 3:2, dismisses as 'altogether unconvincing' the suggestion that it should be understood as a subjective genitive (*Romans,* p. 203).

through this faith that we experience the atoning power of his blood (Rom. 3:25); or, as John puts it, only those who believe 'in him' will have eternal life (John 3:16). However much, then, we give thanks for the life of Christ, and for his faithfulness, and even for his faith, it is in the cross of Christ that faith glories; and this is not a faith which someone else, even Christ, can exercise for us, vicariously. It has to be *my* faith, with all its weaknesses and fluctuations, and all its own great need of forgiveness and cleansing: not Christ believing for me, or Christ believing within me, but I myself believing, just as surely as the life I now live by faith in the Son of God is my life, and not his.

But what is the relation of this faith, my faith, to the faith of Jesus, and indeed to Jesus himself? Clearly (and Torrance does stress this) his faith does not dispense with the need for my faith. Equally, however, my faith has no intrinsic worth of its own. It is weak, sometimes in abeyance ('Where is your faith?' Jesus once asked the disciples, Luke 8:25) and always tainted with sin. This means that we can never put our faith in our own faith. Does it also mean that the deficiencies of our faith must be covered by the perfection of Christ's faith? Possibly, to a degree, but only insofar as Jesus' faith is itself an element in his total obedience. This cannot detract, however, from the fact that the central, decisive element in his atoning work was his death. The blood covers the deficiencies of our faith as it covers the deficiencies of all else. Galatians 2:20 is itself sufficient to remind us of that. Our faith is not in the Son of God who *believed for us*, but in the Son of God *who gave himself for us*: 'God forbid that I should glory, save in the cross of our Lord Jesus Christ' (Gal. 6:14, KJV).

But it is also true that of ourselves we are incapable of believing. Faith is a divine gift. Yet the gift is not Christ's faith offered to us in place of our own, nor is it a gift we possess simply because as part of Christ's inclusive humanity we are included in his believing and trusting; nor, again, is it ours as a result of an ontological union between ourselves and Jesus, as if we were one being with him. It is a gift because the life and death of Jesus secured for us the ministry of the Holy Spirit, who produces faith within us by bearing witness to Jesus in the depths of our fallen human hearts. As we have already noted from Augustine, the Spirit gives us the faith which he commands us to have.[44] It is his gift, yet it is also my free decision, stamped with my personality and marked by time, place and circumstance. The mystery is (and it is even more of a mystery if we believe that Christ had a vicarious and inclusive humanity) that the gift is not given to all. St Paul had it, but the only explanation he can offer is that God 'set me apart from my mother's womb, and called me by his grace' (Gal. 1:15).

---

44. Augustine, *Confessions*, X: xxix.

10. REDEMPTION: SETTING THE PRISONERS FREE

With the concept of redemption we move to consider the effect of the cross on sinners. Not surprisingly it permeates the New Testament, but whereas the concepts of expiation, propitiation and reconciliation are each linked to one specific word-group, the concept of redemption is conveyed by means of a much wider and more vivid range of terminology.[1]

The most basic of these terms is the verb *lyō*, with the primary meaning 'loose' or 'set free from bonds'. Associated with this are the compound form, *apolytroō*, and the corresponding noun, *apolytrōsis*, both of which suggest the idea of 'release on payment of a ransom'; and the ransom itself is denoted by the term, *lytron*, the means or price of deliverance and liberation.

Secondly, there is the verb, *agorazō*, 'I buy'. This is linked to the *agora*, the marketplace, and describes redemption in terms of purchase. Here, again, the idea is intensified by a compound form, *exagorazō*, 'I buy back'. The Latin equivalent is *redimere*, whence the English 'redeem' and 'redemption'. The interesting thing with regard to these verbs is their deployment in connection with

---

1. For helpful introductions see B. B. Warfield, 'The New Testament Terminology of Redemption', in *The Person and Work of Christ* (Philadelphia: Presbyterian and Reformed, 1950), pp. 429–478; and Morris, *The Apostolic Preaching of the Cross*, pp. 9–59.

the liberation or manumission of slaves. Such manumission had to be purchased, either by the slave himself or by a benefactor, and for this there was a clearly recognized procedure. The money was paid to a god (by being deposited in his temple), and when the appropriate sum had been fully lodged it was handed over to the slave-owner; the slave became the property of the god, and he was therefore 'free of all men'.[2]

The third basic verb is *eleutheroō*, 'set free'. In secular usage this, too, was closely linked to the emancipation of slaves, and the emancipation itself turned the slave into an *eleutheros*, a free man. The Christian is similarly free: 'It is for freedom that Christ has set us free. Stand firm, then, and do not let yourselves be burdened again by a yoke of slavery' (Gal. 5:1).

These three verbs have a generally negative connotation: to loose from, to buy back from, to liberate from. The fourth verb, *peripoieomai* (middle voice) is emphatically positive, meaning 'I buy for myself' or 'I make my own'. The redeemed sinner is now the property of the Saviour who bought her, and can say, in the language of the Heidelberg Catechism, Answer 1: 'I, with body and soul, both in life and in death, am not my own, but belong to my faithful Saviour, Jesus Christ.'

Running through this terminology is a constant theme: bondage and liberation. Humanity is enslaved, and Christ has come to set it free. The Old Testament provides its own paradigm, the exodus: 'I will redeem you,' said the Lord, 'with an outstretched arm and with mighty acts of judgment' (Exod. 6:6). Similar language occurs in Deuteronomy 7:8, where Moses speaks of the Lord redeeming Israel from the land of slavery; and centuries later, Isaiah comforts Israel with the words, 'Do not fear, for I have redeemed you; I have summoned you by name; you are mine' (Isa. 43:1). Such expressions abound in the Old Testament, and the comparison between the work of Christ and the deliverance from Egypt is reinforced by, for example, the portrayal of Christ as the Passover Lamb (1 Cor. 5:7) and as the rock which accompanied the church in its journey through the wilderness (1 Cor. 10:4). Heaven is compared to Canaan (Heb. 4:8–11), and Jesus described as a prophet like Moses (Acts 3:22).

The exodus paradigm throws into clear relief the idea of redemption as an act of divine deliverance. Life in Egypt meant not only forced labour and slavery, but a world of enforced idolatry and blasphemy, and of subjection to a reign of terror under an oppressor bent on genocide (Exod. 1:16). From such bondage the Jews could never have delivered themselves. Yahweh himself had to come

2. See William Barclay, *New Testament Words* (London: SCM Press, 1964), p. 191.

down to rescue them (Exod. 3:8). From this point of view, the redemption from Egypt is the supreme Old Testament demonstration of the power of God. Yet, running through the narrative there is also what Geerhardus Vos called a clear 'expiatory strand': 'Grace could not, notwithstanding its sovereignty, be exercised without an accompanying atonement.'[3] This appears clearly in the inauguration of the Passover. On the night when all the first-born males of Egypt were to die, every Israelite household was to sacrifice a lamb and sprinkle its blood on the doorposts and lintels of their home. 'The blood,' said the Lord, 'will be a sign for you on the houses where you are; and when I see the blood, I will pass over you' (Exod. 12:13) Behind the blood all Israel's first-born were secure. Otherwise, they, too, would have been destroyed.

God did more, however, than deliver his people from Egypt. He brought them to Canaan, the Promised Land. This was not, as modern Liberation Theology suggests, a merely earthly utopia from which political oppression, exploitation of the poor, and structural injustice had all been banished. These things mattered, of course; indeed, they mattered enormously, not least because God himself loves justice and laid down stringent regulations with regard to the rights of the alien, the widow, the orphan and the needy (Exod. 22:21–27). But the real hope, which Canaan merely prefigured, was of a heavenly country; and the wealth of that country consisted not of milk and honey, but of 'every spiritual blessing in the heavenly places' (Eph. 1:3, ESV). The biblical concept of redemption never held out the promise of rest or freedom in this world. The exodus and the Promised Land, impressive and suggestive though they are, were but a pale shadow of a world-embracing redemption which would be consummated only when the first heaven and the first earth had passed away (Rev. 21:1).

Redemption from sin

At its most generic and comprehensive, redemption consists of deliverance from sin. It was for such a redemption that the Apostle John gave thanks in the great opening doxology of Revelation: 'To him who loves us and has freed us from our sins by his blood, and has made us to be a kingdom and priests to serve his God and Father – to him be glory and power for ever and ever! Amen' (Rev. 1:5–6). The verb rendered 'freed' is the aorist participle of *lyein*, to loose,

---

3. Geerhardus Vos, *Biblical Theology: Old and New Testaments* (Grand Rapids: Eerdmans, 1959), pp. 134–135.

and its use here presupposes that we were slaves of sin.[4] The same word is used in its literal sense in John's account of the raising of Lazarus, who emerged from the tomb still bound in his grave clothes. 'Loose him, and let him go,' said Jesus (John 11:44, KJV).

In Ephesians 1:7, we find the compound form, *apolytrōsis*, and its meaning is clarified by the addition of an explanatory phrase: 'In him we have redemption through his blood, the forgiveness of sins.' The word for forgiveness is from the verb *aphiēmi*, which has the primary sense of dismissing or sending away. If on the one hand redemption means being loosed from sin, on the other it means being separated from sin, and this imagery accords well with the symbolism of the scapegoat, which carried the sins of Israel away into the desert. It also agrees with John the Baptist's reference (John 1:29) to Jesus bearing away the sin of the world, and again with the language of Peter, when he speaks of Jesus carrying our sins in his own body to the tree (1 Pet. 2:24). But the most vivid imagery with regard to forgiveness occurs in Micah 7:19, where God, incomparable as a pardoning God, is described as hurling all our iniquities into the depths of the sea. 'Buried at sea' might be sin's final epitaph.

But if redemption from sin is the generic idea, what are the details?

First of all, redemption means deliverance from liability to punishment. This point is made most graphically in St Paul's letter to the Galatians: 'Christ redeemed us from the curse of the law' (Gal. 3:13). As is often pointed out, Paul refrains from writing, 'the curse of God', calling it simply the curse of the *law*. However, God is the lawgiver, and it is he who has pronounced a curse on sin: 'Cursed is everyone who does not continue to do everything written in the Book of the Law' (Gal. 3:10). These words are a direct quotation from Deuteronomy 27:26, but in Jeremiah 11:3 almost identical words are attributed to the Lord himself: 'Tell them that this is what the LORD, the God of Israel says: "Cursed is the one who does not obey the terms of this covenant".' Here, Yahweh does not distance himself from the curse. Indeed, it is the fact that it is the curse of a personal God rather than of an impersonal law that makes redemption possible. Not the least awesome part of the original statement is that the curse is pronounced not on the sinner who has violated the *whole* law, but on the sinner who has violated the least part of it. The law is inexorable. It requires complete and perpetual obedience, and pronounces a curse on the slightest infringement:

---

4. Many later manuscripts (and several early versions) have the reading *lousanti*, which would give the meaning, 'to him who *washed* us from our sins'. The reasons for preferring the reading *lysanti* are briefly summarized in Metzger, *A Textual Commentary on the Greek New Testament*, p. 729.

'For whoever keeps the whole law and yet stumbles at just one point is guilty of breaking all of it' (Jas 2:10).

This may seem draconian, but even in modern society individuals find themselves with a 'criminal record' not only when they commit a major crime, but when they commit even a minor offence. At a more solemn level, the doom pronounced on sin is one with which the enlightened conscience has no quarrel. To be a sinner is to be accursed, and to be accursed is to be devoted to destruction.

The symbol of this accursedness, says Paul in Galatians 3:13, citing Deuteronomy 21:23, is the cross: 'Cursed is everyone who is hanged on a tree' (ESV). We cannot, however, reduce the idea of the accursedness of Christ to the fact that he was nailed to a tree. He was not cursed because he was hanged. He was hanged because he was cursed: under a divine imprecation as the one who was carrying the sin of the world. Indeed, he *was* the sin of the world (2 Cor. 5:21).

But here, too, we need to be careful. We cannot enter into what Christ suffered by merely examining the word *katara* (curse). Instead, we have to deduce the meaning of *katara* from what Christ suffered. He died the death which sin deserves, but it was more than mere death as we understand it. It was what Paul elsewhere calls death with a 'sting' (1 Cor. 15:56): not simply the separation of soul and body, but the black hole of separation from God and abandonment by his Heavenly Father; the overwhelming sense of being 'sin', naked and unprotected, in the presence of the Holy. It was the descent into hell, which, contemplated in Gethsemane, almost unmanned him. It was the abyss, the absolute zero, of his *kenosis*. In his own eyes, he was forsaken; in human eyes, he was a reject; in God's eyes, he was such as the divine could not look on or listen to or deliver.

It was from this that Christ redeemed us, so that we shall never suffer what our sins deserve or stand where he stood or descend to the depths and darkness he had to endure. What should have been our end, he made his.

Yet this redemption from the punishment due to sin was not an end in itself. It was in order for something else: 'that the blessing given to Abraham might come to the Gentiles through Jesus Christ, so that by faith we might receive the promise of the Spirit' (Gal. 3:14). This is the redemption *to* that corresponds to the redemption *from*, and it highlights once again the organic link between the forensic and the ontological. The cross secures not only a change of status but a change of heart. It puts us right with God, and it puts us right. We are, indeed, not forgiven on the basis of being 'spiritual', but the ultimate goal of the removal of the curse is that we should receive the Holy Spirit and experience him as a Spirit of empowerment and transformation. Wherever there is forgiveness, communion with God is restored, and wherever communion is restored spiritual recovery begins, to be completed at last by our being conformed to the image of God's own Son (Rom. 8:29).

This link between redemption and transformation is equally clear in Titus 2:14: Christ 'gave himself for us to redeem us from all wickedness and to purify for himself a people that are his very own, eager to do what is good'. Here, what we are redeemed from is not merely the curse due to sin, but sin in the widest possible sense (*anomia*, lawlessness). But closely linked to this is the idea of purification. The redemption is in order to a *katharsis*, and those who experience it are distinguished by their zeal for good (lit., 'beautiful') works. This is not simply a matter of moral influence, as if our purity were no more than our grateful response to redemption. Purity is the object of redemption, secured and provided by the cross itself. Christ gave himself in order that we should be purified. This is reminiscent of Paul's language in Ephesians 5:25–27, where he speaks of Christ giving himself for the church precisely in order to cleanse and wash her, till at last she is radiant, holy and blameless. Sin is pollution as well as guilt, and the redeemed have to bathe in 'the washing of rebirth and renewal' (Titus 3:5) as well as be sprinkled with the blood (1 Pet. 1:2). The renewal, no less than the sprinkling, was part of God's design from the beginning. Indeed, it was the ultimate objective. There must be no disjunction between the forensic and the transformational.

Redemption from the dominion of darkness

Another aspect of redemption *from* is highlighted in Colossians 1:13: 'He has rescued us from the dominion of darkness and brought us into the kingdom of the Son he loves.' It is important to note that the agent referred to here is not Christ, but God the Father; the one to whom we are said in verse 12 to offer joyful thanks (*eucharistoun*). It is he who has rescued us, and what he has rescued us from is the dominion or authority of darkness. This clearly presupposes that in our unredeemed state darkness controlled us. In Ephesians 5:8 Paul even goes so far as to say that we *were* darkness. He uses similar language in Acts 26:18, where he describes the aim of his evangelistic preaching as being to turn the Gentiles 'from darkness to light, and from the power of Satan to God'. The power of darkness is the power of Satan, and the apostle's language reminds us that the dark and satanic not only influence, but control, us. They hold us in thrall, as slaves and subjects of an organized and coherent empire of evil. But God has made an incursion into this enemy territory, and rescued us.

So far, however, the passage contains no explicit reference to the idea of redemption. Yet there is a clear link. God has not only rescued us from the dominion of darkness, he has transported us into the kingdom of 'the Son he loves' (lit. 'the Son of his love', Col. 1:13), and that kingdom is emphatically a kingdom of the redeemed, because in that Son we have 'redemption, the forgiveness of sins' (Col. 1:14). The rescue, the relocation and the redemption are all of a piece, the forgiveness of sins inseparable from the deliverance from the darkness.

It is this same doctrine that Paul sets forth, though in different terminology, in Romans 6. Here the stress falls not on the cross as such, but on our union with the crucified Christ. This union, the apostle insists, secures not only forgiveness and justification, but our death to sin (Rom. 6:3). Christ, though without sin, once lived in the realm of sin. Now he lives in it no longer. He died to it on the cross, and in the resurrection he rose to a new life. This pattern is replicated in believers. They can no longer live in sin (Rom. 6:2), because they are united to the crucified Christ, and in his death sin lost its authority over them as surely as it did over him. They are no longer its slaves. Instead, united to the risen Christ they have been freed or justified (*dedikaiōtai*, v. 7) from sin and live a new life in which sin no longer has mastery over them. To enlist their faculties in its service would now be a betrayal of their new master (Rom. 6:13).

In all these passages the stress falls on the negative aspect of redemption, emphasizing what we have been redeemed *from*: the punishment due to sin, the pollution of sin, enslavement to sin. But through all of them there also runs a clear positive strain. Redemption means that we receive the Spirit of promise, that we become Christ's people, that we are relocated into his kingdom and that our lives are raised to a new spiritual level. This positive emphasis becomes even clearer in such a passage as Acts 20:28, where Paul gives his solemn charge to the elders of the church in Ephesus: 'Be shepherds of the church of God, which he bought with his own blood.'[5] The verb *periepoiēsato* ('bought') conveys the idea of 'making one's own'. This is the motivation Paul offers to the Ephesian elders: God has bought the church for himself, he has paid for it with his own blood, and to pastor it is both an awesome responsibility and a breathtaking privilege.

What is true of the church as a whole is equally true of each individual believer: 'You are not your own; you were bought at a price' (1 Cor. 6:19–20). The church is the new Israel, God's very special people. This is brought out with particular force and beauty in 1 Peter, a letter addressed to people who,

---

5. As the NIV margin points out, many manuscripts have the alternative reading 'the church of the Lord [*kyriou*]'. See Metzger, *A Textual Commentary on the Greek New Testament*, pp. 480–481.

though they were God's elect, were stateless aliens scattered throughout the provinces of Asia Minor. In human terms, they were 'not a people' (1 Pet. 2:10), but now they are the people of God: elect, royal, priestly and holy, called into being in order to proclaim the virtues of the God who had called them (1 Pet. 2:9). Paul strikes a similar note in Ephesians 2:11–22. Once complete outsiders as far as God's family was concerned, the Ephesians have now been brought in to enjoy full citizenship in the divine commonwealth and full membership in the family of God. Nor is this family some small homogeneous unit. It is a multitude too vast to count (Rev. 7:9), transcending all distinctions of nationality, race, language, class and gender; and within this family every barrier erected by ancient hatreds and religious pride has been broken down. Even the age-old boundary-markers between Jews and Gentiles have been demolished (Eph. 2:14–18).

Emancipation and freedom

But as God's one, worldwide kingdom, they are also God's children, and this introduces yet another aspect of the Christian understanding of redemption. It means emancipation and freedom. Peter refers to this in 1 Peter 1:18. The blood of Christ, he says, has redeemed you from 'the empty way of life handed down to you from your ancestors'. Whether Jews or Gentiles, Peter's original readers had all been victims of onerous and futile religious traditions: in thrall to priests, rituals, superstitions and taboos. But the blood of Christ had ransomed them from all that, and now the only rite of purification is obedience to the truth (1 Pet. 1:22).

The full import of this becomes clearer in Paul's extensive treatment of this theme in Galatians 4:1 – 5:1. The key statement is in chapter 4: 'God sent his Son, born of a woman, born under law, to redeem those under law, that we might receive adoption to sonship' (Gal. 4:4–5). Here, the aim and object of redemption is emancipation from the law, but this has two further implications.

First, the redeemed are no longer slaves, forced to gain their master's favour (or at least to avoid the lash) by cringing obedience to endless regulations, whether those of rabbinical law or those of their Gentile equivalents (covered by Paul's word, *stoicheia*, 'the elemental spiritual forces of the world', Gal. 4:3).[6]

---

6. Besides the *stoicheia* of the world there are also God's *stoicheia*. See, for example, Heb. 5:12, 'you need someone to teach you the *elementary truths* of God's word all over again'.

Some of these *stoicheia* were trivial and hair-splitting; others, harsh and oppressive. Whichever, they are no longer the prescribed way to God's favour. The
Christian experiences what no slave ever experienced: grace.

Secondly, the redeemed are no longer minors. As Paul envisages the position
of Jews before the coming of Christ, they were not slaves, but children, and, as
such, heirs to all the promises of God. But they were children under age, and
although they would one day inherit the whole estate, so long as they remained
minors they were no better off than slaves. Indeed, they were actually entrusted
to a slave in the form of a *paidagōgos*, whose duty it was to function as a tutor or
guardian; slave though he was, he had authority over the child. This, as Paul
understood it, was the function of the Torah. It was the *paidagōgos* of the Old
Testament church, put in charge of them till the Messiah should come (Gal. 3:24).

But from this *paidagōgos* Christ has redeemed us. It may seem to us, who have
not experienced it, a small thing. To those who had to live under it, however, the
law was all-present, oppressive and impossible. The cultic requirements involved
daily, weekly, monthly and annual sacrifices; the mandatory fasts and festivals
meant constant disruption; the endless regulations on ritual purity affected even
the minutest details of life; and on all this the rabbis had superimposed their own
huge corpus of additional regulations. No wonder that Peter, addressing the
Council of Jerusalem, described the Law as a 'yoke that neither we nor our
ancestors have been able to bear' (Acts 15:10)! And Jesus, doubtless, had this
very yoke in mind when he extended the great invitation recorded in Matthew
11:28, 'Come to me, all you who are weary and burdened, and I will give you rest.'

Now, with the coming of Christ, the church has come of age. He has
redeemed us from both slavery and nonage, and as adults we no longer need a
paidagōgos. Believing Jews and believing Gentiles alike are free from the yoke of
the Torah (and from the 'beggarly elements' prescribed by the ethnic religions).

The problem is, however, that we find it hard to be grown-up, and would
often prefer to live under a regime of micro-regulation (and to impose it on
others). This is what Paul saw among the Galatians: 'How is it that you are
turning back to those weak and miserable forces? Do you wish to be enslaved
by them all over again?' (Gal. 4:9) Too often the answer is, 'Yes!' Being free is
difficult. It brings responsibilities. But then Paul reminds us that our freedom
was dearly bought. Christ subjected himself to the law to which the slaves were
in bondage so that the slaves might go free (Gal. 4:4–5). 'Stand fast therefore
in the liberty wherewith Christ hath made us free,' proclaims the apostle, 'and
be not entangled again with the yoke of bondage' (Gal. 5:1, KJV).

This is the foundation of the Protestant doctrine of Christian liberty, set forth
memorably in chapter 20 of the Westminster Confession: 'God alone is Lord of
the conscience, and hath left it free from the doctrines and commandments

of men which are in any thing contrary to his word; or beside it, if matters of faith or worship.' This does not mean that conscience is autonomous. God is its Lord, and we are bound by every expression of his will. But equally, God alone is its Lord. We are his children, and no-one else has authority to meddle in his family, either by laying down extra-biblical taboos or by imposing rites, rituals and regulations undreamed-of in Scripture. It is, indeed, one of the Father's rules that we are to obey all lawful human authority, lawfully exercised. But when the state forbids what God commands or commands what God forbids, the Christian conscience is not bound; and though we owe due submission to the presbyter-bishops who are 'over us in the Lord' we owe them no allegiance when they try to impose as matters of conscience liturgical and theological traditions for which there is no warrant in Scripture.

The redemption-price

The most important element in the New Testament doctrine of redemption still remains: there is always a redemption-price, and it is always God himself who pays it, in Christ.

This appears clearly even when the word for 'redeem' is the simple verb, *lyein*, to loose. We find it in, for example, Revelation 1:5, where Christ is said to have redeemed (loosed) us from our sins 'by his blood'. The precise phrase John uses is 'in his blood' (*en tō haimati autou*), a common expression for 'at the price of'. In Revelation 5:9 the same phrase is linked to the verb 'to purchase': 'with your blood you purchased for God persons from every tribe and language and people and nation'. The price of our redemption was the slaying of the Lamb.

This idea of cost is intensified in the noun *lytron*. The default meaning of this word, according to Liddell and Scott's *Greek-English Lexicon*, is 'price of release', and this could refer to the release of slaves, hostages, prisoners of war or even debtors.[7] Closely linked to this was the idea of 'ransom'

---

7. Cf. Deissmann's comment, 'when anybody heard the Greek word *lutron* , "ransom", in the first century, it was natural for him to think of the purchase-money for manumitting slaves' (Adolf Deissmann, *Light From The Ancient East: The New Testament Illustrated by Recently Discovered Texts of the Graeco-Roman World*, tr. Lionel R. M. Strachan [London: Hodder and Stoughton, 1910], pp. 331–332). He adds: 'The union of the idea of manumission with the idea of sacrifice was made easier for the ancient Christians by the fact that sacral manumission, *e.g.* at Cos, was not complete without sacrifice' (p. 334).

or 'ransom-money'. One of the most suggestive instances of this concept occurs in Numbers 3:44–50, where Yahweh is laying down instructions for the redeeming of Israel's first-born. In view of the fact that the first-born of Israel had been spared when the Lord struck down all the first-born of Egypt, he claimed all Israel's first-born as exclusively his own. This was modified to the extent that he accepted the Levites in their place, but there remained the problem that there were more first-born than Levites: a short-fall of 273, in fact. These had to be redeemed, and this was to be done by the payment of a redemption-price of five shekels a head: the sum to be paid to Aaron and his sons as *lytra* (LXX) for the ransoming of the first-born.

Jesus himself provides the supreme instance of the New Testament use of *lytron* when he declares, 'Even the Son of Man did not come to be served, but to serve, and to give his life as a ransom [*lytron*] for many' (Mark 10:45). This echoes the language of the greatest of Isaiah's Servant Songs: the Servant, numbered with transgressors, and bearing the sin of many, will pour out his life unto death (Isa. 53:12). The precise import of this is made clear in verse 10, which speaks of Yahweh as making the Servant's life a sin offering (*'āsām*). Read against this background (and the allusions to Isaiah cannot be accidental), Jesus' words in Mark 10:45 clearly imply that his life, precisely because it is offered as a sin offering, is the redemption price of his people: the ransom which secures their deliverance.

In 1 Timothy 2:6 we find the stronger form, *antilytron*: Christ Jesus in his capacity as mediator 'gave himself as a ransom for all people'. The addition of the prefix *anti* would justify the translation 'substitutionary ransom', but even without this refinement the substitutionary element is clear. The redemption price is accepted, the sinner goes free.

In 1 Peter 1:18 we again find the root *lytron*, but this time in the form of the verb, *elytrōthēte*: 'you were redeemed'. In this passage, the idea of price is not only present, but predominates. It was paid, however, not in the ordinary currency of human commerce, or even in the currency of normal diplomacy, but in the extraordinary currency of God's plan of salvation, 'the precious blood of Christ' (1 Pet. 1:19); and this blood was shed not accidentally or even in some ordinary act of martyrdom, but in the solemn liturgical context of sacrifice. Jesus was the sacrificial lamb, 'without blemish or defect'.

The result of the payment of the *lytron* is set forth in the word *apolytrosis*: a very rare word outside the New Testament, but used by the apostolic writers as the standard term for redemption. There is a long history of attempts to show that this word means only deliverance in a general sense, without any reference to a price.[8] However, the core of the word *apolytrōsis* is *lytron*, a ransom, or price of release; the standard meaning of the corresponding verb *apolytroō* in literary Greek is 'release on payment of a ransom'; and in the key New Testament instances of the noun *apolytrōsis* the cost is made unmistakeably clear. There is a specific redemption price, the blood of Christ, as Paul makes clear in, for example, Ephesians 1:7, where he refers to Jesus as the one in whom 'we have redemption through his blood'. The same connection occurs, though less directly, in Romans 3:24–25. Here, redemption (*apolytrōsis*) is the basis of justification, but redemption itself also has an underlying basis, the sacrifice (*hilastērion*) of Christ. As we have seen, there is some debate as to whether we should read 'God presented him as a sacrifice of atonement through faith in his blood' (NIV 1984) or, 'whom God has set forth as a propitiation by his blood, to be received by faith' (ESV). Either way, our redemption came at the price of the blood of Christ, the expiation for our sin.

The same emphasis on a costly redemption appears in Hebrews 9:15. Those who are called receive the promised eternal inheritance only because Christ died 'as a ransom' (*eis apolytrōsin*). This passage highlights both the capacity in which Christ died and the purpose for which he died. He died as 'the mediator of a new covenant', and he died to secure his people's release from transgressions. In this particular context, where the writer is addressing Hebrew Christians, the redemption refers specifically to transgressions of the first or Mosaic covenant, but this can hardly mean that there is one redemption for Jewish sinners and another for Gentiles. Jews had their own troubled consciences and Gentiles theirs, but the one redemption avails for both; and what achieved that redemption, that release, was the death of the Mediator, who obtained eternal redemption by entering the Most Holy Place with his own blood (Heb. 9:12).

Even if we were to take the term *apolytrōsis* as meaning in itself no more than deliverance in some general sense, it is plain that the deliverance which the New Testament envisages is the result of some great, epoch-making event; as to what event that was, there can be no doubt. It was the death of Christ, between the

---

8. See, for example, the discussion of the arguments of Albrecht Ritschl in Warfield's essay, 'The New Testament Terminology of Redemption' (Warfield, *The Person and Work of Christ*, pp. 461–468). Cf. the remarks on *apolytrōsis* in Ernest Best's comment on Ephesians 1:7. Best concedes that in non-biblical Greek it normally has the meaning 'release, e.g. of a prisoner, where a price is paid', but argues that in biblical Greek it usually means only 'deliverance in a general way' (Ernest Best, *A Critical and Exegetical Commentary on Ephesians*, International Critical Commentary [Edinburgh: T&T Clark, 1998], p. 130).

third hour and the ninth hour on Good Friday, just outside Jerusalem: not his teaching, not his example, not the social impact of his message, not the changed lives of his followers, but the sacrificial shedding of his blood as a great, climactic act of worship, obedience and self-surrender. That blood, a great atoning moment the like of which had never occurred before, and which never needed to be repeated, was the price that set the slaves, the prisoners and the doomed, free.

The idea of price is even more prominent in the two remaining redemption-words, *agorazō* and *peripoieomai*. *Agorazō* has the straightforward meaning, 'I buy'. Paul uses it in 1 Corinthians 6:20, and reinforces the idea of purchase by linking it with the word *time*, price: 'You were bought at a price.' The precise price is not specified, but the implication is clear enough, and the result is spelt out clearly. We are not our own, but belong to the one who bought us. The background, again, is the manumission of slaves. As we have seen, the classical practice maintained the fiction that the slave was bought by a deity, became the property of that deity, and thus was no longer the property of his original master. In Christian manumission, the fiction is no longer a fiction. God pays the real redemption price, and the redeemed become his. The point is made explicitly in 2 Peter 2:1: apostates deny the Lord who *bought* them. Here, once again, the verb is *agorazō*, but the word for 'Lord' is not the usual *kyrios*, but *despotēs*, a master, particularly of slaves. Christians do not belong to themselves, but to their *despotēs*, who bought them at a great price. Therefore, to revert to Paul, we must honour God with our bodies (1 Cor. 6:20), and all the more so because of the cognate truth that the Master, by his Spirit, dwells within us (1 Cor. 6:19).

In Galatians 3:13, Paul uses the compound form, *exagorazō*: 'Christ redeemed us from the curse of the law by becoming a curse for us'. The prefix (*ex*) does not seem to add significantly to the meaning, though it may hint at the idea of 'buying *out of*', but *exagorazō*, too, was commonly used of the manumission of slaves. Here in Galatians 3:13 the primary thought, once again, is the idea of deliverance: deliverance from the curse of the law, that is, from the curse due to violations of the law. Paul, probably from reasons of reverent sensitivity, shrinks from describing it as 'the curse of God', but the curse of the law can be none other than the curse pronounced by the lawgiver, and we have already seen enough to be clear that God cannot be distanced from what happened on Calvary: 'it was the LORD's will to crush him and cause him to suffer' (Isa. 53:10).

What stands out, however, is that our deliverance from this curse was secured only at a price. Christ became a curse for us. The nature of that curse cannot be understood abstractly (for example, by scrutinising the word *katara*). It can be understood only from what Christ suffered. The original curse was that if we disobeyed we should certainly die (Gen. 2:17), and Christ certainly suffered that: as the sin-bearer, his life was forfeit. But the curse went deeper than that.

He was crucified 'outside the city gate' (Heb. 13:12), a symbol of his being cut off from the covenant people. He became the ultimate, absolute outsider, whom men must forsake and disown, and whom the Holy City must reject. Above all, he was forsaken by God his Father: delivered up by him, ignored by him, crushed by him, condemned by him. This was the 'hell' (on earth, and in life) into which he descended, the death which he uniquely, had to taste (Heb. 2:9). Nor was this simply the result of his solidarity with us as if, like a soldier in the First World War, he had volunteered to share with others the misery of the trenches. He did not come to share the curse with us, but to deliver us from it; and he delivered us from it by suffering what we shall never suffer. He became the Reprobate One, doomed to dishonour and wrath for our sin; or, as Isaiah says of the Servant, 'the LORD has laid on him the iniquity of us all' (Isa. 53:6) This is the ultimate expression of the principle that 'grace is free, but it is not cheap'. God in Christ bestows his gifts on sinners freely, but the cost was immeasurable. We scarcely dare let our imagination dwell on the paradox that God himself became a *katara* in place of us, enduring himself the curse due to *our* violations of *his* law.

But the price covered not only deliverance from the curse. It also, as we have seen, secured for us, whether Jews or Gentiles, the blessing promised to Abraham (Gal. 3:14). There is a direct link between Christ being made a curse and our receiving the gift of the Holy Spirit, and the link appears even more clearly in Galatians 4:4–5, where Paul once again uses the verb *agorazō*: 'God sent forth his Son, born of woman, born under the law, to redeem [*exagorasē*] those who were under the law, *so that we might receive adoption as sons*' (ESV, italics mine). Here, those who are redeemed are seen as having been originally slaves under the law, and the price paid for their manumission corresponded to that: their redeemer redeemed them by making himself a debtor to the law. But the liberated slave is not simply told that he is now a free man, at liberty to go his own way. He is told that he now belongs to God and will be cared and provided for by him as if he were his very own son or daughter. Nor is this all: the liberated are changed from the inside. The Spirit comes, assuring them of God's love, giving them confidence even in the presence of the Holy, and enabling them to call him not only *kyrie* ('Lord'), but *Abba* ('Father'). All this was paid for on Calvary, and it means that believers must no longer think of themselves as slaves, or go back to the gods they once served, or submit ever again either to the burdens of the Mosaic code or to the 'weak and miserable' taboos of the ethnic religions and rabbinic regulations. They are no longer slaves of a harsh, ungrateful, relentlessly demanding master. Their Father is their only master, and neither circumcision nor uncircumcision matter one iota. All that matters is faith, expressing itself through love (Gal. 5:6).

The idea of price appears equally clearly in the remaining redemption-word, *peripoieomai*, which, as we have seen, means, 'I purchase for myself'. This is the word Paul uses to describe the church in his address to the Ephesian elders. It is 'the church of God, which he bought with his own blood' (Acts 20:28). This is not some vague, general deliverance. It is a purchase, as a result of which the church belongs to God. This is what the pastors must never forget. They have been charged with the care of a flock that belongs to someone else, in this case to God himself; and it belongs to him not merely because he is Lord of all and owns even the cattle on a thousand hills (Ps. 50:10), but because he has bought it, and fully paid for it. How much? His own blood! Specifically, of course, it was the blood of Christ, but although this blood was human blood it was the blood of a divine person, the Son of God, who had taken human nature, and who had, in and through that nature, suffered and died. This is the solemnity of the elders' position. They have the care of people so precious to God that he paid with his blood to make them his own possession. Sometimes they are, indeed, very 'peculiar' people, but even then they are peculiarly *his* people, objects of his extra-special love and concern. Calvin even carries this the length of suggesting that negligent pastors are guilty of sacrilege, 'because they have profaned the blood of the Son of God, and have made useless the redemption acquired by him, as far as they are concerned'.[9]

To whom was the ransom paid?

The New Testament does not directly ask the question, 'to whom was the price paid?' It would certainly have had little patience with the position of Irenaeus who, according to Gustav Aulén, always regarded the ransom as paid to the powers of evil, to death and to the devil.[10] This reflects the danger of 'illegitimate totality transfer', as if we must read into the New Testament concept of ransom every detail of our human usage of the same idea. The New Testament avails itself of the metaphors of ransom and manumission only to highlight two facts: the fact of deliverance and the fact of price. It does not avail itself of other details common to human ransoming, such as negotiation with the

---

9. *The Acts of the Apostles 14-28*, tr. John W. Fraser, ed. David W. Torrance and Thomas F. Torrance, Calvin's New Testament Commentaries (Grand Rapids: Eerdmans, 1995), pp. 183–184.

10. Gustav Aulén, *Christus Victor: An Historical Study of the Three Main Types of the Idea of the Atonement*, tr. A. G. Herbert (London: SPCK, 1965), p. 30.

party holding the hostage, or the identity of the one who to whom the ransom is paid.

Yet we must be equally careful not to reduce the idea of redemption to a mere metaphor. There is a real deliverance, and there is a real price. Besides, there is total clarity as to what the price was. It was the sacrificial self-offering of Christ. But to whom did he offer himself? Again the answer is clear: he 'offered himself unblemished *to God*' (Heb. 9:14, italics mine). This immediately creates a paradox, particularly if we view the atonement as exclusively a divine act: God pays the price of redemption, and God pays it to himself. But a similar paradox applies to every aspect of the atonement. In expiation, God covers our sins from himself; in propitiation, God appeases himself; in reconciliation, God makes peace with himself. Now, in redemption, God himself meets the cost of liberating moral and spiritual debtors; and he pays it to himself, because it is to himself the debt is owed.

But is this not a problem of our own making? Clearly, the divine initiative and the divine cost-bearing are crucial aspects of the atonement, but we must be careful not to emphasize the divine side at the expense of the human. Christ is a high priest taken from among men (Heb. 5:1); he obeys as the Last Adam (Rom. 5:12–21); and he mediates as the man Christ Jesus (1 Tim.2:5). From this point of view the act of atonement is external to God: God hangs on the cross not as God in naked deity, but as the God-man; not in the one nature of the eternal Logos, but as the Logos made flesh; not in his own name, but in our name, as the representative of man, offering himself as man to the One of whom he says, 'the Father is greater than I' (John 14:28). It is to this 'greater' that Jesus pays the price of our liberation; to the God to whom his people's lives were forfeit, just as in an earlier, typological age the forfeited lives of the first-born were redeemed by the five shekels of the atonement money.

The idea of a redemption price being paid to the Judge of all the earth is no absurdity. It is his prerogative to decide whether it is right to let the condemned go free; and if so on what terms. He has set his heart on forgiveness; but he has also laid down that without the shedding of blood there can be no forgiveness (Heb. 9:22)

Crude commercialism?

But does this notion of a redemption-price not introduce an incongruous element of commercialism into the doctrine of the atonement? Sometimes, it has to be admitted, popular presentations of the cross have strayed in this direction. Some have spoken of the covenant of redemption as a 'bargain';

some have spoken of the 'infinite value' of the sufferings of Christ; some have suggested that because of the dignity of his person, one drop of his blood would have been a sufficient atonement; some have even compared the atonement to a set of scales where the evil of sin on the one side was exactly balanced by the sufferings of Christ on the other.

All such talk is inappropriate, if not, indeed, downright irreverent. Salvation was not preceded by negotiation between God and the sinner (like independent business partners), nor did God the Father and God the Son close a bargain to save the world, each making sure he did not lose out in the resulting deal. Any such nuances were peripheral to Protestant theology. More important, they formed no part of the biblical doctrine of the atonement. Commercial arrangements are in their very nature pecuniary, but any such element is utterly alien to Calvary. As Peter explicitly pointed out (1 Pet. 1:18), we were not redeemed with silver and gold. Granted, the background to much of the New Testament language of redemption is the manumission of slaves, which did involve the payment of money to a god who in turn paid it to the slave-owner as the price of the slave's freedom. The Christian doctrine retains both the idea of emancipation and the idea of price, but expressly excludes the idea of an exchange of money. Instead, we have been redeemed by the blood of Christ, but even here there is no room for a crass literalism, as if what mattered was the quantity of blood or the bloodiness of the sacrifice. In reality, the death of Christ was not particularly bloody. Instead, the blood is metonymy for the death which we as sinners deserved and which Christ died in our place; and at the same time it is a symbol of his vicarious obedience. He obeyed, and he loved, even to the extent of shedding his blood. That blood had no pecuniary or quantifiable value. Its whole value lay in the glory of a vicariously sacrificed life.

The background to the cross is not commercial, but judicial, and as judicial, it is rooted in the very nature of God. God is a judge, but he is never a merchant. Sin is lawlessness, God is the lawmaker, and as such his displeasure is inevitable. Even in human justice, however, it is not the purpose of a penal system to ensure an exact correspondence between a crime and its punishment, as if, for example, the exact physical injuries inflicted in a case of mugging must be inflicted on the mugger. Instead, the right punishment is the one prescribed by the law, and while that punishment must be proportionate to the crime, it can seldom be its exact equivalent. In the case of sin, and by the decree of the Judge of all the earth, the punishment for sin is clear: 'the wages of sin is death' (Rom. 6:23). This, in all its depth and awfulness, is what Christ suffered, and its 'value' lies not in the agonies of the cross being quantitatively equal to the pains of hell, but in the fact that this was the doom prescribed by the law. It was the statutory sentence.

Yet, although the nature of the punishment is entirely the prerogative of God as sovereign, it is not arbitrary. Sin is our human defiance of boundaries; death is the ultimate boundary: the final, non-negotiable demonstration of human finitude, and the *reductio ad absurdum* of the satanic promise, 'you will be like God' (Gen. 3:5). But sin is also the rejection of God. It repudiates him as our *summum bonum* and banishes him to the margins of our lives. It makes him an outsider. The divine response to the sin of the first Adam was that he 'drove out the man' (Gen. 3:24, KJV). The divine response to the sin borne by the Last Adam was to forsake him; and that was the curse. The sinner becomes the outsider. Sin is at its heart relational: a repudiation of both the lordship and the fatherhood of God. Its punishment, too, is relational. Light can have no fellowship with darkness.

This makes it impossible to introduce quantitative comparisons into the doctrine of the atonement. Love and hate, justice and mercy, cannot be measured. Even less, however, can we portray God as a Shylock demanding his pound of flesh. Grace runs through the whole narrative of God's dealings with fallen man. No sooner has the forbidden fruit been eaten than God moves in to assert his control of the situation. The human pair are not immediately destroyed as they deserved (and probably feared). Nor does God at once pronounce them cursed. The serpent is cursed, and the ground is cursed: Adam is told only that labour will now be transformed into toil, and Eve is told only that she will give birth in sorrow. But at the same time God gives hope. A Seed will come who will destroy the serpent and give the final victory to the woman's seed.

None of this accords with the picture of a God intent only on securing exact retribution. As we have seen repeatedly, the atonement is rooted in the divine love, and everything flows from his initiative. It is grace that defers judgment. It is grace that allows that the One shall stand for the many. It is grace that provides the One. And, above all, it is grace that agrees to become the One. The whole cost is borne by God, who becomes man for the sole purpose of putting himself in a position where he is personally able to pay the redemption-price of his people.

It is this grace – this grace and no other – which becomes the basis of the justification of the ungodly. We have nothing to offer: nothing that matches the redemption price. Our whole confidence lies in what God did for us on the cross of Calvary. There, he paid in full; and there, our chains fell off.

11. VICTORY: DISARMING THE POWERS

The theme of victory is central to the Christian doctrine of atonement. Indeed, it was the note sounded in the very first word of hope spoken by God to fallen man. The serpent had defeated the woman, but one day her seed would utterly destroy him (Gen. 3:15). As revelation unfolded, this emphasis was never lost. For example, in connection with the exodus Yahweh declared, 'I will bring judgment on all the gods of Egypt' (Exod. 12:12). Similarly Psalm 2 warns the rulers of the earth that if they oppose the messianic king he will dash them in pieces (v. 9); and Psalm 72 promises that 'he will crush the oppressor' (v. 4). Even in Isaiah's fourth Servant Song (Isa. 52:13 – 53:12), where the predominant note appears to be one of suffering, the whole is set in the context of victory. The opening lines declare, 'See, my servant will act wisely; he will be raised and lifted up and highly exalted'. And the concluding stanza sounds the same note: 'Therefore I will give him a portion among the great, and he will divide the spoil with the strong' (Isa. 53:12).

There is no muting of this note when we come to the fuller Christology of the New Testament. Here, Jesus is repeatedly spoken of as a victor and conqueror. In Luke 11:21 he himself hints unmistakeably that he has already overpowered 'the strong man' (Beelzebub), otherwise he would never have been able to break into his house and cast out his demons. According to John 12:31, the cross is fatal for Satan and his kingdom: 'now the prince of this world will be driven out'; according to Colossians 2:15, Christ disarmed the powers and authorities; according to the writer to the Hebrews he destroyed the one who held the power of death (Heb. 2:14); according to St John, the very purpose of Christ's mission was 'to destroy the devil's work' (1 John 3:8); and according to the book of Revelation, the 'great dragon' has lost his place in heaven, been bound with a great chain, and thrown into the abyss (Rev. 12:7–8; 20:1–3).

Clearly, then, the messianic victory is no peripheral biblical theme. It is central to the promises of God, the work of the Messiah and the purpose of the cross. Gustav Aulén claims that Protestant theology after Luther completely suppressed this emphasis on the atonement as a divine conflict and victory.[1] The truth is quite to the contrary. According to Calvin, for example, the fruit of Christ's death is that, 'he has freed us from a diabolical tyranny', with the result that we now have to deal only with an adversary who has no power against us: 'the devil himself has been laid so low as to be of no more account, as if he did not exist.'[2] But quite apart from comments such as these, the emphasis on the threefold office of Christ as prophet, priest and king ensured that the ideas of conquest and rule never dropped out of sight. It was a key part of the Redeemer's work that he ruled and defended his people, and restrained and conquered all their enemies.[3] Linked to this was a holistic view of the mediatorial role. Christ was no less a king during his life on earth than he is in his post-resurrection state in heaven, and his cross was no less a kingly than a priestly act. This is why the Scottish theologian, Hugh Martin, can speak of the cross as simultaneously an 'altar of priestly agency, a throne of powerful action, and a chariot of victory and triumph'.[4] 'The cross itself,' Martin continued, 'is glorious; not from the subsequent resurrection and enthronement, but glorious from itself. It is itself a chariot of triumph. There is more agency and power in Christ's cross, than in all His work as Creator of the universe.'[5]

This all accords with the portrayal of Christ as not only a lamb, but a lion (Rev. 5:5–6), and it is surely as 'dramatic' as anything Aulén can glean from Irenaeus, Luther and others whom he cites as exponents of a so-called 'classical' view which allegedly held the field before the theory of Anselm became the orthodoxy of the Western church. In reality, the motifs of conquest and victory are not alternatives to expiation, propitiation, reconciliation, satisfaction and

---

1. Aulén, *Christus Victor*, p. 132.
2. *The Epistle to the Hebrews and The First and Second Epistles of St Peter*, p. 31 (on Hebrews 2:14).
3. See Shorter Catechism, Answer 26.
4. Martin, *The Atonement*, p. 82.
5. Ibid., p. 74.

redemption. None of these can stand alone; and none can claim priority or dominance over the others. The cross secures its victory precisely because it expiates sin, propitiates God and ransoms the sinner. Stripped of these priestly effects it can have no kingly effects. Nor as a victory and a conquest is it a separate action from his dying. It was the very death that atoned for sin that destroyed the devil (Heb. 2:14).

The 'victory passages' also highlight, however, that the triumph of the cross was the joint action of both the Father and the Son. The Son's involvement needs no proof, but just as we have seen that the Father was involved in the sacrifice of his Son, so he was involved in his victory. This mutual involvement might, of course, be inferred from the general principle that all the outgoing acts of God are acts of all three trinitarian persons. It might also be inferred from Jesus' disclaimer in John 5:30, 'by myself I can do nothing', and from his claim, later in the same gospel, 'it is the Father, living in me, who is doing his work' (John 14:10). The words of Luke 11:20 likewise point in the same direction: 'If I drive out demons by the finger of God, then the kingdom of God has come upon you.' This clearly indicates that Jesus' deliverance of the demon-possessed was effected in association with the Father. How much more his final triumph on the cross!

But it is not a matter of mere inference. The point is made explicitly in Colossians 1:13, where it is expressly God the Father who is said to have rescued his people from the power of the darkness. It is also the most probable reading of Colossians 2:15. It is tempting at first glance to assume that it was Christ who 'disarmed the powers and authorities', but this assumes an unheralded change of subject in the middle of the paragraph (Col. 2:13–15). It was God the Father who made us alive with Christ, forgave us all our sins, and cancelled the written code that was against us. It may be that in verse 15 the apostle slips imperceptibly from speaking about the Father to speaking about Christ, but this is far from certain; and if there is no change of subject then it was God the Father who disarmed the powers and authorities. Paul adds, however, that he did this *en auto*. Unfortunately, this phrase is slightly ambiguous. It can mean either 'by *him*' (Christ) or 'by *it*' (the cross). Either way, it is clear that Christ was the agent or instrument of the Father's conquest. Like the triumphant believers in Revelation 12:11, God overcame by the blood of the Lamb.

Yet, careful as we must be not to dissociate the work of Christ from the work of the Father, Calvary was in a preeminent sense the victory of the incarnate Son, and both the Father and the Spirit would wish us to see it as such. Indeed, as Hebrews 2:14 makes clear, it was for this very purpose that the Son took flesh and blood: so that he could destroy the one who had the power of death. From this point of view, Christ's body was the sword with which he conquered; and, if one may use a conceit sometimes used by Scottish theologians, in his death he takes this sword out of its scabbard (separating his body from its soul), returning it to its scabbard in the resurrection.[6]

Behind the language of victory there lies a clear biblical dualism: on the one hand, God; on the other, the forces of darkness. The dualism, however, is not symmetrical, as if there were two forces equally ultimate and equal in might. Satan is not eternal, and he is neither god nor demigod. The forces of darkness are creatures, albeit personal creatures. Created holy, they are now in a state of rebellion against their Maker; and in that rebellion they are led by their prince, Satan. It was he who encompassed the fall of the first human pair; he who from the outset sought to frustrate the ministry of Jesus; he who put it into the heart of Judas Iscariot to betray him; he who orchestrated those forces of malice and injustice which nailed him to the cross. And it is his forces, organized by the Parliament of Pandemonium, who, age after age, seek to overthrow the church (Matt. 16:18). By him believers were ruled while in their unconverted state, by him they are still relentlessly pursued (1 Pet. 5:8), and with him (and not merely with flesh and blood) they have to struggle day by day (Eph. 6:12).

These demonic forces are not the 'planetary bodies' which fascinate astrologers (though, as Best points out, the names of the planets show their association with pagan gods),[7] but superhuman, personal, intelligent forces led by a great mastermind implacable in hatred, unwearying in scheming and terrifying in ferocity. Wherever there is evil, it is his work. Wherever there is good, it provokes him to fury. Sometimes he is violent as a lion, sometimes wily as the serpent, and sometimes as plausible as an angel of light. But though he and his demons are infinitely adaptable, his strategy remains ever the same: victory over the Maker, whatever the cost; the destruction of the church, however long it takes; the establishment of hell on earth.

This was the adversary that Christ had to confront and conquer, and he emerged victorious in his every encounter: in the three great temptations in the wilderness; in the poor demonized men and women who accosted him regularly throughout his ministry; in those 'works of the devil' (disease, disability and death) which posed him a challenge at every turn; and, above all, in the last great conflict on the cross of Calvary. Here, once and for all, Christ overthrew the dominion of Satan.

This clearly implies a faultline running through human history. Before Calvary, Satan reigned; after Calvary, he rages but no longer reigns. Jesus himself

---

6. See, for example, Martin, *The Atonement*, p. 86.

7. Best, *Ephesians*, p. 593.

acknowledged the reality of satanic power when he referred to him as 'the prince of this world' (John 12:31; 16:11), and he implied it when he compared himself to a housebreaker who had broken into Beelzebub's premises and was now carrying away the spoils (Luke 11:21). The Apostle Paul spoke in similar vein when he described Satan as 'the ruler of the kingdom of the air' (Eph. 2:2).

But what power did the devil really possess? He never had absolute dominion. Even in the moment of man's first transgression God was able to pass immediate judgment on the serpent and to announce his inevitable overthrow (Gen. 3:14–15). The Maker still remained lord of the whole earth. Every creature owed him obedience: light and darkness, heaven and *sheol*, were subject to his dominion, and he gave its name to every star (Isa. 40:26). None could resist his will (Rom. 9:19).

Satan, then, had no absolute, or even legitimate, authority. But he did have a usurped one. Mankind, by sinning, became the slave of sin, and as the slave of sin they were the slaves of Satan. It is primarily because his spirit is at work in us that we are all by nature children of disobedience (Eph. 2:2). The world is *his* world. This is why it hated Christ, this is why it hates his church and this is why we are forbidden to love it (1 John 2:15). Indeed, God has ordained that to the end of time a state of war shall exist between the seed of the woman and the seed of the serpent (Gen. 3:15).

Hebrews 2:14–15

But Calvary brought a revolution. It was a glorious *coup d'état*. The clearest statement of this is Hebrews 2:14–15, which states categorically that Christ destroyed the devil and that he did it by his death. But we are still left with pressing questions.

First, in what sense did the devil have the 'power' of death? The reference is not to authority (Gk *exousia*) but to strength (Gk *kratos*). The devil did not have the authority to introduce death. It was God's sentence on human sin, and it was no afterthought: 'you must not eat from the tree of the knowledge of good and evil, for when you eat of it you will certainly die' (Gen. 2:17). Yet the devil had the power of death in the sense that he was able to fill the earth with violence (Gen. 6:11), and he also has the power of death in that he is the great instigator of persecution. It was probably from this perspective that the writer to the Hebrews viewed him. Many of his readers had been exposed to insult and persecution (Heb. 10:33), others had stood side by side with those who had been so treated, and at the time of writing many members of the community were in prison. They clearly had grave cause to fear this roaring lion and his power to devour. The same perspective appears in Revelation, where the souls of the martyrs cry out, 'How long until you avenge our blood?' (Rev. 6:9–10).

Yet what we are told in Hebrews is not merely that the devil had lost the power of death. What we are told is that he has been destroyed. He still exists and he still roars and he still attacks and schemes. But he has been reduced to nothing, his kingdom fatally undermined. He is no longer the power in the world. He has fallen from heaven (Luke 10:18) and is already an outcast (John 12:31).

The second question is, how can the one who holds the power of death be said to have been destroyed when death still reigns even over believers?

It is indeed true that apart from those who will still be alive at the parousia all the redeemed taste death, the writer to the Hebrews himself included. Yet Christ has transformed death. One reflection of this is that the New Testament never describes believers as 'dying'. Instead they 'fall asleep'. This is how, for example, the book of Acts describes the martyrdom of Stephen: he 'fell asleep' (Acts 7:60). Paul uses similar language when he writes to comfort the Thessalonians, grieving over the death of Christian friends. Their loved ones, he says, 'have fallen asleep in [Jesus]' (1 Thess. 4:14). Death, he tells the Corinthians, has lost its sting (1 Cor. 15:55–57). It is no longer accompanied by the curse demanded by the law, and for that reason it has lost its terror.

Old Testament believers dreaded going down to *šĕ'ōl*, where faculties were so attenuated that no one remembered God and no one praised him (Ps. 6:5). To them, death was a land of darkness and oblivion, without love or care (Ps. 88:11–12). The attitude of New Testament believers is completely different. Not only have they been redeemed from the fear of death, they look forward to it as a relief from labour and struggle, and as the gateway to something better. This is why Paul can declare, 'I desire to depart and be with Christ, which is better by far' (Phil. 1:23). Even where he registers a degree of anxiety about the disembodied state (2 Cor. 5:4) he can still say, 'we would prefer to be away from the body, and at home with the Lord' (2 Cor. 5:8). In 2 Timothy 4:8, he views death as the end of his fight (Gk *agōna*): the moment when he slips his moorings, casts off from this world and sets off for his coronation. And far from viewing death as a state of feeble, shadowy existence with only attenuated faculties, he sees it as a state where we put childish things behind us and see God face to face, and where faith, hope and (above all) love achieve perfection (1 Cor. 13:11–13).

But how can all this be ascribed to the death of Christ? The paradox here is that Christ destroyed the devil with his own weapon. As we have already seen, no man (or devil) took Jesus' life from him. He laid it down voluntarily, in effect assuming to himself the power of death, and choosing the time, the place and the manner in which it would be used against himself. From one point of view, his death was a triumph for Satan. It was his 'hour'. In reality, the expiatory and propitiatory power of the cross was Satan's destruction. The atonement broke his power. Where the blood was sprinkled, God could no longer condemn; where God could not condemn, the devil could not accuse; where he could not accuse, he could no longer hold; and where he could no longer hold, men and women transferred their allegiance from Satan to the Son of God. The Crucified, having bought and rescued them with his blood, sat down at God's right hand (Heb. 1:3); Satan was thrown into the abyss (Rev. 20:3).

But how can we maintain this when so few have actually transferred their allegiance and the vast majority are still the devil's slaves? Part of the explanation is the tension between the 'already' and the 'not yet'. Jesus' reign has been inaugurated, but not yet consummated; the devil has received his deathblow, but not yet met his final doom.

However, there is another avenue to explore here: the cosmic implications of the cross, and the possibility that Christ may be said to have redeemed *collectively* the whole creation. According to 2 Corinthians 5:19 God reconciled 'the world' to himself. Colossians 1:20 puts it even more strongly: through Christ he has reconciled to himself 'all things, whether things on earth or things in heaven, by making peace through his blood, shed on the cross'. The same note is sounded in Philippians 2:10: at the name of Jesus every knee will bow 'in heaven and on earth and under the earth'.

This, yet again, takes us back to basics. The disobedience of the first Adam had implications for the whole creation, and so, too, has the obedience of the Last. He bore the sin of the world, shed his blood for it, bought it. Now it has his name on it. In Adam, the dust of the earth was discredited. In Christ, it covers itself in glory. This is why in Revelation 5 the whole universe joins the church and the angels in singing the praise of the Lamb:

> Then I heard every creature in heaven and on earth and under the earth and on the sea, and all that is them, singing:
>> 'To him who sits on the throne and to the Lamb
>>> be praise and honour and glory and power,
>> for ever and ever!'
> (Rev. 5:13)

Clearly, however, this cosmic reconciliation cannot mean that the demonic ultimately makes peace with God. On the contrary, as far as the devil and his demons are concerned the reconciliation takes the form of a pacification; and his destruction is a key element in that pacification. Yet destruction is not annihilation. It is banishment. In the story of the fall, God drove humanity out of Eden (Gen. 3:23). In the story of redemption, God takes humanity back, but he drives

Satan out of his cosmos. He puts him 'outside' (Rev. 22:15) in the place of outer darkness (Matt. 8:12) where there is no *cosmos* (a world of ordered beauty), but only the darkness and chaos of the pit that serves as the cesspool of the universe. The new heaven and the new earth will contain only righteousness, because the great inventor and embodiment of evil will have been banished from it for ever.

Yet we must not forget the tenses of salvation. The redemption of the world is a work in progress. The universe *has been* saved, the universe *is being* saved, and the universe *will be* saved.

Colossians 2:15

Another key passage is Colossians 2:15. The powers and authorities referred to here are the same as those Paul mentions in Ephesians 6:12, where he distinguished them from 'flesh and blood', refers to them in the same breath as he speaks of the devil, and clearly means us to understand them as the agents through whom Satan implements his wiles. The reason the Christian needs the whole armour of God is precisely that these are superhuman spirits whose natural sphere is 'the heavenly realms' (Eph. 6:12). When Paul describes them as rulers, authorities and powers he does not intend us to see them as distinct ranks of angels. He is not giving us an angelology. His concern is that we should know the strength of the enemy. They have pedigree, authority, strength and cunning. They are indeed world powers (*kosmokratoras*, Eph. 6:12).

But now, according to Colossians 2:15, they have been 'disarmed'. There is some debate as to the meaning of this verb (*apekdysamenos*). It is in the middle voice, and if we were to give this its full value it would mean 'to strip off from oneself', and would refer most naturally to Jesus, who shook off the principalities and powers who pursued him relentlessly. Grammatically, however, the subject of the paragraph (Col. 2:13–15) is not Jesus, but God, who made us alive with Christ, forgave us all our sins and cancelled the written code that was against us. It is natural, then, to assume that God is still the subject of *apekdysamenos* in verse 13. Whatever action it points to, it was God who performed it, but it is very difficult to think of the evil powers clinging so closely to the Almighty that he had to strip himself of them.

There is good precedent, however, for not giving the middle voice its peculiar, reflexive value, and this would leave us free to take the verb as an active one. Taken in this way, it was used, for example, of stripping a captured soldier of his armour and his weapons. This would make perfect sense in the context of Colossians 2:15, and this is how it was understood by Jerome, who translated it *exspolians*. The KJV ('having spoiled principalities and powers') followed

Jerome, and the NIV follows the same tradition ('and having disarmed the powers and authorities, he made a public spectacle of them').

But how did he disarm them? According to the NIV he disarmed them by the cross. The original, as we have seen, is more ambiguous. The Greek phrase is *en auto*, which may mean either 'by it' or 'by him'. It makes little practical difference. The cross was *his* cross and God acted in him primarily through the cross. Either way, Christ crucified was God's agent in disarming Satan, and the cross was his instrument.

The preceding context gives us more detail. God's action, according to verse 13, was twofold: he raised us together with Christ, and he forgave our sins. The 'raising' referred to presupposes that we were dead in sins (Eph. 2:1), but God made us alive in Christ, raised us up and put us where Satan cannot reach us: seated in the heavenly realms with Christ Jesus. This is why Paul can speak of our lives being hidden with Christ in God (Col. 3:3). There, Satan can exercise no dominion, and there he cannot destroy; or, to adopt the language of Jesus himself, no power can now snatch us out of the Father's hand (John 10:29).

The second element in God's action was that he forgave all our sins, and this was linked inextricably to the cross. The essence of the forgiveness was that God cancelled the written code that was against us. This code (*cheirographon*) may be either a bond which we had failed to honour or a law we had failed to keep. Either way, God cancelled it. He erased the writing, blotting it out completely. But that was not all. He nailed it to the cross. This may well be an allusion to the *titulus* which Pilate nailed to the cross of Jesus. If so, then the symbolism here is that the indictment on which Jesus was condemned was 'our sins': our broken bond. But God did not merely cancel it. He took it away (Col. 2:14). Taken together, these amount to a powerful threefold description of the way that God disarmed Satan: he cancelled the indictment, he nailed it to the cross, and he took it away. Our guilt, our broken bond, was Satan's title to enslave us and drag us down to hell with himself, trophies of his victory over the Maker. The cross cancelled the bond, and not only rescued us from Satan but made us heirs of 'the inheritance of his holy people in the kingdom of light' (Col. 1:12).

The result, says Paul, is that the powers and principalities were disgraced. God made a 'public spectacle' of them (Col. 2:15). The same word (*deigmatizō*) is used of Joseph in Matthew 1:19. When he learned that Mary was pregnant he wanted to divorce her quietly, so as not to 'expose her to public disgrace'. But public disgrace was precisely what God wanted for the forces of darkness. At one level, of course, it applies to the politicians and judiciary who had condemned Jesus. They thought that if they could bring about his death neither he nor his movement would ever be heard of again. In reality, by crucifying him they disgraced themselves and released forces which neither the Jewish leaders nor the imperial might of Rome would ever be able to control. But deeper still was the disgrace of the devil himself, destroyed by what he thought was his masterstroke. Confident that the cross would secure his victory, he was outwitted by the wisdom of God: neutralized and conquered by divine weakness.

Now, in Paul's final picture, he and his demons are part of God's victory parade. The Crucified One marches in triumph through history, Satan tied to Christ's victory car, his bedraggled army in chains, half-dragged, half-running in view of the whole moral universe, on their way to execution (Jude 6).

Paul gives a complementary picture in 2 Corinthians 2:14: 'But thanks be to God, who always leads us ... in Christ's triumphal procession.' In the first instance the reference here is to the apostles, through whom Christ spreads 'the aroma of the knowledge of him'. But need it be confined to them? Are not all believers the Redeemer's trophies: spoils plundered from Satan's kingdom? God displays us proudly: once his enemies, now his friends; once slaves of sin, now liberated; once doomed to die, now destined for life eternal. 'They are led in with joy and gladness, they enter the palace of the king' (Ps. 45:15). Thanks be to God!

Yet once again we have to remember the 'already' and the 'not yet'. Even though God has disarmed the spiritual forces of evil we are still at war with them; sometimes the battle is so fierce that we make little progress, and it takes us all our strength to hold our ground (Eph. 6:13). We may still assure ourselves, however, that we are fighting an already-conquered foe, stripped of his main weapons and fully aware that defeat is inevitable. This is precisely the point Oscar Cullmann made when he alluded to the contrast between D-Day and Victory Day: 'The decisive battle in a war may already have occurred in a relatively early stage of the war, and yet the war still continues. Although the decisive effect of that battle is perhaps not recognised by all, it nevertheless means victory. But the war must still be carried on for an undefined time, until "Victory Day".'[8] Satan now fights with depleted strength, furious but demoralized. He no longer has the power to separate us from the love of God (Rom. 8:38–39). Instead, it is we who shall be hyper-conquerors (Rom. 8:37).

Revelation 20

When we turn to Revelation 20 we realize at once that we are in the realm of apocalyptic: notoriously difficult territory, where every interpreter must proceed

8. Oscar Cullmann, *Christ and Time* (rev. ed., London: SCM Press, 1962), p. 84. Cf. Anthony A. Hoekema, *The Bible and the Future* (Exeter: Paternoster Press, 1979), p. 21.

warily. A book where locusts look like horses (9:7), horns have heads like lions and a woman sits on all of seven hills, tempts our ingenuity, and ingenuity is a dangerous tool for the exegete. At the same time, literalism looks scarcely less dangerous; and if the Apocalypse as a whole is an area into which we venture at our peril, the twentieth chapter is the most hotly contested area of all, not least because it embodies concepts which are unique to itself and correspondingly hard to understand, and yet have such appeal and such *prima facie* clarity that to many they are the shibboleths of biblical orthodoxy. Here alone we meet the concept of the 'second death' (Rev. 20:6), here alone we meet the concept of the 'first resurrection' (v. 6), and (above all), here alone we meet the concept of the millennium, the thousand-year earthly reign of Christ and his saints (vv. 2, 4, 6–7).

One serious consequence of the millennialism which has been built on these texts is that it has bred an extremely pessimistic view of the present in order to enhance the glory of the future. Yet it is hard to reconcile such pessimism with what we have already seen of the destruction of the devil (Heb. 2:14) and the disarming of the demonic powers (Col. 2:15). Assuming the coherence of Scripture, we must bear these passages in mind when we read in Revelation 20 of the binding of Satan. Pessimism will suggest that this cannot be a present reality (the world is in too much of a mess) and millenarian belief may require us to argue that the binding can refer only to a future period towards the end of Christian history. It is easy to be sceptical about the idea of a bound devil when we think of all the evil so manifestly present in the world. Yet the whole tendency of the book of Revelation is to take us behind the phenomena in order to give us a glimpse of the invisible spiritual realities which are operating behind the scenes and determining the course of history. This is why, in Revelation 4, before we see anything of wars and famines and bloody martyrdoms, we see the throne and the One who sits on it. This is why in Revelation 5 we see the Lamb standing in the very centre of the throne. And this is why we are told that it is the Lion of the tribe of Judah who holds and unseals the scroll, controlling the sequences of history (Rev. 5:7).

Is any of this logically consistent with the present dreadful state of the world? No! No more than it is consistent with the existence of God, or at least the existence of a wise, powerful and benevolent God! But it is the reality: the reality that faith sees and lives by. Satan is not on the throne. He is not in charge of the scroll. On the contrary, an angel has come, clapped him in irons, thrown him into the abyss and turned the key. Of course this interpretation has fuzzy edges. How can we explain the fact that he will be released for 'a short time' (v. 3)? I'm not sure, unless it means that he will be released a little: given a little freedom to prowl, though always chained. Besides, as there have been times of revival when the Spirit has come in extraordinary power, so there have been times when the roaring lion has been given the freedom to behave with extraordinary ferocity. But the idea that Satan is now bound, and that the cross of Calvary is 'the great chain', is consonant with the tenor of the entire New Testament. There, the prince of this world has had his hour, and has been judged and thrown out (John 12:31). The King who came to Bethlehem now reigns, and 'the kingdom of the world has become the kingdom of our Lord and of his Messiah, and he will reign for ever and ever' (Rev. 11:15). There is nothing opaque or uncertain about such a statement.

But in what sense can we speak of Satan as 'bound'? The clearest hint is given in verse 3: 'to keep him from deceiving the nations any more'. The key to understanding this lies in the word *ethnē*, here translated 'nations'. The same word occurs in Galatians 3:14, where it is rendered 'Gentiles': 'that the blessing given to Abraham might come to the Gentiles'. It occurs in the same sense earlier in the book of Revelation itself: when the seer was told to go and measure the temple he was ordered to exclude the outer court, 'because it has been given to the Gentiles' (Rev. 11:2). Consistency suggests it be given the same meaning in Revelation 20:3. Satan is bound in order to keep him from deceiving *the Gentiles* any more; and this inaugurates a new era in redemption history. In the whole period before the coming of Christ Satan kept the Gentiles in darkness. Only in Israel was the light. Yet throughout the Old Testament there had been hints of a different day to come: a day when God's salvation would be known among all nations and all the ends of the earth would fear him (Ps. 67:7); a day when the earth would be full of the knowledge of the Lord as the waters cover the sea (Isa. 11:9); a day when all the earth would shout for joy to the Lord (Ps. 100:1). Micah had foretold a time when 'many nations will come and say, "Come, let us go up to the mountain of the LORD, to the temple of the God of Jacob"' (Mic. 4:2); and Joel had proclaimed that in the last days God said, 'I will pour out my Spirit on all people' (Joel 2:28). It was as the fulfilment of this promise that Peter understood the Day of Pentecost: 'this is what was spoken by the prophet Joel' (Acts 2:16). Paul set his own mission in a similar context. The era of Gentile exclusion was over, and God had sent him to 'open their eyes and turn them from darkness to light, *and from the power of Satan to God*' (Acts 26:18, italics mine). This, he tells the Ephesians, was the great 'mystery' hidden from previous generations but now revealed by the Spirit: 'This mystery is that through the gospel the Gentiles are heirs together with Israel, members together of one body, and sharers together in the promise in Christ Jesus' (Eph. 3:6).

This marks the great divide, the caesura, in redemption history (and indeed in world history). On the far side lie 'the former days'; on the near side lie 'the last days'. These days are pre-eminently the age of Gentile mission, and the great prerequisite of that mission is the binding of Satan. Were the nations still trapped in his web of deceit, Gentile mission would be futile. Now that he is bound we can set out with confidence. We shall return later to this link between the victory of Christ and the imperatives of worldwide evangelism.

New management

But the victory of Christ means more than mere destruction and conquest. It means that the world is now under new management. Christ reigns, and to this the New Testament bears abundant witness. Jesus himself declared that all authority over the universe had been given to him (Matt. 28:18). Paul told the Ephesians that God had raised Christ from the dead, set him above all rule and authority and dominion, and appointed him head over everything (Eph. 1:20–22). And in the Apocalypse, as we have seen, the Lamb, once crucified between two thieves, now stands in the centre of the throne (Rev. 5:6).

The first thing to note here is that this new administration refers specifically to the supremacy of the Lamb *as mediator*. The authority has been 'given' to him (Matt. 28:18). As the eternal Logos (designer, creator and preserver of all things) he had reigned from the beginning. This is why John can declare (John 1:11) that when he came into the world he came to what was 'his own'. Even when the world gave allegiance to its own 'prince' it still belonged to its Maker. Yet, just as sin prompted God to expel humanity from paradise, so it prompted him to withdraw in a measure from his own creation. Apart from Israel 'he let all nations go their own way' (Acts 14:16). But now, in Christ, the King has come, walking among men as once he walked in the Garden of Eden; and not only has he come, but he has come in our nature: the Word made flesh (John 1:14). In that nature he enjoyed a human's eye view of the world. In that nature he was pursued by Satan, suffered and died. And now in that nature he reigns, bringing to bear on his administration all the compassion and sensitivity he had learned while he dwelt among us, sharing our situation and limited to our resources.

But he not only reigns *as* man; he reigns *for* man. He did not draw a line under his work as redeemer when he cried on the cross, 'It is finished!' Far from withdrawing from the field and (for example) leaving it to the Holy Spirit to continue where he himself left off, he remains fully engaged and fully committed. Even his lying under the power of death for three days was part of the work of redemption: he had to 'taste' death (Heb. 2:9). With his resurrection he actively resumes his redeeming work, dedicating his exalted state to giving glory to God the Father (Phil. 2:11); and if you were to ask him, in subordination to that, 'what is the policy of your administration?' he would reply, 'to give eternal life to as many as the Father has given me' (John 17:2).

He is still an en energetic, proactive Saviour, fully involved in every conversion, shepherding every single sheep and tending to every single lamb. This is what he does with the power given to him.

The second thing to note is that this enthronement and empowerment of Jesus is a direct result of his obedient self-sacrifice. The clearest statement of this is in Philippians 2:8–9, where the death on the cross is expressly linked to the exaltation by Paul's 'therefore': 'he became obedient to death – even death on a cross! *Therefore* God exalted him to the highest place.' The same connection appears in Hebrews 1:3: 'After he had provided purification for sins, he sat down at the right hand of the Majesty in heaven.' This is echoed in Revelation 5:6, where it is not simply as the risen Lord that Jesus stands in the centre of the throne, but as the sacrificial Lamb, already slain and still bearing the marks of his suffering and death. He is worthy to open the scroll precisely because he was slain, and because with his blood he purchased people for God (Rev. 5:9).

Such language clearly suggests the idea of reward. The Father's exaltation of his Son is his response to the wonder of his obedience (Phil. 2:9), and as the obedience was the greatest imaginable, offered by one who did not personally owe it, and carried to the extreme of deliberately laying down his life, so the exaltation is hyper-exaltation. The resurrection body of Jesus is as glorious can God can make it, his position the highest it is in God's power to bestow, the submission of the entire universe complete.

But it is not merely reward. He is enthroned for the sake of his work, which he now prosecutes not from a position of weakness but from a position of strength. He can now build his church confident that the power and wisdom of hell will never prevail against it. He can pour forth his Spirit to empower his people for mission (Acts 1:8) and he can move heaven and earth for the conversion of a single sinner. An earthquake becomes a link in the chain of events leading to the salvation of a jailer in Philippi (Acts 16:26); a storm and a shipwreck help carry his servant, Paul, to preach the gospel in Rome (Acts 28:14). He has the whole world in his hands.

We note, thirdly, that the supremacy of Christ is universal. Part of this universality we have already seen: Christ's supreme power over the devil and his demons. But its scope is wider still. He reigns over the whole of time, the whole of space, and over everything contained in them.

Temporally, the dominion of the Son of Man is 'an everlasting dominion that will not pass away, and his kingdom is one that will never be destroyed' (Dan. 7:14). Corresponding to this is the vision of Revelation 22:3: even when the old heaven and the old earth have passed away 'the throne of God and of the Lamb' is the citadel of New Jerusalem. This is not compromised in any way by what Pauls says in 1 Corinthians 15:24, where he speaks of Christ handing over the kingdom to the Father and God becoming all in all (1 Cor. 15:28). This marks the completion of the redeeming work of Christ, but it is clear that this is but the end of the beginning: the end of one dispensation of the reign of Christ, not the end of his reign as such. He remains for ever the leader of his redeemed people. In Hebrews 2:5–9, for example, it is plain that the world to come, no less than the present one, is to be subject to Christ. After all, it is only in association with him that the saints can reign for ever and ever (Rev. 22:5). Yet they serve as well as reign (Rev. 22:3) and he, too, reigns as servant, as the Last Adam, as heir to the creation mandates to colonize and subdue the earth and exercise dominion over every creature (Gen. 1:28). Even then, however, he has a pastoral, as well as a royal, role: the Lamb at the centre of the throne will be our shepherd (Rev. 7:17).

Spatially, Christ's dominion extends to all the nations (Matt. 28:18), regardless of whether they acknowledge it, and this fact should be a key element in our evangelism, especially in an age which, as Dietrich Bonhoeffer pointed out, can no longer be approached on the basis of a religious *a priori*.[9] At the heart of the old approach lay the idea that people have conscious religious concerns and personal spiritual needs to which Christ is the answer: some God-shaped void, for example, or a guilty conscience, or a sense of emptiness and lack of fulfil-ment because of the vanity of all things temporal. But what if people feel no such needs? What if, to use the language of Bonhoeffer, they are 'religionless'? 'How can Christ become the Lord of the religionless?'[10] In the light of Philip-pians 2:11 this question answers itself. Christ *is already* the Lord of the religionless, and Christian proclamation is a summons to recognize that fact. The imperious call that every knee must bow extends to the non-religious: to those who have given God no thought, who have no God-shaped void in their hearts and feel no emptiness in their lives. The obligation to bow the knee does not rest on any subjective state of the individual human heart but on the great, unvarying objective fact that Jesus Christ *is* Lord, a fact which is true for all, always and everywhere.

In a very special sense, however, Jesus is Lord of every believer, and we, conversely, are his servants (*douloi*). Yet this is more than a binding 'legal' rela-tionship with all the obligations which such a relationship entails. Christ reigns in our hearts and in our affections, as Peter reminded his readers, 'though you have not seen him, you love him' (1 Pet. 1:8). It is this love that creates the great

---

9. Dietrich Bonhoeffer, *Letters and Papers from Prison*, ed. Eberhard Bethge (enlarged ed., London: SCM Press, 1971), p. 280.
10. Ibid.

primal longing to see him as he is (1 John 3:2). But Christ also reigns in the sense that he holds spiritual sway in the very depths of our souls. Where once Satan reigned, Christ is king. This cannot mean that believers are sinless, but it does mean that sin is no longer the master (Rom. 6:14). Led by the Spirit, we have declared war on it, and the war will be a fight to the death (Rom. 8:13); and distressing though the remaining outbursts and eruptions of sin certainly are, we are no longer caught in the grip of that spiritual impotence which left us totally incapable of faith, hope or love. Now, by the grace of the indwelling Christ, we are capable of all three, and despite constant frustration and frequent defeat we bear the fruit of the Spirit (Gal. 5:22).

But the sovereignty of Christ is not confined to the spiritual and inward. It also extends to the material creation. As the eternal Son, the image of the invisible God, he never let go of it. All things were created by him (Col. 1:16) and in him all things hang together.

Now he has gone further, uniting himself to the material creation by taking the dust of the earth into personal union with himself and by reconciling the world to God by his blood. The universe is his by a double right as its Maker and as its Redeemer. In the interim between his first and second advents he carries it (Heb. 1:3), not by continuous creation nor yet as a detached observer of its evolutionary progress, but as the one who energizes, preserves and governs its every movement, macrocosmic and microcosmic.

In the end, he will recreate it. 'I saw,' said John, 'a new heaven and a new earth, for the first heaven and the first earth had passed away' (Rev. 21:1). There is no prospect of our creating through human strength and ingenuity our own utopia or making our own way back to paradise. Nor will the new world evolve by the unguided operation of forces already present within the cosmos. Such forces would carry us only to a state of entropy and inertia. But when the God who said, 'Let there be light!' finally says, 'Let there be a new universe!', then New Jerusalem will come down from heaven from God (Rev. 21:2): regenerated by cataclysmic divine *fiat*, not by evolution. Even then, the transformation remains in the closest possible connection with redemption. He who regenerates the soul and raises the body will also recreate the universe. This is the 'total eschatology' proclaimed by Scripture: a new soul in a new body in a new universe. Then God will see all that he has recreated, and it will give him infinite satisfaction: 'Very good!'

But if it is beyond us to build New Jerusalem it is also beyond us to imagine it. We cannot extrapolate from our present to that future, projecting into the world to come our own favoured features of the present one. We cannot even construct a model of the heavenly city from the pictures given to us in Scripture. Even when we have collated all that the Bible says it remains that,

No eye has seen,
  no ear has heard,
no mind has conceived
  what God has prepared for those who love him.
(1 Cor. 2:9, NIV 1984)

What we can say is that it will be a world from which evil has been banished, doomed to exist only 'outside'. Conversely, it will be a cosmos in which even more splendidly than in the present one the heavens declare the glory of God (Ps. 19:1–6) and in which humanity, shepherded by the Lamb, will at last achieve its destiny, reigning over its environment but also, sharing in the care of it. The world belongs to its Saviour, and precisely for this reason we owe it, now and for ever, a duty of care commensurate with the price he paid for it.

Lordship and mission

Finally, the inseparable connection between the lordship of Christ and the worldwide mission of the church. That link lies at the heart of Jesus' parting words to his disciples as recorded in Matthew 28:18–20. There is a clear, categorical imperative, 'make disciples of all nations' (v. 19). But that imperative rests on a great indicative: 'All authority in heaven and on earth has been given to me' (v. 18). Everywhere the missionary goes, Jesus is Lord. Nor does this fact stand alone. Not only is Jesus lord, but Satan is bound. The Gentiles are no longer his to hold fast in the bonds of ignorance and delusion. This is not how things look, of course. The mighty empires of Islam and Hinduism seem impervious to the gospel. Yet Christ is Lord of India as he is of Iona; and Satan is as bound in Riyadh as he is in Canterbury. Besides, there is a great third factor. The Holy Spirit has come: 'You will receive power when the Holy Spirit comes on you; and you will be my witnesses in Jerusalem and in all Judea and Samaria, and to the ends of the earth' (Acts 1:8) Yet once again appearances belie it. We preach with 'poor, lisping, stammering tongues',[11] and while not ashamed of the gospel we are often ashamed of the way we proclaim it. But by God's grace, as Paul discovered, our stammerings become the saving power of God (Rom. 1:16). There is no heart the victorious Christ cannot open.

---

11. 'There is a fountain filled with blood', William Cowper, 1772.

Conclusion

We live, then, in the age of a regnant Christ, a bound devil and an ever-present Spirit. It is in such an age that we hear the call to tell every man, woman and child, 'I have good news for you'; and it is in such an age that we hear the call to place the socially-transforming power of the Messiah at the heart of every culture on earth. Our commission is not merely to save individuals but to disciple nations (Matt. 28:19).

If we have eyes to see, we can already see the Lamb on the throne; and if we have ears to hear, we can already hear the music of an exultant universe:

> To him who sits on the throne and to the Lamb
> be praise and honour and glory and power,
> for ever and ever!
> (Rev. 5:13)

FOR FURTHER READING

BERKOUWER, G. K. (1965), *The Work of Christ*, Grand Rapids: Eerdmans.

CALVIN, JOHN, *Institutes of the Christian Religion*, 2 vols., ed. John T. McNeill, tr. Ford Lewis Battles, Philadelphia: Westminster Press, 1960, Bk. II. XV-XVII. [Vol. 1, pp. 494–534.]

DENNEY, JAMES (1951), *The Death of Christ*, ed. R. V. G. Tasker, London: Tyndale Press.

JEFFERY, STEVE, MIKE OVEY and ANDREW SACH (2007), *Pierced For Our Transgressions: Rediscovering the Glory of Penal Substitution*, Nottingham: IVP.

LETHAM, ROBERT (1993), *The Work of Christ*, Leicester: IVP.

MCGRATH, ALISTER E. (1987), *The Enigma of the Cross*, London: Hodder and Stoughton.

—— (1994), *Christian Theology: An Introduction*, Oxford: Blackwell, pp. 337–368.

MARSHALL, I. HOWARD (2007), *Aspects of the Atonement: Cross and Resurrection in the Reconciling of God and Humanity*, London: Paternoster.

MORRIS, LEON (1960), *The Apostolic Preaching of the Cross*, London: Tyndale Press.

—— (n.d.), *The Cross in the New Testament*, Exeter: Paternoster Press.

MURRAY, JOHN (1989), new ed., *Redemption: Accomplished and Applied*, Grand Rapids: Eerdmans.

PACKER, JAMES I. (1973), *What Did the Cross Achieve?: The Logic of Penal Substitution*, Tyndale Biblical Theology Lecture, 1973, repr. in *The Collected Shorter Writings of J. I. Packer*, 4 vols., Carlisle: Paternoster Press, 1998–99, vol. 1, pp. 85–124.

REYMOND, ROBERT L. (1998), *A New Systematic Theology of the Christian Faith*, 2nd ed., Nashville: Nelson, pp. 623–702.

STOTT, JOHN R. W. (1986), *The Cross of Christ*, Leicester: IVP (20th anniversary edn 2006).

TORRANCE, THOMAS F. (2009), *Atonement: The Person and Work of Christ*, Milton Keynes: Paternoster, pp. 1–200.

WARFIELD, B. B. (1950), *The Person and Work of Christ*, Philadelphia: Presbyterian and Reformed, pp. 325–530.

BIBLIOGRAPHY

Anselm, *Anselm of Canterbury: The Major Works*, ed. Brian Davies and G. R. Evans
(Oxford: Oxford University Press, 1998).

Aquinas, Thomas, *St Thomas Aquinas Summa Theologica*, 5 vols., tr. Fathers of the English
Dominican Province (Notre Dame: Ave Maria Press, 1981).

Athanasius, *First Discourse against the Arians*, 39 (NPNF, Second Series, vol. IV).

———, *The Incarnation of the Word of God*, tr. A Religious of C.S.M.V. (London: Geoffrey
Bles, 1944).

Augustine, *Homilies on the Gospel of John*, Tractate CXIX, 6 (NPNF, vol. VII).

———, *On the Holy Trinity*, IV.2 (4) (NPNF, First Series, vol. III).

———, *Saint Augustine: Confessions*, tr. Henry Chadwick (Oxford: Oxford University Press,
1992).

Aulén, Gustav, *Christus Victor: An Historical Study of the Three Main Types of the Idea of the
Atonement*, tr. A. G. Herbert (London: SPCK, 1965).

Baillie, Donald M., *God Was In Christ: An Essay on Incarnation and Atonement* (London:
Faber and Faber, 1948).

Barclay, William, *New Testament Words* (London: SCM Press, 1964).

———, *The Plain Man Looks at the Apostles' Creed* (London: Collins, 1967).

Barth, Karl, *Church Dogmatics*, 4 vols., eds. G. W. Bromiley and T. F. Torrance (Edinburgh:
T&T Clark, 1956-75).

Baxter, Richard, *Universal Redemption of Mankind by the Lord Jesus Christ* (London: 1694).

Best, Ernest, *A Critical and Exegetical Commentary on Ephesians*, International Critical
Commentary (Edinburgh: T&T Clark, 1998).

Bethge, Eberhard, *Dietrich Bonhoeffer: A Biography*, rev. and ed. Victoria J. Barnett
(Minneapolis: Fortress Press, 1989).

Betz, Hans Dieter, *Galatians* (Philadelphia: Fortress Press, 1979).

Bloesch, Donald G., *Jesus Christ: Saviour and Lord* (Carlisle: Paternoster Press, 1997).

Bonhoeffer, Dietrich, *Letters and Papers from Prison*, ed. Eberhard Bethge (enlarged ed., London: SCM Press, 1971).

Brown, Joanne Carlson, and Parker, Rebecca, 'For God So Loved the World', in Joanne Carlson Brown and Carole R. Bohn (eds.), *Christianity, Patriarchy and Abuse* (New York: The Pilgrim Press, 1989).

Brown, Raymond E., *The Gospel According to John (XIII-XXI): Introduction, Translation, and Notes*, The Anchor Yale Bible (New Haven: Yale University Press, 1970).

Burton, Ernest De Witt, *A Critical and Exegetical Commentary on the Epistle to the Galatians* (Edinburgh: T&T Clark, 1921).

Bushnell, Horace, *The Vicarious Sacrifice* (London: Strahan and Co., 1871).

Calvin, John, *The Acts of the Apostles 14-28*, tr. John W. Fraser, ed. David W. Torrance and Thomas F. Torrance, Calvin's New Testament Commentaries (Grand Rapids: Eerdmans, 1995).

———, *Commentary on the Last Four Books of Moses arranged in the Form of a Harmony*, vol. 2 (Edinburgh: Calvin Translation Society, 1853).

———, *The Epistles of Paul the Apostle to the Galatians, Ephesians, Philippians and Colossians*, tr. T. H. L. Parker (Grand Rapids: Eerdmans, 1996).

———, *The Epistle of Paul The Apostle to the Hebrews and the First and Second Epistles of St Peter*, tr. William B. Johnston, ed. David W. Torrance and Thomas F. Torrance, Calvin's New Testament Commentaries (Grand Rapids: Eerdmans, 1994).

———, *The Epistles of Paul the Apostle to the Romans and to the Thessalonians*, tr. Ross Mackenzie, ed. D. W. Torrance and T. F. Torrance (Grand Rapids: Eerdmans, 1995).

———, *The Gospel According to John 11-21 and the First Epistle of John*, tr. T. H. L. Parker, Calvin NT Commentaries (Grand Rapids: Eerdmans, 1994).

———, *A Harmony of the Gospels of Matthew, Mark and Luke, Volume III, and the Epistles of James and Jude*, tr. A. W. Morrison, Calvin's NT Commentaries (Grand Rapids: Eerdmans, 1995).

———, *Institutes of the Christian Religion*, 2 vols., ed. John T. McNeill, tr. Ford Lewis Battles, Library of Christian Classics (Philadelphia: Westminster, 1960).

Campbell, John McLeod, *The Nature of the Atonement* (repr. 2nd ed., Edinburgh: Handsel Press, 1996 [1867]).

Campbell Morgan, G., *Hosea: The Heart and Holiness of God* (London: Marshall, Morgan and Scott, n.d.).

Carson, D. A., *The Gospel According to John* (Leicester: IVP, 1991).

Cavanagh, Lorraine, *Making Sense of God's Love: Atonement and Redemption* (London: SPCK, 2011),

Chalke, Steve, and Mann, Alan, *The Lost Message of Jesus* (Grand Rapids: Zondervan, 2003).

Chalmers, Thomas, *Select Works of Thomas Chalmers*, ed. William Hanna (Edinburgh: Constable, 1856).

Clifford, Alan C. (ed.), *Christ for the World: Papers Delivered at the 2006 Conference of the Amyraldian Association* (Charenton Reformed Publishing: Norwich, 2007).

Cranfield, C. E. B., *The Epistle to the Romans*, vol. 1, International Critical Commentary (2 vols., Edinburgh: T&T Clark, 1975).

——, *The Gospel According to Saint Mark: An Introduction and Commentary* (Cambridge: Cambridge University Press, 1959).

Cullmann, Oscar, *Christ and Time* (rev. ed., London: SCM Press, 1962).

Dale, R. W., *The Atonement* (21st ed., London: Congregational Union of England and Wales, 1900).

Deissmann, Adolf, *Light From The Ancient East: The New Testament Illustrated by Recently Discovered Texts of the Graeco-Roman World*, tr. Lionel R. M. Strachan (London: Hodder and Stoughton, 1910).

Denney, James, *The Death of Christ*, ed. R. V. G. Tasker (London: Tyndale Press, 1951 [1902]).

Dickson, David, *A Brief Exposition of the Evangel of Jesus Christ according to Matthew* (repr., Edinburgh: Banner of Truth, 1981 [1647]).

Dodd, C. H., *The Bible and the Greeks* (London: Hodder and Stoughton, 1935).

——, *The Epistle of Paul to the Romans* (London: Collins [Fontana], 1959).

——, *The Interpretation of the Fourth Gospel* (Cambridge: Cambridge University Press, 1968).

——, *The Meaning of Paul for Today* (repr., London: Collins [Fontana], 1958 [1920]).

Dunn, James D. G., *A Commentary on the Epistle to the Galatians* (London: A & C Black, 1993).

Edwards, Jonathan, *The Works of Jonathan Edwards*, rev. Edward Hickman, 2 vols. (repr. Edinburgh: Banner of Truth, 1974 [1834]).

Fairweather, Eugene R., *A Scholastic Miscellany: Anselm to Ockham*, Library of Christian Classics (London: SCM Press, 1956).

Fitzmyer, Joseph A., *Romans: A New Translation with Introduction and Commentary*, Anchor Bible, vol. 33 (London: Geoffrey Chapman, 1993).

Franks, R. S., *The Work of Christ* (London: Thomas Nelson, 1962).

Fung, Ronald Y. K., *The Epistle to the Galatians* (Grand Rapids: Eerdmans, 1988).

Gibson, David, and Gibson, Jonathan (eds.), *From Heaven He Came and Sought Her: Definite Atonement in Biblical, Historical, Theological and Pastoral Perspective* (Wheaton: Crossway, 2014).

Grane, Leif, *The Augsburg Confession: A Commentary*, tr. John H. Rasmussen (Minneapolis: Augsburg Publishing House, 1987).

Green, Joel B., and Baker, Mark D., *Recovering the Scandal of the Cross: Atonement in New Testament and Contemporary Contexts* (Bletchley: Paternoster, 2000).

Grudem, Wayne, *Systematic Theology: An Introduction to Biblical Doctrine* (Leicester: IVP, 1994).

Hartley, John E., *Leviticus*, Word Bible Commentary, vol. 4 (Dallas: Word Books, 1992).

Hengel, Martin, *Crucifixion in the Ancient World and the Folly of the Message of the Cross* (Philadelphia: Fortress Press, 1977).

Hoekema, Anthony A., *The Bible and the Future* (Exeter: Paternoster Press, 1979).

Hick, John (ed.), *The Myth of God Incarnate* (London: SCM Press, 1977).

Hodge, Archibald Alexander, *The Atonement* (repr., Grand Rapids: Baker Book House, 1974 [1867]).

Jeremias, Joachim, *The Eucharistic Words of Jesus* (London: SCM Press, 1966).

Kitamori, Kazoh, *Theology of the Pain of God* (repr., Eugene, Oregon: Wipf & Stock, 2005 [1965]).

Kittel, G., and Friedrich, Gerhard (eds.), *Theological Dictionary of the New Testament*, 10 vols., tr. and ed. Geoffrey W. Bromiley (Eerdmans: Grand Rapids, 1965–76).

Lampe, G. W. H., *God As Spirit: The Bampton Lectures, 1976* (Oxford: Clarendon Press, 1977).

Lennox, John C., *God's Undertaker: Has Science Buried God?* (Oxford: Lion, 2009).

Lewis, C. S., *Mere Christianity*, C. S. Lewis Signature Classics Edition (London: HarperCollins, 2012).

———, *They Asked for a Paper: Papers and Addresses* (London: Geoffrey Bles, 1962).

Lightfoot, J. B., *The Apostolic Fathers, Part I: S. Clement of Rome* (repr. Grand Rapids: Baker, 1978 [1890]).

———, *St Paul's Epistles to the Colossians and Philemon: A Revised Text with Introductions, Notes, and Dissertations* (8th ed., London: Macmillan, 1886).

Luther, Martin, *Luther's Works*, 55 vols., tr. and ed. Various (Saint Louis: Concordia Publishing House, 1955–86).

———, *Werke: kritische Gesammtaugabe* (Weimar: Hermann Böhlau, vol. 5, 1892).

Macleod, George F., *Only One Way Left* (Glasgow: The Iona Community, n.d.).

Martin, Hugh, *The Atonement: In Its Relations to the Covenant, the Priesthood, the Intercession of Our Lord* (repr. Greenville: Reformed Academic Press, 1997 [1870]).

McGrath, Alister E., *Iustitia Dei: A History of the Christian Doctrine of Justification* (2nd ed., Cambridge: Cambridge University Press, 1998).

Marshall, I. Howard, *The Gospel of Luke: A Commentary on the Greek Text* (Exeter: Paternoster Press, 1978).

Mascall, E. L., *Whatever Happened to the Human Mind: Essays in Christian Orthodoxy* (London: SPCK, 1980).

Metzger, Bruce M., *A Textual Commentary on the Greek New Testament: A Companion Volume to the United Bible Societies' Greek New Testament* (3rd ed., London/New York: United Bible Societies, 1975).

Moberly, R. C., *Atonement and Personality* (London: John Murray, 1901).

Morris, Leon, *The Apostolic Preaching of the Cross* (2nd ed., London: Tyndale Press, 1960).

———, *The Gospel According to Matthew*, Pillar NT Commentary (Grand Rapids: Eerdmans and Leicester: Apollos, 1992).

Motyer, Alec, *The Prophecy of Isaiah* (Leicester: IVP, 1993).

Moulton, James Hope, and Milligan, George, *The Vocabulary of the Greek Testament Illustrated from the Papyri and other Non-Literary Sources* (London: Hodder and Stoughton, 1952).

Mozley, J. K., *The Impassibility of God: A Survey of Christian Thought* (Cambridge: Cambridge University Press, 1926).

Murray, John, *Collected Writings of John Murray, Volume Three: Life of John Murray; Sermons & Reviews* (Edinburgh: Banner of Truth, 1982).

——, *The Epistle to the Romans: The English Text with Introduction, Exposition and Notes*, vol. 1 (Grand Rapids: Eerdmans, 1959).

——, *Redemption Accomplished and Applied* (Grand Rapids: Eerdmans, 1955).

Nicole, Roger, 'C. H. Dodd and the Doctrine of Propitiation', in *Standing Forth: Collected Writings of Roger Nicole* (Fearn: Christian Focus Publications, 2002).

Olson, Roger E., *Arminian Theology: Myths and Realities* (Downers Grove: IVP Academic, 2006).

Owen, John, *The Works of John Owen*, 24 vols., ed. William H. Goold (repr., London: Banner of Truth Trust, 1967 [Edinburgh, 1850–53]).

Pannenberg, Wolfhart, *Jesus: God and Man* (London: SCM Press, 1968).

Plummer, Alfred, *A Critical and Exegetical Commentary on the Gospel according to S. Luke*, International Critical Commentary (5th ed., Edinburgh: T&T Clark, 1922).

Preston, John, *The Breast-plate of Faith and Love* (London: 1634).

Ramsey, Arthur Michael, *The Glory of God and the Transfiguration of Christ* (London: Longmans, Green and Co., 1949).

Ramsey, Ian T., *Religious Language: An Empirical Placing of Theological Phrases* (London: SCM, 1957).

Rashdall, Hastings, *The Idea of Atonement in Christian Theology* (London: Macmillan, 1919).

Ratzinger, Joseph, *Introduction to Christianity*, tr. J. R. Foster and Michael J. Miller (San Francisco: Ignatius Press, 2000 [1969]).

Rutherford, Samuel, *Fourteen Communion Sermons by the Rev. Samuel Rutherford*, with a Preface and Notes by Rev. Andrew A. Bonar (Glasgow: Charles Glass & Co., n. d.).

Schaff, Philip, *The Evangelical Protestant Creeds*, vol. 3 of *The Creeds of Christendom with a History and Critical Notes*, 3 vols. (New York: Harper, 1882).

Smeaton, George, *The Doctrine of the Atonement According to the Apostles* (repr., Peabody: Hendrickson, 1988 [1870]).

Stibbs, A. M., *The Meaning of the Word 'Blood' in Scripture* (London: Tyndale Press, 1947).

Taylor, Vincent, *The Atonement in New Testament Teaching* (3rd ed., London: Epworth Press, 1958).

Torrance, James B., 'The Vicarious Humanity of Christ', in Thomas F. Torrance (ed.), *The Incarnation: Ecumenical Studies in the Nicene-Constantinopolitan Creed* (Edinburgh: Handsel Press, 1981).

Torrance, Thomas F., *Atonement: The Person and Work of Christ*, ed. Robert T. Walker (Milton Keynes: Paternoster, 2009).

——, *Juridical Law and Physical Law* (Edinburgh: Scottish Academic Press, 1982).

——, *The Mediation of Christ* (Grand Rapids: Eerdmans, 1983).

——, *Scottish Theology: From John Knox to John McLeod Campbell* (Edinburgh: T&T Clark, 1996).

——, 'Karl Barth and the Latin Heresy', *Scottish Journal of Theology* 39, no 4 (1986), pp. 461–482.

Vos, Geerhardus, *Biblical Theology: Old and New Testaments* (Grand Rapids: Eerdmans, 1959).

——, *Redemptive History and Biblical Interpretation: The Shorter Writings of Geerhardus Vos*, ed. Richard B. Gaffin (Phillipsburg: Presbyterian and Reformed, 1980).

Warfield, B. B., *Critical Reviews* (London and New York: Oxford University Press, 1932).

——, *The Plan of Salvation* (rev. ed., Grand Rapids: Eerdmans, n.d.).

——, 'The New Testament Terminology of Redemption', in *The Person and Work of Christ* (Philadelphia: Presbyterian and Reformed, 1950).

Wesley, John, *Sermons on Several Occasions,* 5 vols. (London: Wesleyan Conference Office, 1876).

Westcott, Brooke Foss, *The Epistle to the Hebrews: The Greek Text with Notes and Essays* (London: Macmillan, 1889).

Wolterstorff, Nicholas, *Hearing the Call: Liturgy, Justice and World* (Grand Rapids: Eerdmans, 2011).

INDEX OF NAMES

INDEX OF SCRIPTURE REFRENCES